Encounter with Anthropology

ENCOUNTER WITH ANTHROPOLOGY

by

ROBIN FOX

HARCOURT BRACE JOVANOVICH, INC., NEW YORK

Copyright © 1968, 1973 by Katellian Trusts

Printed in the United States of America

The author and publisher acknowledge permission to reprint, in whole or in
part, the following essays: 3, in *Ciba Foundation Symposium: The Family and
Its Future*, K. Elliott, ed., copyright The Ciba Foundation 1970; 4 (as "Parenté
et Mariage"), in *L'Ethnologie*, O. Herrenschmidt, ed., Librairie Larousse, 1973;
6, *New Society*, 1962, copyright © New Society 1962; 7, in "The Living Past
in Donegal," *Clare Market Review*; 8, in "Structure of Personal Names on
Tory Island," *Man*, 1963, copyright © 1963 Royal Anthropological Institute,
and in "Kinship and Land Tenure on Tory Island," *Ulster Folk Life*, 1966,
copyright © Ulster Folk Museum 1966; 9, in "Cochiti Indians of America,"
New Society, 1963, copyright © New Society 1963; 10 (as "Pueblo Baseball:
A New Use for Old Witchcraft"), *Journal of American Folklore*, 1961, copyright © American Folklore Society, Inc. 1961; 11 (as "Veterans and Factions
in Pueblo Society"), *Man*, 1961, copyright © 1961 Royal Anthropological Institute; 12 (as "Witchcraft and Clanship in Cochiti Therapy"), in *Magic, Faith
and Healing*, Ari Kiev, ed., The Free Press, copyright © 1964 by The Free
Press of Glencoe, a Division of Macmillan Publishing Co., Inc.; 13 (as "Multilingualism in Two Communities"), *Man*, 1968, copyright © 1968 Royal Anthropological Institute; 14, in "North America," *Historia Religionum*, vol. 2:
Religions of the Present, C. J. Bleeker and G. Widengren, eds., copyright ©
1971 E. J. Brill and Co.; 15, in *Man and Beast: Comparative Social Behavior*,
J. Eisenberg, ed., Smithsonian Institution Press, copyright © 1971 Smithsonian
Institution. The first two essays originally appeared in *The New York Times
Magazine*.

Library of Congress Cataloging in Publication Data
Fox, Robin, 1934-
   Encounter with anthropology.
   Includes bibliographical references.
   1. Ethnology.   2. Race. I. Title.
GN315.F68   301.2   73-12873
ISBN 0-15-128793-7

First edition

B C D E

For Katherine, Eleanor, and Anne

Contents

Contents

Language and Religion

Man in Nature

Epilogue: Anthropology Tomorrow 341

Encounter with Anthropology

Anthropology as a Vocation

Anthropology is, with music and mathematics, one of the few true vocations; and the anthropologist may become aware of it within himself before ever he has been taught it.

—Claude Lévi-Strauss, *Tristes Tropiques*

Let us then give to the word biology the very wide meaning it should have, and will perhaps have one day, and let us say in conclusion that all morality, be it pressure or aspiration, is in essence biological.

—Henri Bergson, *The Two Sources of Morality and Religion*

THIS IS A BOOK about anthropology by a puzzled anthropologist who does not know quite how he fits into his discipline any more. And judging by the book reviews of some of his colleagues, the discipline has *its* doubts about the relationship. Something is wrong somewhere. This would not matter if the field were, say, art history; there would be no excuse for thrusting another book at a public already over-burdened with books. No disrespect is meant to art history, but somehow anthropology catches the public imagination in a different way. Only psychiatry can rival it as an attention getter. Everyone knows our splendid elder statesmen, like Ashley Montagu and Margaret Mead; and while Louis Leakey, Robert Ardrey, and Desmond Morris may be pooh-

3

poohed by the profession (unjustly), they do ensure that some of our subject matter gets a wide airing. Bronislaw Malinowski's *Sexual Life of Savages* has never gone out of print.

People are as fascinated by anthropology as anthropologists are fascinated by people. The anthropologist makes us take a new look at ourselves; he shows us the alternatives to our own secure and petty lives—or insecure and grandiose lives, for that matter. Such men are dangerous, thinking too much about how else we might do it—although, as will be seen, few anthropologists want to rock the boat. Anthropologists tantalize, titillate, shock, and even amaze. But they do not really threaten, since it was all in another country and besides the wench is dead. They are, by and large, gentle folk, well liked for their jests. But every good jester is a philosopher gone mad—at least in Shakespeare—and you never know when he might bite instead of smile. Anthropologists are the custodians of the unconscious of the human race, and perhaps, like the psychiatrists, dangerous fellows at that.

If you meet an anthropologist and decide to ask him a question, you will probably pick one of three topics: primitive people, early man, or race. If you know there is to be an article by an anthropologist in a Sunday magazine, you assume it will be about one of these three things. If it isn't, then you assume that it will bring the perspective suggested by these three topics to whatever it *is* about. An anthropologist might write about the presidential inauguration, or Bob Hope's command performances at the White House, but he would probably want to compare the former to installations of tribal chiefs in Africa, and the latter to sacred clowning among the Pueblos of New Mexico. The trick here is usually for the anthropologist, trained to cast a quizzical eye on other and, to most people, more exotic cultures, to turn that same eye on his own odd customs and weird ways. We can thus see ourselves as others see us, and Fox's first law —that all foreigners are funny—comes easily into operation, and we laugh at ourselves. The anthropologist's trick of making the familiar seem exotic and amusing by showing it to be a tribal custom makes him something of a social success. Whereas most of us take our institutions for granted and see other people's institutions as progressively (or regressively) more bizarre as they deviate from ours, the anthopologist looks at all institutions (including those most familiar to him) from the same distance. They cannot be taken by him as God-given. They have to be explained (even "we" are, after all, just another tribe). They are usually "explained" by being put into comparative perspective. "Inauguration is another example of installation ceremonies the purpose of which is . . ." "Privileged jesting at the expense of rulers is another example of 'inversion rituals' the purpose of which is . . ." Different anthropologists would end each of these sentences differently, and fight to defend their endings as the right ones. But whatever their conclusions, their premises would be much the same and would include as an irreducible minimum the use of data from primitive tribes.

But what happened to early man and race? Embarrassed anthropologists, accosted by laymen eager to have the word on Leakey's latest species of fossil man, will often have to confess that they don't know one fossil from another. They are *social*, or *cultural*, anthropologists, they will explain, and they don't know about fossils. "Funny sort of anthropologist!" one irate old Devonshire man flung at me in 1961 after I confessed that I had no idea what little simian beast it was that had been unearthed in an Italian coal mine. (*Oreopithecus*, I now know—but that's another story.) He might well be angry, for the public has a right to expect those who profess and call themselves anthropologists to be able to pronounce on human origins and all that. A long lecture on the history of modern social/cultural anthropology and its relative lack of connection with physical anthropology will not satisfy anybody who *knows* that anthropologists were onto that Piltdown thing but weren't saying anything out of embarrassment, or are keeping the Yeti hidden in the University of Calcutta because it spoils their theories, or have been persecuting Professor Raymond Dart for telling the unvarnished truth about our murderous origins in South Africa, of all appropriate places (*pace* Mr. Ardrey). The social anthropologist's disdain of these matters, his invocation of tribal gods with names like Émile Durkheim and A. R. Radcliffe-Brown, will not help. A funny sort of anthropologist he will remain.

But the same eager inquirers might well get the opposite rebuff. Cornering their anthropologist and moving in for the kill, they get in a rapid series of questions about the missionary position in the Marquesan sex act (they read about it in a Sunday supplement), or why the Samoans don't have puberty (they do, but no one ever gets that one quite right), or the latest "lost tribe" that has just been "found" (although *it* knew it was there all the time). "Sorry," they will be told, "but, you see, I'm a *physical* anthropologist and that stuff is strictly for the social/cultural boys. Now, about the genetics of skin color, *Oreopithecus*, or the osteodontokeratic conjectures of Professor Dart . . ." Well, our listener, all agog for the latest news from the comparative sexuality battlefront ("Is it true that Africans buy their wives?"), will be perhaps inclined to think that he has here a funny sort of anthropologist. What ever happened to queer customs and beastly practices?

On the other hand, he might be lucky and hit upon that know-all character, the *general* anthropologist. This Renaissance figure could go on at length about blood types, art styles, sexual mores, fossil skulls, flint flakes, peasant folk tales, chimpanzee intelligence, the caste system, African law, agglutinative languages, economic development, beaker people, voodoo death, primitive mythology, et cetera. Both at dinner parties and in the middle-range middle-brow press, the general anthropologist is a winner. I know. I was one for a while.

His problem is that, while obviously conversant with all that makes the anthropologist such a splendid social asset— if a rotten social critic—he seems as fragmented as his knowledge itself. "But what does all this tell us about the human condition, Mr. Anthropologist?" At such questions he either quails or is genuinely embarrassed. They are the scope of philosophy or theology but not of "science," in which the general anthropologist takes refuge as surely as a hunted man once sought sanctuary in church. But the listener wants to know. He presses. "All this incredible erudition— how is it put together? What framework encompasses it all? How does it combine—this knowledge of evolution, of archaeology, of human biology, of comparative custom, of linguistics—to ask and answer the Great Questions?" The general anthropologist will not have a coherent answer. But his more narrow-minded colleagues might: the social anthropologist might argue that his perspective is humbling in its view of the relativity of cultural values; the physical anthropologist might argue for the awesomeness of a view of man in evolutionary time as part of nature, or he might argue about the unity of man, the cant of racism. The general anthropologist, having no particular perspective, would clumsily have to try to put these two views side by side. He would not be able to produce a linkage to satisfy his listeners in their genuine interest or even justify his own thinly spread and seemingly disparate accumulation of knowledge in the first place. To say that this knowledge is all about "man" is not good enough—so is comparative literature, history, mathematics, economics, et cetera. Why not throw those in, too? What is the general anthropologist doing with all this knowledge if he can't put it together somehow?

Newton practiced alchemy along with genuine science—but he had to go a separate way with each. The general anthropologist is in much the same position: he can no more produce a theory to link his knowledge of physical anthropology with social anthropology than Newton could to link black magic with the law of gravity. And the reasons are very similar. By embracing the principles of empirical science, Newton cut himself off from magic—yet he practiced both. The general anthropologist has cut off the social and cultural universe from the physical, yet he continues to insist on studying both social and physical anthropology. Most physical anthropologists, feeling perhaps that they are "real" scientists, just leave the social and cultural alone. But many cultural anthropologists, with that "craving for generality" that Ludwig Wittgenstein identified as a basic human motive, try to embrace the necromancy of skulls and genes and fossil sequences. Indeed, in the textbooks on general anthropology, these sections might as well be about the philosopher's stone for what relevance they have to the rest of the book. "Thank God that's over. Now let's get on with the strange customs."

Yet something in us warms to the Newton of the hopeless, Faustian wizardry, and, by the same token, to the gallant fight of the general anthropologist to float lead on water. Newton sensed that there were mysteries that the second law of thermodynamics knew nothing of, and at least some of us sense that there must be a link, however mysterious, between those skulls, chromosomes, and flints on the one hand, and those queer customs on the other: that what man *does* must be related to what man *is*.

But before we can pursue the mystery we must unhoist ourselves from our own petard. We have banished the physical from the cultural; we have hauled culture out of nature, and we must shove it back again, even if it protests. For here is the paradox: the general anthropologist is one of those who proclaim most loudly man's cultural emancipation from physical nature while at the same time insisting that every genuine anthropologist should know about both. At least the physical and cultural anthropologists *in sensu stricto* are consistent. Each just ignores the other. But the general anthropologist can't have it both ways. Students, at least, are beginning to ask awkward questions. Why should they learn all the physical stuff and the archaeology if none of it is relevant to human behavior? Why indeed? Newton may have had his private perversions, but he didn't try to write them into the college curriculum; and if he had announced that science had superseded—indeed, was inimical to—necromancy, but that students had to qualify in both in order to graduate as "real" scientists, he might have been pelted with apples from more than natural sources.

Science made up its mind about necromancy, but cultural anthropology can't seem to make up its mind about physical anthropolgy. An intellectual history of the subject is neither possible nor necessary here. Suffice it to say that as an academic discipline anthropology took its impetus from the idea of evolution and the consequent search for origins, both social and physical. One looked for fossils to confirm physical origins and evolution, and to "primitive" man for clues to social origins and evolution. Also, the diversity of human types raised the question of whether, in the course of evolution, we had developed as one species or as more than one; a question now obviously settled, but one that was genuinely problematical to our ancestors. Since language seemed a uniquely human attribute, and since the comparative method in linguistics had been so successful—and, further, since most of the huge number of unrecorded languages were those of "primitive" peoples—linguistics was taken into the anthropological maw. Thus the great "four-field" system that now dominates American anthropology was developed: cultural (social) anthropology; archaeology (prehistoric—the classicists had grabbed classical archaeology); linguistics; physical anthropology (largely the study of race and fossil man). Origins were the object, comparision the method, and, after 1859, Charles Darwin the inspiration.

It all sounds fine. So what happened? Well, at least some of the offspring of the great founding fathers decided that the marriage of these topics was forced, miscegenous, or just plain embarrassing. The great parental idea of Darwinism itself—that the human species is just another animal species that has gradually emerged from the rest of nature but retained its kinship with it—lost the power to bind together the restless offspring. This was partly due to the dynastic development of an autonomous sociology under Émile Durkheim, which heavily influenced British anthropology, and to an antihistorical development in America under Franz Boas. But it was also because even the Darwinians had to wait for the maturity of genetics as a science, and population genetics in particular. It was not until the 1930's that evolutionary biology came into its own with R. A. Fisher, J. B. S. Haldane, Sewall Wright, and with Julian Huxley's new synthesis. It was not until the 1950's that the genetic code was broken and ethology, the science of the evolution of animal behavior, made any headway against the prevalent Pavlovian behaviorism. Until these developments it was hard for Darwinian ideas to be applied as successfully to human behavior and society as they had been to human anatomy and physiology. And by that time the damage was done and social/cultural anthropology, along with the other social sciences, had ditched Darwin as surely as natural science had ditched necromancy. As a consequence, the amazing discoveries in the biological sciences—in endocrinology, in behavior genetics, in primatology, in ethology, in molecular and population genetics, in neuroscience, and so on—are passing anthropologists by like a train in the night, while they sleep securely wrapped in their doctrine of the "superorganic"—that human behavior cannot be reduced to explanation by biological principles.

But do we really care if the anthropologists cannot put their house in order? Do we need to do anything but laugh at the schizoid Ph.D. programs with their built-in contradictions? I once gave a paper at a celebrated anthropology department in which I argued for the integration of the subject in a Darwinian framework. The students in the audience were more or less on my side. Afterward, a physical-anthropology professor came up to me almost in tears. "You've saved my generals," she said, referring not to her staff officers but to the forthcoming general examinations for graduate students. "I've had a hell of a time getting them to take it all seriously. Now I think they understand why they have to do it."

But does this matter? If the trainload of new knowledge passes them by and leaves them snugly in their superorganic siding, what is lost? I think a great deal. Anthropology is more than just another academic discipline; it is the *only* academic discipline capable of grasping the new knowledge, putting it into the old Darwinian framework, and coming out with a view of man that might be a more satisfactory basis not only for research, but also for a critical re-examination of human values. If anthropology fails us now, the fragmentation of knowledge will continue and biology and behavior will drift even further apart. Those who study behavior will be helpless against the claims of the biologists;

those who study biology will not appreciate the consequences
for behavior of their tinkering with genetic material.

And tinker they will. The biological time bomb is already
going off. Experiments at the genetic level that might lead to
genetic engineering in the very near future are already going
on. Yet the people doing these experiments have no training
and little interest in the subtle interplay between biology and
behavior that goes into the construction of our social orders.
At the same time, the students of social behavior are busily
denying that any such interplay exists, thus leaving the field
wide open for the biological Nosy Parkers to work their little
schemes—or for whoever is dealing out the instructions to
the biologists to work *theirs*. If anthropology, which has stubbornly kept a foot on each side of the divide between the
social and natural sciences, does not grasp the opportunity
to do what is after all its job—investigate the nature of man
—then it may never be done. The manipulators of people's
lives have an easy enough time of it as it is, without being
handed the actual weapons. Some form of genetic tinkering
may well suit them beautifully. Given the general awe of
science, they can blind man to what they are doing to his
genes as easily as they blind him to what they are doing with
scientific hardware for "defense" and other noble ends. If
man has no way of saying "What you are doing will disturb
the process of being human in such and such a way," then
on what grounds can the case be argued? If it is insisted that
biology and behavior are not linked fundamentally, how
can, for example, the use of "helpful" drugs—such as the
drugs given children to speed their learning, or oral contra-
ceptives—be assessed?

All this gives rise to a very curious paradox that surpasses
even the academic split mind already encountered. Most of
the anthropologists who protest the loudest against the "neo-
Darwinian" approach to behavior do so not on intellectual

but on ideological grounds. They are "liberals," believing in progress, reform, the perfectibility of man—or at least in his social improvement. To them, curiously, neo-Darwinism is a version of neo-Fascism. By claiming that biology enters into the determination of behavior, they say, Darwinists encourage racism. Darwinists are also supposed to support the *status quo*, because it is all too easy to claim that whatever exists is simply a reflection of human nature—the distinction between the roles of men and women, for example, or the pervasiveness of social inequality. On the other hand, if one doesn't believe in human nature in the first place, there is no necessary *status quo*; men can learn anything, including better social institutions, greater equality, et cetera. The argument has been ventilated often—by John Stuart Mill, for example—and always to show that any notion of the innate was reactionary: such a notion leads people to think that men just are the way they are (aggressive, acquisitive, et cetera) and that nothing can be done about it.

A damaging accusation if it is true. But, paradoxically, it really works the other way around. If there is no human nature, any social system is as good as any other, since there is no base line of human needs by which to judge them. If, indeed, everything is learned, then surely men can be taught to live in any kind of society. Man is at the mercy of all the tyrants—be they fascists or liberals—who think they know what is best for him. And how can he plead that they are being inhuman if he doesn't know what being human is in the first place? If, however, man can establish what the basic human satisfactions and needs are—if he knows what the human social nature is and what kinds of social systems are compatible with it—he can make a stand against the brainwashers, genetic tinkerers, totalitarians, and utopian liberals who would knock us into shape. Man does, in fact, have some intuitive knowledge of what is human and what is not—

and what is human is not always "nice," by any means—
and he does protest when this is abused and infringed upon,
although a basic fact of human nature is a capacity to put up
with almost anything. The liberal ideologues, in their anxiety
to protect their own view of human behavior, may be betray-
ing man to the manipulators. At least B. F. Skinner is honest
about this—tell us what kind of social behavior you want, he
says, and we will produce it, and none of that nonsense about
Freedom and Dignity, please; they have already cost us too
much. But perhaps the problem with Freedom and Dignity is
like the proverbial problem with Christianity: they haven't
been tried.

That anthropologists should be at their best as amusing
social commentators rather than as serious social critics is a
sad commentary on the profession that has more data about
human frailty and nobility at its command than any discipline
other than history. Even history is handicapped, since it
rarely moves beyond the confines of "civilization"—a peculiar and recent episode in human affairs. This failure on
the part of anthropology is doubly odd, since, in the eighteenth century, it was the great French social critics—
notably Rousseau—who looked to the "savage" for enlightenment. And, distorted as it was as a version of Darwin's real
theories, social Darwinism in the nineteenth century, with its
doctrines of progress, survival of the fittest, and *laissez faire*,
was at least an intellectual force. It obviously owed more to
Herbert Spencer than to Darwin, but Spencer, too, was one of
the great comparative sociologists and tried to marry the
comparative method in anthropology with evolutionary
theory, and to marry both to biology and social policy. But it
was the very collapse of such grand schemes, and also the
failure of social revolution to bring total happiness to mankind, that led to the disillusion about such knowledge and to

its fragmentation, and to the retreat from responsibility. Anthropology, like the other social sciences, ceased to be a subject for questing intellects who wished to understand the Nature of Man and to effect the Betterment of Mankind. It became a profession. That is to say, it became something that any fool with enough persistence and the right training could master—as long as he kept out of "grand theory" and social revolution. A self-effacing modesty, appropriate to a profession, overtook the subject: "We don't really know very much, but we know what we do know very well indeed." As for any idea of involvement in the Fate of Mankind, since mankind had ceased to be the subject matter, then so had its fate. (There was, and is, something called "applied anthropology," which has been "the discipline in the nation's service," as Woodrow Wilson might have put it—a kind of tropical-social-work venture mainly concerned with getting recalcitrant savages and peasants to behave like middle-class Euro-Americans in preparation for the millennium that "aid" and "modernization" would bring.) So modest did anthropologists become that not many of them wanted to be answerable for more than their own few square miles of tribal territory. Over this they ruled, and anyone who has been unlucky enough to have to listen to an anthropologist tell what he did on his vacation (he calls it "field work") will have noticed how he refers royally to "my people." For social anthropologists, in both England and America, field work came to replace scholarship—and even thought—as a boy-scout mentality swept the discipline. An anthropologist was no longer someone who wrestled with the Nature of Man or the Universal History of Mankind; he was someone who had done field work—gone off to live with the natives for a year or two to learn their customs firsthand.

Now this is fine. As Malinowski said, field work is to anthropology what the blood of the martyrs is to the church. But field work is in danger of succumbing to Gresham's law: the mediocrity of mere field workers is threatening to swamp the vocational nobility of anthropology as a science in the service of mankind. Field work is not an end, but merely a means; it is the collection of necessary data—we go on from there. But to most anthropologists, even if they acknowledge other ideals, field work is the end. And someone who has not done field work is not a real anthropologist—and probably would have difficulty getting a job. More and more is heard about "trained anthropologists," as though they were dentists or circus ponies. Yes, there they are—hordes of them—all clutching their field notes, writing their articles, putting out their monographs, and training more animals for a part in the great anthropological circus. I will probably be drummed out of the profession for saying so, but I believe that this obsession with field work as an end in itself—as the mark of a real anthropologist—and the professionalization of the subject are the bases for the decline and stultification of anthropological ideas. Anthropology as taught is not hard to do. As a profession it attracts a few brilliant intellects and many little talents. It is in danger of becoming an intellectual slum with its own culture of poverty, a growth industry as mindless as a corporation seeking an expansion of its markets. But its raw material—the natives who inhabit the fields, or whatever, where the work of the profession is done —is rapidly becoming exhausted. "Savages" will soon be irrelevant in a world that is changing daily into a new and terrifying social order that will take the class struggle out of individual nations and on to a global scale. "Natives" are part of the depressed populations of the third world who are getting poorer and more numerous and more restless. It's going to take more than applied anthropology to satisfy their restlessness and to solve their problems. It all begins to look suspiciously like intellectual imperialism to some critics within the profession itself. The only problem with these self-appointed keepers of the radical conscience is that they are as sunk in pseudo-Marxism, para-Maoism, or fanatical feminism as the rest of the profession is in its retreat into field work and modesty. They are radical anthropologists, but their anthropology does not inform their radicalism—they could as well be dentists—except to allow them to make pious statements about racism, colonialism, or sexism, and to persecute free thought that does not conform to their own rigid notions of the good and the true. A real radical anthropology must first make a radical change in the whole make-up of the subject so that it becomes a powerful tool for the analysis of human nature through the incorporation of the material of the biological sciences in a neo-Darwinian framework; and this analysis itself must be the basis for a new attack on social policy, a new attempt to define the human in human nature, and the social in social systems.

The fate of mankind has to be someone's concern, and can we trust the politicians or the physical scientists or the generals or the businessmen or the revolutionaries? They all have too much of a vested interest in their own versions —including the liberal humanitarian anthropologists whose good consciences get in the way of hard thinking. Robert Heilbroner quotes an example of good socialist thinking that begs completely the question of what is natural in human behavior. After the revolution in Cuba, the new government found that some fifty-five thousand ex-revolutionary heroes had set themselves up in small trading enterprises from which they were making small profits. They were all expropriated and punished for their treachery to the revolution and for their sellout to bourgeois ideals. But, asks Heilbroner—himself a radical critic of economics and the economy—how do we know that it was not a normal aspect of human behavior and had nothing to do with reactionary treachery?

Only the doctrine that man's consciousness is *wholly* shaped by social conditions would assume otherwise, and with no proof. Directly or indirectly, by acts of law or social indifference, millions are daily punished for being human and millions more rewarded for being inhuman. Anthropology is the one science with even half a chance to get at what really is human: How did human social behavior evolve and what are the consequences of that evolution? Instead, it goes on producing field workers, moans and groans about the disappearance of the "primitive," and preaches that everyone is good unless taught to be evil.

There is a wave of urgent anthropology conferences at the moment that deal endlessly with ways of trying to get in the information on the last remaining truly primitive peoples before they go down under epidemics, exploitation, bombing, and progress generally. But, as my colleague Lionel Tiger pointed out, the really urgent anthropology should be done in the White House, the Pentagon, and the offices of the international corporations, since it is their policies that are responsible for the disappearing act in the first place—and for the disappearance of all of us in the not so very long run.

Of course, anthropologists have a mandate to gather the data on primitive man, since this is their special corner of the behavioral-science market and their moral responsibility to the intellectual community as well. But, sadly, this obsession serves only to emphasize the field-work aspects of the subject as ends in themselves; meanwhile, the train is roaring off into the darkness. It is just as urgent to have anthropologists working in the laboratory jungle as in the Amazon. If they don't get aboard the train soon, they'll be left doing their little war dances and playing with their glass beads and wondering where everybody has gone and why they aren't listening any more.

Anthropologists emasculated themselves as social critics.

18

They cut loose from biology and from the nature of man, and they embraced behaviorism and relativism. All cultures were as good as all other cultures. Customs had to be interpreted according to the role they played in their own cultures, and not according to some abstract standards imported from the outside. "Our" values did not apply to "theirs." This is all very well as a counter to condescension and even attack from supposedly superior cultures. Ethnocentrism used to be the cardinal sin of anthropology. "They" were to be seen on their own terms, as "functioning entities" in which every custom played its appointed part. Kurt Vonnegut, Jr., gently ridicules this stance. In *Slaughterhouse Five* he alludes to his time as a student of anthropology:

I think about my education sometimes. I went to the University of Chicago for a while after the Second World War. I was a student in the Department of Anthropology. At that time they were teaching that there was absolutely no difference between anybody. They may be teaching that still.

Another thing they taught was that nobody was ridiculous or bad or disgusting. Shortly before my father died, he said to me, "You know—you never wrote a story with a villain in it." I told him that was one of the things I learned in college after the war.

Within the profession some protested. If this doctrine were followed through, on what basis could the Nazis be condemned? And how could attacks on such cultures be justified except in terms of pure *Realpolitik?* If an elegant, functional explanation of cannibalism could be given, then why couldn't the same be done for Dresden and Hiroshima, for genocide and selective extermination? The answer is that it could. But it is one thing to explain the functions of such practices, another to approve them. Unfortunately, this distinction has not always been clear to anthropologists whose lack of philosophical sophistication is second only to their enthusiasm for field work. But given the anti-human-nature bias, given that all is learned and hence anything is possible, on what basis could anthropologists criticize inhumanity even if they wanted to? These limitations did not stop them, of course.

The professionalization of anthropology, its fragmentation, the embracing of behaviorism and cultural relativism, the obsession with field work as an end—all these have wrecked a discipline that is perhaps the only hope for a science not only *of* humanity but *for* humanity. Economics, political science, sociology, psychology have little basis on which to do this, although there have been creditable attempts. Anthropology alone among the behavioral sciences can easily grasp the chance offered by the new biology to go back to Darwin and start again, and to get to the root of what is human. But to do this anthropologists have to revolutionize the subject as it now stands. They have to produce marginal anthropologists, in the same way that society produces marginal people who, in turn, become its anthropologists. Self-satisfied members of the Establishment rarely want to question the society of which they are a part. Things are, to them, what they seem to be. It is the marginal man who questions, who is restless and dissatisfied, who looks beneath the surface. Anthropology is now itself a smug establishment.

The field-work strangle hold must be broken. Not that the anthropologist of the future should not do field work—although I hope he does not get involved in the undignified scramble to find substitute savages in slums. But field work should not be an initiation rite into the discipline; it is merely one way of getting data on human social behavior. The problem with initiations (and this is also their strength) is that the initiate tends to identify with the system in proportion to pain he suffers in the initiation. And field work can be a painful experience. Having gone through an ordeal, the initiate has truly too much to lose by bucking the system that demanded all this of him. Anyway, he is amply rewarded

20

—and the more he has suffered, the more his prestige. Anthropologists remain obsessed with their "people," unable to think of the world except through the spectacles of the Bongo Bongo. What ever happened to mankind? Well, there are comparativists, but they deal with societies at such an abstract level that they lose as much as they gain.

Anthropology is not one subject now, but a rag bag of odds and ends held together by sentiment and dynastic interest. Perhaps the best that can be hoped for is that the center will not hold, since the center is a hollow reed anyway, and that those anthropologists who really care can return to anthropology as a vocation and quit the nonsense about professionalism. They can be the mad amateurs foraging in the dawn of new discoveries. They can have strange ideas and indulge in unprofessional conduct of all kinds without let or hindrance. They can traffic in biology and ruminate on human nature without being accused of ideological unsoundness. They can concern themselves with the fate of mankind without being attacked as propagandists. They can roam about the whole intellectual landscape at will without being out of bounds. Come to think of it, that's what they do anyway. Since anthropology is so amorphous, there will always be some who will sit around the frontiers like intellectual barbarians, occasionally making raids into the interior but just as fruitfully going off in other directions—unless they are caught up in the mediocre professionalism that has hold of the discipline. They will always be the enemies of professionalism—probably because it is inhuman and not part of the inherited repertoire. It appeals to the sense of, and need for, order and predictability and security of the unadventurous; but it leaves no room for the predatory madness that is the source not only of general mayhem but also of discovery and invention.

For the layman, anthropological subject matter—all those

fossils and queer customs—is fascinating, but anthropological theory is a long yawn. The average freshman in biology is handling theory and method of a greater degree of sophistication than the most advanced anthropology professor. Given the secure foundation of evolutionary biology, the biology freshman and his professor are remarkably free to move across the intellectual landscape—a freedom they might not use, but which is there. Until anthropology has the same built-in freedom, until it stops arguing about what its subject matter is, let alone what to do with it, it will remain an easy prey for the mediocre careerists and other scavengers of the dying body of a discipline.

2.

The essays that follow are, in the truest sense, an encounter with anthropology. I have saved "The Cultural Animal" for the end because it takes up some of the themes in this introduction and develops them into a position that represents more or less where I stand today. The essays, not in chronological order, can be read as one man's attempts to get hold of some of the areas of a rambling subject. There is no steady development, but, rather, a series of excursions into various fields: evolution, race, kinship, marriage, religion, language, witchcraft, curing, factions, legends, conflict, groups, and so on. The variety of subjects itself makes a point, for it is clear to me on looking these essays over that I have spent fourteen years groping about trying to define what I was doing and how to do it. My problem has been, I suppose, that since I was never properly initiated into anthropology I have never totally identified myself with its prevailing ideology. Nor, for that matter, have I had to undo a lot of firmly entrenched damage that I might have suffered if I had been brought up in the four-field system (plus cultural relativism) in America, or in the English system of intensive field work combined with ignorance of physical and archaeological anthropology. I managed to do some of both but not much of either and a lot else besides. Perhaps I am not really an anthropologist at all, and I should just leave those who are to get on in peace with what they are doing. If I have an intellectual lineage, it would go back to the French *philosophes*—Montesquieu, Rousseau, Condorcet; to the English political philosophers—Hobbes and Locke; or to the Scottish Enlightenment thinkers—Ferguson, Hume, Smith, Stewart; and to the fathers of sociology—Pareto, Comte, Spencer, and Marx. Not that I follow all their doctrines; that would involve outright contradictions. It is their spirit of inquiry I admire.

What is this spirit? It is the willingness to deal with the problem of the nature of man directly, and to ask what consequences this nature has for our moral and social lives. It is the willingness to explore what *is* to discover what *ought to be*. It is, in other words, a commitment to moral exploration. There are better and worse ways of organizing our social and moral lives—what are these? What are the alternatives? What are the limitations? What are the possibilities?

Like Kant, all of us who grasp this philosophical nettle have to face up to the skepticism of Hume. Can *ought to be* ever be derived from *is?* Can any amount of knowledge of how things are tell us how they should be? Before Darwin, that was a difficult question to answer. But since Darwin, it is known that organisms are adapted in certain ways and that there is in a real sense a range of behavioral possibilities that are natural to any species. It is fairly easy to recognize when this natural behavior is being distorted and to watch the deleterious effects on the animals concerned. Surely the same is true for man? He is what he is because he has adapted successfully to changing environments and selection pressures. There is a range of behavior that is natural to him, and that, if thwarted, will produce detrimental results. For this range to become clear, all the varieties of social order that man has produced must be carefully looked at. This is the first clue. This is also where the comparative anthropologist comes in. Fossil evidence must be examined to see what the stages of development of the human animal have been in order to see how man was molded in the evolutionary process. This is where the physical anthropologist comes in. The actual biological make-up of man as it affects his behavior should be the next focus. This is where the new bio-anthropologist would come in if he were not banned from the club. The final consideration should be man in the context of his mammalian inheritance, of his relatedness to other forms of life, so that the unique features of human social behavior can be winnowed out. This is where the comparative ethologist and especially the primatologist come in, and where another hybrid, the anthropological ethologist, might well serve his turn, if he existed and were respectable.

With this battery of information the range of possible behaviors and social orders that were recognizably human could be established. Outside this range would be those behaviors and organizations that were clearly forced on the creature— not part of his pattern of adaptedness. Truly, Hume's logical point could never be overcome; there is no logic whereby any *is* can decide for us what ought, or ought not, to be. This is a decision anthropologists must take. But it is open to any of them to urge that the decision be taken in terms of what can be strictly defined as human. After all, except for a few psychopaths and dabblers in human misery, the vast majority of anthropologists is on the side of the human—they simply disagree on what it is. As the great but neglected philosopher Morris Ginsberg always stoutly argued in the teeth of logical positivism and other skepticisms, most moral argument *is* about facts, and the disagreements are not irrational and emotive, but factual. Anthropology, with its unrivaled source of information on the human condition and its evolution, could be—should be—at the center of moral philosophy.

This view of anthropology as a branch of ethics is not exactly fashionable. And given the training most anthropologists have had, it is hard to see how any of them might have arrived at it. So, embarrassing as intellectual autobiography can be, I must engage in it for a moment to provide the context for the essays that follow. Perhaps I have only just come to realize that my "career" has not really been that of an anthropologist, but of a renegade philosopher who has made various excursions into anthropology and, for all practical purposes, passed successfully as an anthropologist. But being, in this sense, a marginal anthropologist, I am perhaps better able to probe beneath its surface pretensions and delusions.

Why did you become an anthropologist? was once a much more common question than it is today, because there used to be only a few of us and we were regarded as relatively amiable oddballs. Now, alas, this is not so. A young man seeking my advice recently told me that he was unsure whether to, as he put it, "pursue a career" in medicine, law, or anthropology. He wanted to know what the "career opportunities" were in anthropology. I hope my pain was not obvious to him. There was a time when people went into anthropology—and it was highly risky and not very rewarding—in order to escape the world of "career opportunities" and professionalism generally. They went into it to *find things out,* and not because it was an alternative to dentistry and had better prospects for promotion than computer programing. But I shouldn't complain, because I got into anthropology by mistake and against my better judgment.

It all started, I suppose, during what would now be called

my "teens" (in those days we were just "schoolboys"), when I was having a bad fit of religious doubts. Nowadays, teen-agers have sex problems. I don't remember any of my peers in that Yorkshire grammar school (in the 1940's and '50's) having what might be called "sex problems." Or, if we did, we didn't know that that was what they were. Not that we weren't interested in sex, in a surreptitious way, but the culture had somehow managed to persuade us to sublimate so cleverly that repression was not needed. (We wrote a lot of bad poetry.) Nor did we have political problems, although we were all interested in politics and some of us very active. Neither sex nor politics caused us misery. Religion still was a problem, inasmuch as our parents were conventionally re-ligious and we had been brought up in conventional middle-class Anglican homes, in which the truths of the Church of England version of Christianity were not even a recognized subject of discussion. Might as well discuss the truth of the law of gravity. But, for a number of us, the discovery that all was not as neat and tidy in the C. of E. garden as we had thought was truly painful. To repudiate religion would have been so shocking to our parents and our society that it bordered on the unthinkable. Yet, at the same time, we were afflicted with the adolescent virus of integrity and could not accept religion as merely a meaningless set of social forms. Headmasters told us we could just be cynical; that no one in his right mind would confuse the Church of England with religion or even, for that matter, with Christianity. But to no avail. It is hard to convey to young people today, concerned as they are with Vietnam and ecology, just what this was all about, but it was real enough to us. And, of course, we searched for allies, for comfort in literature, for a feeling that we were not alone. We discovered the Rationalist Press Association and Bertrand Russell; Voltaire and anticlerical-ism; Spencer and agnosticism; Huxley and evolutionism;

Bernard Shaw and Shavianism—and above all, for me, Sir James Frazer and *The Golden Bough* (via, in my case, T. S. Eliot and *The Waste Land*). It was a heady time—but rocky. I might never have made it, because I hated school and was not inclined to put myself out anywhere but on the rugby field. Not that I was anti-intellectual (for a long time I cast the school in *that* role); I was simply anti.

World War II came almost on my fifth birthday. My father, an army reservist, was called up immediately, and my mother and I went off to follow him about the country. Stationed as he was with antiaircraft units, he was posted wherever the blitz was worst, except for brief interludes in Somerset and Norfolk. In consequence I rarely ever went to school—I certainly don't remember any schools. They were mostly being used as hospitals, refugee camps, or barracks. School did not open the day after a night raid, and there were raids most nights. I learned from reading books—by gutting the local libraries—and from the BBC, which provided the best education possible and on which I am forever imprinted. When the war ended and I had to face the prospect of school, I was already too far gone. I had spent my time almost wholly in the company of adults and did not know what to do with hordes of children. I could not get used to the idea that I had to learn what I was told to learn and not question it. I became what we now call a "behavior problem"; then I was a troublemaker (the terms change, and the remedies along with them). No one counseled me much. I didn't take any tests, but I did take several beatings. I was always marginal to school. The prospect of escaping to the free atmosphere of the university, where I could pursue my antireligion studies in the company of men dedicated to the search for knowledge, kept me sufficiently in line that I even became a prefect, school captain, and positive pillar of society. Even so, I kicked against doing English or history at

Oxford or Cambridge—the fate reserved for bright boys who could write. I decided instead that I wanted to go to London University, largely because it was in London, and to study economics, largely because of my interest in politics. This included a burgeoning dislike of socialism, partly derived from old-fashioned Tory parents and partly from a dislike of the authoritarianism of the postwar Labour party. (Was it a coincidence that so many Labour party leaders were ex-school-teachers?) To smite religion hip and thigh and thwart the socialist takeover became my two obsessions—about as incongruous a pair of obsessions as the imagination of a confused teen-ager could come up with.

I was not led to the university by conventional middle-class ambitions; my grip on the middle class was more tenuous than that on the school system. Although I had grown up in a middle-class atmosphere (church choir, grammar school, tennis club, rugby team, young conservatives, et cetera) I was middle class only by adoption. My father was a private soldier who had served seven years in India and returned in 1933 to a depression economy that had no room for his services as a signaler. My mother, coming from a successful family of Irish immigrants that included police inspectors, headmasters, and sanitary engineers, was nevertheless the child of the black sheep of the family, who, gassed in World War I, atheistic, anticlerical, argumentative, and determined to buck the conventions, had become a coal miner. My mother learned her middle-class values as a nanny; my father went along. He was a Tory of a kind not uncommon in the north. He admired the aristocracy and the "officer class" generally, as is the way with many old soldiers who were proud of their trade and nostalgic for better times. I suppose technically I was in the working class, but I was never of it. I missed all the initiations, and once at the grammar school I was already most of the way elsewhere. But I was not truly middle class, either. Perhaps I was an Anglo-Irish, socially mobile, dis-affected, marginal man? It is a pleasant thought. I always felt a kinship with Branwell Brontë, who died in disgrace where I was born; indeed, a number of teachers prophesied for me a similar end to his.

At the London School of Economics a new world did open up. But economics wasn't very satisfying. I got the early impression that it did not have the answers to much. I think I was right. And then I found what must have been one of the best degree programs ever invented, but which has never been sung as such: the B.Sc. degree in sociology. This course allowed and encouraged us to try not only sociology, but also philosophy, statistics, demography, psychology, economics, criminology, and, as a special option, social anthropology. I approached Maurice Freedman of the anthropology department (now professor at Oxford), who did his best to deter me. "What have you read that is relevant?" he asked. *"The Golden Bough,"* I replied, "—abridged edition." He was skeptical and told me if I thought *that* sort of thing was what I would be doing I was mistaken. Nevertheless, I transferred to the social anthropology option of the sociology degree. We didn't do much of *The Golden Bough,* it was true. We did a lot about lineage systems and some of the other things that follow in this book, and I was not enchanted. I had been seduced by philosophy: by Karl Popper, Ernest Gellner, Morris Ginsberg, Donald Macrae, and, at University College, by A. J. Ayer. Also I had begun to take existentialism seriously and to see its likeness to logical positivism in the ethical realm: they were both amoralisms. But I did learn two valuable things in my undergraduate career: to understand the properties of the normal curve, and to know a metaphysical statement when I saw one.

Anthropology I did not find difficult, but neither did I find it stimulating. I spent most of my time on Hampstead

Heath and in various furnished rooms in North London reading philosophy and wrestling with statistics. My political ideas changed a little and I caught up with sex problems, but I completely lost interest in the whole religious issue; in the cosmopolitan atmosphere of London it suddenly became a tediously provincial concern. Even so, the study of primitive religion continued to fascinate me more than any other aspect of anthropology. After graduation, in 1957, I was attracted to America for a reason that must strike younger readers as sublimely ironic: I was a draft dodger. Like many of my contemporaries, I was angered by the Tory government's policies in Cyprus and particularly in Egypt. The Suez crisis of 1957 brought us all out on the streets and got me clubbed by the police. I would have refused the draft anyway; but, with the crisis over, the prospect of going into the army, while it did not present any moral problems concerning Egypt and Cyprus, nevertheless seemed a terrible waste of time. I was determined to fake ill health; but, if that failed, I had to have an alternative. As exemptions were granted for higher education, I decided to continue mine at a safe distance. By this time I was convinced that I should be a philosopher. I had been ill in 1956, when I should have graduated, and had to repeat my final year. That year's grace had enabled me to start in on the ambitious thesis I hoped eventually to loose on the world. It was called "The Role of the Behavioral Sciences in the Establishment of a Rational Ethic." I obtained the promise of a teaching assistantship at Cornell, which had the best philosophy department in America at the time. I also had the promise of a place in the Department of Social Relations at Harvard—they were studying "values" there, and I might be able to squeeze my philosophical obsessions in without anyone noticing. At the last moment Cornell reneged, so I went to Harvard, to the Department of Social Relations, hoping for the best.

"Soc. Rel." was a strange business. It was put together under the inspiration of Talcott Parsons and his theory of action, and was, in its way, a pioneering attempt to break down the conventional barriers in the social sciences and produce an integrated science of behavior. But professionalism was killing it. There were four fields (there may still be, for all I know): sociology; social psychology; clinical psychology; social anthropology. Everyone had to do a bit of each plus statistics. But the trouble was that the end product did not fit well into the job market. What was he—a psychologist, an anthropologist? No one was sure. Consequently, those responsible for each field tried to cram their students with extra knowledge so that they could fit into a conventional job in a conventional department somewhere. Those of us who opted for anthropology not only had to master the major fields; we also had to satisfy some minimum requirements in physical anthropology, archaeology, and linguistics—so that we would be employable. Not unpredictably, there was chaos. I was often rushing about: from a session on the interpretation of Rorschach tests to a class in nonparametric statistics to a session on stratigraphy in the Peabody Museum cellar to a lecture on attitudes and prejudice to a rat-running session in the basement of Memorial Hall to a seminar in Middle American ethnology to a class in phonetics to a lecture on Weber, and so on round all the combinations thereof. It was, in its way, exhilarating, except that there was no time to learn anything, and, since I was not sure that I wanted to be a "professional anthropologist" anyway, all rather pointless. There was little to remind me of philosophy except linguistics, to which I took with a measure of enthusiasm that surprised my teachers.

Looking back, I don't regret it. I picked up a good deal of out-of-the-way knowledge and I learned an immense amount from my fellow graduate students. At last one of them suggested to me that since I didn't need a Ph.D. anyway, why didn't I just relax and take a few courses until I found out what I did want? So I decided not to go for the Ph.D.

My teachers were sympathetic and tolerant. They found me a job as a tutor at Leverett House and also as an associate at the Laboratory of Social Development under John Whiting. I argued and wrangled with Whiting for a glorious year, in which I read most of Freud and the psychoanalysts, and a hefty amount of Pavlov, Watson, Hull, Skinner, and the behaviorists in general. If I reject them now it is certainly not out of ignorance, for I was well drilled. However, my teachers wanted me "into the field"—which, they rightly reckoned, would shut me up. So it was arranged, and while I still hankered after philosophy, I could see it was relentlessly slipping away from me. I compromised. I would go into the field, but to do linguistics. I was packed off for the Southwest and the Pueblo of Cochiti, where a gracious anthropologist, Charles Lange, agreed to share his field with me; part of the outcome can be seen in the essays on Cochiti that follow. I did work on the language—I still have notebooks packed with stuff I have not looked at since—and my first publication was in linguistics. But when I returned to Harvard after my second summer in the Southwest, I knew I would either have to go on for the Ph.D. or get out. At that point a job offer came from England. The little University of Exeter in the West Country wanted a sociologist who could teach social anthropology.

I was still a reluctant sociologist—for that is what I was now officially designated. Somewhere, I felt, I would find a place to write my philosophical book. But I found myself teaching in a small department where we had to be Jacks of every trade, and this took up so much time that there was no room for the rational ethic. I played cricket and croquet indifferently badly, became a proud father, and tried to decide where to go from there. Partly to satisfy a craving for some understanding of my Irish roots and partly for pure relief, I started some field work in Donegal on Gaelic-speaking Tory Island; some of the results are laid out here. Language was again the chief attraction, because I was taken with Benjamin Lee Whorf's hypothesis about the relationship between language, thought, and reality. What happened when people spoke two very different languages in the same community? What I would be doing was a kind of philosophy.

As so often happens, things turn up. My old teacher at LSE, Raymond Firth, had followed such anthropology as I had been doing, and offered me a position there in his department. To be back in London, after even such a pleasant provincial exile as Exeter, was tempting.

I had another reason for accepting. One of my first publications had been on the incest taboo. I picked up this interest from Maurice Freedman, who once in a tutorial flung at me in his brusque and incisive way: "Why can't we have a sexual free-for-all within the family and still have marriage out of it?" As usual, he went to the heart of the matter, and I spent many hours wrangling with that one. But, in reading all the literature on incest, I became convinced that something was going on that belonged to the nature of the beast and not to abstract social functions. I began, tentatively, to look at zoological material, to think about imprinting. My first formulations had been heavily behaviorist. When I was at Harvard, it was understood that if one wanted a causal explanation of anything, one had to come up with a reinforcement schedule of some kind. So, for me, incest—or, rather, the reaction to incest—was explained by "negative reinforcement." However, this came to seem less and less plausible. In London, I felt, I would be in contact with a wider range of scientists, including zoologists, who could provide me with a different way of looking at the problem. My colleague there, Burton Benedict, was a Fellow of the Zoological Society—largely out of his nostalgia for the private zoo he had as a child, I think—and he introduced me to those scientists. That was another beginning.

To my horror, I was assigned, as the junior in the department, to teach the subject everyone wished to avoid: kinship—"advanced kinship," it was called. I had never had much interest in the topic, although I had gone through the standard paces of collecting genealogical information in Cochiti and on Tory. Now I had to master it in a hurry. The only way to do this, I found, was to cut through the enormous amount of verbiage to some first principles on which kinship systems seemed to rest. In my attempt to do this, I evolved a way of teaching the subject that students responded to with great enthusiasm, since previously, they said, it had been a jungle of conflicting facts or facile generalizations. Falling back on my philosophical "training," I treated kinship as a problem in deductive logic. There had, then, to be premises. I found four from which kinship systems could be derived: that women have the children; that men impregnate women; that men exert control; and that there is an incest taboo. I spun the lectures out from there to include all known systems—although I now see I was quite wrong about some of these. I was persuaded to make this into a book, which appeared in 1967 as *Kinship and Marriage: An Anthropological Perspective*. Like it or not, and despite my pleasure in the logical side of the problem, I was becoming an anthropologist proper—and, what is more, in its most prestigious, difficult, and esoteric area: kinship theory. In the meantime, under pressure from a desire to go back to the United States, I wrote a Ph.D. thesis. I saw that my Cochiti material conflicted with the accepted account of the Pueblos in the great standard work by Fred Eggan, *Social Organization of the Western Peublos*. I proceeded to do a grand revision of his whole theory, a kind of whodunit in which a careful sifting of the evidence revealed the truth by eliminating the alternatives. Then I reconstructed the crime. The whole thing was decidedly odd by British social anthropological standards because it involved a pseudohistorical reconstruction of the development of a kinship system, and this sort of thing was simply not done in functionalist circles. But there was no one who could very well quarrel with it and it was passed. It came out as a book—in 1967 again—called *The Keresan Bridge: A Problem in Pueblo Ethnology.* The peculiar title, with its suggestion of a purely local problem, the exotic series (the London School of Economics Monographs in Social Anthropology) of which it was a part, and the intractable nature of the material have kept it obscurely on the shelves. But it was weighty and impressive and had a lot of diagrams, and I was again firmly established as an "expert" on kinship.

Meanwhile, back at the Zoo, I had been sitting in on seminars with Desmond Morris and the brilliant group of young ethologists around him. I had begun to delve into physical anthropology more deeply after reading Robert Ardrey's remarkable *African Genesis.* I had forced myself to learn genetics, and read much in ethology and zoology. I became a Fellow of the Zoological Society; started a program of symposia at the Royal Anthropological Institute on ethology and anthropology; was made a member of the curious and exclusive Tetrapods Club, where I tried out my incest ideas for the first time on zoologists, and learned a lot from such people as David Attenborough (now head of BBC Television), John Napier, and W. M. S. Russell. I summed up those ideas in 1967, a busy year, when I was asked to give the Malinowski Memorial Lecture at the LSE. It was really very nice of them to ask me, since I was undoubtedly a maverick and wouldn't stick to my kinship last like a good anthropological cobbler. They even let me teach a lecture series called "Man, Race, and Culture," in which I rambled on about territory and aggression and phylogeny and dominance, and showed a lot of monkey movies.

But, more important, in 1965, at a Zoo meeting, I was introduced to Lionel Tiger, over from Canada. The coincidence of our names was remarkable, but the coincidence of our ideas was even more remarkable. We have worked together ever since, and inasmuch as he is a political sociologist by trade, he is no more obligated to the ideology of anthropology than I am—less so. But he had to go back to Canada, and we found that working together was like playing chess by mail. So when, in 1967 (*annus mirabilis*), Rutgers University asked me to come and start a department of anthropology, I accepted, and asked Tiger to join me there.

After eight years in England of groping through various aspects of anthropology, after four years of the eight in London trying to learn from the natural sciences something about the basic nature of man, and now, after five years of setting up a department at Rutgers (with one year off at Stanford Medical School) and writing a controversial book with Tiger, *The Imperial Animal,* I am back to where I was when I set off for Harvard clutching my unfinished thesis and hoping that I could smuggle it past the stern customs men who guard the way into professional anthropology.

I don't think they were wasted years and I am glad I was diverted. The most I could have done in those days was to assert that a rational ethic would be possible if we had a theory of human nature. I know now that we can have one; that we are on the way to one; that it will lead us to revise our values; that it will form the basis for rational social criticism. And if anthropology doesn't want to be on the side of history, then that is its loss. I am, perhaps, a philosophical anthropologist.

Philosophical anthropology will not extract man from

nature, but understand his place in nature. It will go back to Huxley and Darwin for its orientation, and to Montesquieu and Marx for its breadth of concern. It will deal with the moral and political consequences of its findings in a way that will satisfy Ernest Becker's longing for what he calls "the lost science of man": the science of social concern, a moral science. This is relevance on the truly human scale, and not the petty involvement with transient fads that most proponents of "relevant anthropology" are promoting. It will pursue the Rational Ethic, the basis for a critical appraisal of the social order, itself based on a knowledge of the nature of human society as a natural product of natural selection. And to do this it will need all the data and all the analyses that have been poured out from the traditional anthropology departments—and a lot more besides. So no one need tremble for his job. There can never be too much knowledge— even if we have to discard great sheaves of it as useless, some will be pure gold.

Perhaps above all, philosophical anthropology must engage in the study of the evolutionary basis of illusion. Human cultures rest securely on the species' repertoire of social behavior—our behavioral genetic patrimony. But whereas this repertoire provides the invariant form for these cultures, the content or style of the culture can vary enormously and subtly. This follows from the human capacity for illusion. Cultures are massive con jobs, and the variations are as unlimited as the imagination of man itself. But even this has its limits. There are distinct patterns to the delusional systems that characterize most of religion and politics. There are characteristic swings between extremes: between the doctrine of divine rulers and the doctrine of divine democracy, for example, with some polities, like the American, wavering between the two in a positively weird fashion. Extremes of polytheism and monotheism, of worldly and otherworldly orientations, of the idea of the world as good and the idea of the world as evil—all have a pattern and, in fact, work within limits, just as social arrangements, seemingly as multifarious as those in kinship systems, all work within limits. Rather than stressing ideology, illusion, symbolism, et cetera as examples of what *removes* man from the natural world, anthropologists must begin to understand these illusory patterns as themselves *products* of natural selection. Man is prone to some delusions and not to others. There is no necessity to his ideological obsessions any more than to the fundamental patterns of his linguistic ability. They just are that way; they could have been different. And they are that way for the same reason that his anklebone is that way, or that his kinship systems are that way: they are the end product of behavioral evolution. Imagination and mind evolved as surely as the anklebone, and we must understand them as evolutionary products. In 1920, Carveth Read began to explore the role of illusion in the life of the evolving hunting primate—his *Lycopithecus*—and Freud took it further in *The Future of an Illusion*. Anthropologists must return to these explorations and create a very different anthropology of religion from what exists today. And this must have at its center what that older and wiser study of religion—theology—had at its: the question of evil. This is not a question that can be ducked by blaming "circumstances," because men create the circumstances that create the evil. They create evil with ease and with pleasure, they splash about in it and glorify it. It is as human as motherhood or courage and as "real" as lineage systems. But anthropologists react to it as Buddha reacted to his first signs of death, disease, and old age after a childhood deliberately sheltered from any knowledge of them. Part of the delusional system is anthropology itself, as Vonnegut saw so clearly. And this is tragic. There must be a new science of the human capacity for illusion.

To this end, philosophical anthropology will join structural anthropology of the French style, since what Lévi-Strauss and his followers are doing is searching for those innate bases in the human mind that structure our perception of the social world and transmit it in myth. Philosophical anthropology will happily embrace the work of the generative grammarians since Chomsky and his people are searching for the innate properties of mind that enable us to handle grammar and so make possible our most human achievement, articulate speech. It will be a different anthropology in its outcome: it will be avowedly a branch of ethics. But internally it need not change much; specialization is too much with us and there are not many willing to take the risks. All that is needed is the chance—and that a few adventurers come along. Lévi-Strauss once said that he had a neolithic mentality: he went into an area, devastated it, then moved on. Some of us perhaps have a predatory mentality—which fits our theories, anyway. We sit on the borders and raid and plunder where we see the most likely intellectual pickings. Then we make our camp out of the best of everyone else's. In this happy intellectual jungle, however, no one loses anything and all may eventually gain.

Ultimately, there should be an anthropolgy that is simply a division of evolutionary biology, itself a branch of ethics. But this scheme for the reintegration of the sciences of life, behavior, and morals is perhaps a piece of romantic utopianism, a cry for a return to nature as pathetic yet as appealing as the cry of the romantic movement itself. But nature was as important to the eighteenth-century Enlightenment as to the romantics, and even more important to the nineteenth-century evolutionists. Somewhere along the line in the twentieth century we have lost both our emotional and intellectual ties to nature, and with these we have lost our humility and even our chance of survival. Evolution and ethics have to come together again if man is to survive. Perhaps anthropology can still make the marriage—if there is time.

These essays illustrate some of the raw material from anthropology proper—both in data and in theory—that will be drawn upon. They do not by any means cover the whole of anthropology, not even the total range of my own interests. They represent some of my excursions into anthropology and some of the plunder I came back with. Some were light-hearted excursions, others more serious; some were deliberately professional, others deliberately journalistic; some have been previously published, others not. The final essay is a plea, as this introduction is, to begin a search for a center to anthropology; it also provides a few ideas about where to look. To do this will be to follow those who have had a vision of a science of man that would truly be a science of all mankind, past and present, civilized and savage, hominid and protohominid; a vision, that is of course Darwin's, of a science of life that will put man back into nature without robbing him of his dignity. Unlike B. F. Skinner, most anthropologists have not wanted to go *beyond* freedom and dignity but to *achieve* freedom and dignity. And much as I may dislike their methods, I am with them in spirit. It may be a cliché, but anthropologists can say without embarrassment that they are on the side of man. The outlook is not hopeful, and, God knows, he needs all the friends he can get.

Evolution and Race

THE FIRST ESSAY, "The Evolution of Sexual Behavior," takes up one of the themes of the introduction. It is a rendering of the Malinowski lecture I gave at the London School of Economics, and tries to utilize knowledge of human evolution and human sexual behavior by asking how this behavior must have evolved. The answers are speculative; like any serious theorist, I am constantly adjusting the system to meet the demands of new information. Not that I want to hide behind the awful formula found so often in the psychology journals: "My data compel me to conclude that . . ." As though data exercised some coercive force on the poor resisting scientist. More times than not, this should read: "I have compelled my

41

data to conclude that . . ." Intuition is important; somehow you just know that you are on the right track and you stay with it. To switch theories in panic fashion at every new bit of seemingly conflicting evidence is as foolish as to stick rigidly to a theory even when it is totally contradicted. Raymond Dart knew he was right about the hominid status of *Australopithecus,* even though the weight of scientific opinion (yea, even of Lord Zuckerman) was against him for over twenty years. And he *was* right. I have frequently been assailed because the data originally presented on chimpanzees by Dr. van Lawick-Goodall seemed to be in conflict with the baboon data I have relied heavily on here. But it transpires from the later work of Dr. Goodall and her students and co-workers, and from the work of the Japanese primatologists in Africa, that the chimpanzees are not all that unlike the baboons after all, particularly when they get out into the woodland savanna—the baboons' natural habitat. In fact, contrary to the position I have taken, it seems that the chimps may well have once inhabited the woodland savanna as extensively as the baboons do now. They may have spent a large part of their evolution there. For some reason, instead of just staying in the forest, they left it and then retreated to it again.

The second essay, "The Abolition of Race," deals with an explosive topic and has caused me considerable trouble. Apart from the odd feminist attack on the "male chauvinism" of the first essay—as if I had created the world and all that therein is—I have had relatively little nonsense from fanatics. But the race piece produced fury, obscenity, and even actual threats—and from both sides. Since I argue in favor of racial interbreeding, I was assailed by both the right-wing racial purists and the black-power advocates. Clearly you can't have black power if everyone is light brown, so that makes sense. But since this is one of the few pieces of mine that have found favor with the East Coast liberal intelligentsia, I include it out of nostalgia for the days when I was counted one of their number—before my "biologism" put me firmly into the ranks of the damned. It was also pre-Jensen, but the point stands. Arthur Jensen told us nothing new; he merely reminded us of things that had been neglected (twin studies, for example). But when it comes to race and intelligence, he is confused; and while I deplore the outrageous persecution he has suffered at the hands of liberals and radicals alike, I still contest his conclusions.

The whole race question is really a pseudo issue. Human variation operates within fairly strict boundaries, and people everywhere are basically the same in their behavior. One does not have to believe in infinite human plasticity and unlimited cultural diversity to combat racism. One has only to believe—as I do, on good Darwinian grounds—that man is *one* species and that speciation can be demonstrated *not* to have taken place within this unified species. Even when "racial" differences are taken into account, it is estimated that every human shares at least 97 per cent of his physical traits with every other human. At the level of behavior, the same is true, despite cultural differences. What people *do* is much the same, whatever their style of doing it. If you are interested in behavioral evolution the way I am, racial differences become meaningless: the species is the unit.

These two essays represent my attempts to link physical anthropology with ideas on the evolution of behavior. They illustrate a way of thinking that began for me in the mid 1960's, and that has been elaborated at some length by Tiger and me in *The Imperial Animal*. But they also illustrate the range of concerns that are open to an anthropologist if he goes into the subject through the "physical" door. Having gone through that door, I have taken a few turnings that would probably never have been taken by those who want to stay in the main corridor marked "Physical Anthropologists Only." I may not have reached the end of any passage, but I hope that I have at least kept all the doors open.

ONE

The Evolution of Sexual Behavior

HUMAN SEXUAL BEHAVIOR is as much the end product of evolution as human sexual anatomy. But while the idea that the body has evolved has become familiar, we are only beginning to understand the implications of extending to behavior the same kind of analysis that has proved successful with flesh and bone. Indeed, it must seem at first glance that this is an impossible task. The evolution of human anatomy can be studied from the various fossil forms that have been discovered, and the gradual transition from ape man to true man can be discerned with some accuracy. But there is only the sketchiest idea of what these creatures were *doing*, so is it possible to ask about the evolution of their behavior?

Nevertheless, it is known that there must have been such

an evolution. In the same way as there was a gradual transition from apelike to manlike form there must have been a similar gradual transition from apelike to manlike function. Man's body testifies to the first change—as any simple comparison of man with other primates will show. To what extent does his behavior testify to the second?

At least one school of zoologists would claim that the study of the evolution of behavior can be more instructive than that of the evolution of anatomy. The science of ethology —defined by one of its practitioners as the "biological study of behavior"—which has flourished under the leadership of such men as Konrad Lorenz in Germany and Niko Tinbergen in Britain, is one of the youngest branches of zoology. Its stance is neo-Darwinian, and in essence it points up the fact that natural selection operates on the performance of the animal. Structure therefore evolves in order that the creature may function in ways that give it selective advantage in the struggle for survival.

In the case of certain gross motor activities this may seem obvious: speed enables animals to chase and to flee, et cetera. But the ethologists have concentrated mainly on the *signaling* abilities of animals, showing how these social signs serve to enhance threat behavior, inhibit aggression, attract mates and so on. The point about these signals—whether they be structural, such as bright coloring, or purely behavioral, such as specific postures—is that they evolved by the process of natural selection and hence have become part of the genetic repertoire of the animal.

When a black-headed gull is defending its nesting site during the breeding season the presence of any other animal is clearly threatening to it. Male and female black-headed gulls look pretty much alike; so even when a prospective mate lands on the site, the male's aggressive instinct of territorial defense is aroused. However, if the female does not stare at the male but turns her head aside, then the male's aggression is inhibited and the preliminaries of mating become possible.

This looking-away gesture of the gull is only one of many in its total ethogram of postures and gestures, which are as much a part of its genetic endowment as feathers and wings —and just as necessary to its survival and success. The ethologists have found that by careful comparison of closely related species, they can arrive at answers to the question, Why does this particular species behave in this particular way?

Ethologists have, until very recently, confined their attention to lowlier forms of life, such as birds, fish, and small mammals. In these the genetically based behaviors are easy to ascertain. But what of the more complex, higher mammals —and what of man?

Some very careful studies of man's primate cousins over the past decade have produced much-needed comparative material from closely related species. But these species prove to be much more complex than the little creatures familiar to ethology. It is not that they are without genetically programed predispositions, but that their range of behavior is extended by programing to take more advantage of their learning ability than is the case with lower forms.

At the pinnacle of this development stands man, with the greatest learning capacity of all animals. His behavior has evolved, it is true, but this evolution has been toward greater flexibility. To put it paradoxically: man's greatest instinct is the instinct to learn. It is therefore natural to man to be unnatural—to go beyond nature and supplement the genetically endowed predispositions of behavior with cultural forms not built into the chromosomes.

This has been regarded by some observers as the ultimate stumbling block to our understanding of human behavior on ethological lines. And it is true that if the methods of the ethologists are rigidly stuck to, only a limited amount will be learned about man. Nevertheless, things are not so black. What the flexible learning ability of man allows him to do is extend the range of his behavior, but only within well-defined limits. His genetic behavioral inheritance lays down for him a limited number of things to do, but he can vary enormously the ways in which he does them.

For example, as with many other animals, man prefaces the formation of a stable mating arrangement with some form of courting activity. The form of this activity, however, can be extremely varied, and consists of a great many postures, gestures, and sounds that are traditional rather than genetic. The black-headed gull can look away and do a few other things, but it cannot write sonnets, dance the frug, or wear an engagement ring. The difference can perhaps be expressed in a metaphor: animal behavior is like filling in a form; in some animals there are a lot of instructions on the form but only a limited space for answers, while in other animals there is the same number of instructions but the space for answers is large and the range of possible answers is wide. It is not that animals have instincts while man does not, but that man can do more things about his instincts than other animals.

What kinds of evidence exist for looking at the basic sexual behavior of man as the end product of a long process of natural selection? There is the fossil record; the social behavior of related species; the social behavior of the creature itself. With a judicious survey of the evidence from these three sources, it should be possible to reconstruct the evolution of human sexual behavior. (I am confining this analysis to heterosexual behavior.)

It may seem absurd, but perhaps the greatest gap is in the information on the natural sexual behavior of man. A great deal of the knowledge here is inferential; very little is known about sex, despite man's seeming obsession with it. But at a fairly gross level there is enough known to start with, even if the knowledge is not of the detailed kind that the ethologist would need. What, then, are some of the main characteristics of human sexual behavior?

There is the striking fact of the absence of an oestrous cycle in the female: she does not go into heat. This fact is usually phrased as "permanent sexual receptivity" in the human female—which may seem a little extreme and over-optimistic. Such evidence as there is on female receptivity indicates that it is at its height just before and just after menstruation. This is curious in that the peak in other primates comes halfway between menstrual periods—that is, during ovulation. In other words, most nonhuman primate females are most receptive at the time when they are most likely to conceive, while the human primate female is most receptive when she is least likely to conceive. There may be the evolution of some kind of birth-control device lurking here, but it is difficult to see this as being very efficacious unless the female determines the timing of intercourse according to her own physiological state of readiness—an interesting but unlikely theory.

The lack of heat goes along with the lack of a breeding season. This is not peculiar to man, but it does put him into the category of primates that have continual sexual activity. True, there are birth peaks in most societies, which shows that breeding is to some extent seasonal (in Christian countries the peak comes nine months after Christmas, as a rule), but there is no rutting season as such in man. This year-round activity is probably also connected with another feature—namely, the high level of sexual activity and the drive for novelty and variety in sexual experience. Compared, say, with the gorilla, man exhibits a level of sexual activity that is quite phenomenal.

49

Insofar as the end product of sexual activity is offspring—and in man this is not always the case—the "breeding pair" is the most typical unit for this purpose. Like many fish, birds, and mammals that establish "pair bonds," man does not just mate promiscuously and then leave the female to rear the young. Rather he tends to associate regular sexual activity and at least some degree of emotional attachment with the rearing of offspring.

One way of looking at this—favored, for example, by Desmond Morris—is to see the "pair bonding" phenomenon among animals duplicated in man by the process of "falling in love"—a behavioral mechanism for keeping the pair together. Other observers (including this one) see more of a contractual element in the male-female relationship when it comes to the business of forming a family and rearing children. Love and marriage may go together like a horse and carriage, but let us not forget that the horse has to be broken and harnessed.

Strong bonds between mated pairs are certainly common enough in *Homo sapiens,* but this is by no means the whole story. These bonds are not necessarily the result of a primitive pair-bonding instinct and, indeed, seem extremely variable in intensity. They are primarily an adolescent phenomenon and obviously have to do with giving impetus to the breeding process. But once this is under way the relationship becomes complex indeed, and the bond between the pair is as much an outcome of their role as parents as of their role as lovers. The "tenacity of the pair bond," which Morris seems so anxious to establish, is as much a tenacity of the parental bond as anything else. There are obviously good evolutionary reasons for this. But the bond is not exclusive; there is no reason why it should be; and there are many reasons why it could not have been.

The starting point for the analysis of the biological evolution of any human social behavior is obvious: the brain. Apart perhaps from the precision grip of the hand and the bones and muscles devoted to the striding walk, this is man's only major biological specialization.

The question that must then be asked is the familiar one of chicken or egg. Did the growth of the brain lead to the capacity for greater social complexity, or vice versa? I think the answer is undoubtedly that, as certain kinds of animals developed complex social system as weapons in the struggle for survival, there was pressure in the direction of selecting out those animals with the best brains. These were the animals better able to cope with the complexities of life in a social group. But in our particular family of animals, the primates, what kind of social system was involved?

Here another of our three kinds of evidence must be introduced: the social behavior of primates. This is, as might be expected, enormously varied. But certain constant features stand out in those primates that, like man, have an organized social system, and particularly in those that, again like man, have spent a considerable portion of their evolution outside the forest environment in which the earliest primates were nurtured. Typical examples are the baboons and macaques.

A baboon group usually comprises about forty animals that wander about in search of food, always keeping together. This cohesion is of enormous advantage to animals like these, living as they do in open savanna and subject to attacks from predators. A single baboon is not much of a match for the big cats, but a group of baboons stands a pretty good chance of beating off attacks with concerted action.

The social system, however, is anything but democratic. Power in the group lies with the biggest and most successful of the males. These (never more than about six in number, however large the total group) stay at the center with the females and young. Around this central core will wander a number of "cadets"—young males who are candidates for membership in the hierarchy. At the edge of the horde are the "peripheral males"—unsuccessful and immature animals who have not yet made it. Many never will. Some even wander off and become solitaries—the drop-outs of the monkey rat race. These peripheral males act as first line of defense and a kind of living radar for the group. The big males of the hierarchy are the ultimate deterrent; they also keep order within the group, and are especially solicitous of the welfare of the young.

This is a very sketchy account of a "typical" society of ground-dwelling primates. What are its dynamics? How do young males get into the hierarchy and what is the significance of this? The significance is overwhelming in terms of the evolution of the group because *it is only the males of the hierarchy that do the breeding.* While the cadets and peripheral males may get a chance to copulate with a female during her infertile periods, only the hierarchical males mate with the females at the peak of oestrus—that is, during ovulation. Therefore, only these males are going to pass on genes to the next generation. It is of tremendous significance, then, to know what characterizes these successful males.

Before answering this question it must be noted that there is another form of terrestrial primate society that has to be reckoned with: the form represented by baboons living on dry desert savanna, as opposed to those living in woodland savanna. The desert horde is not divided into the components just described, but rather into a series of polygamous families in each of which one male collects a number of females (usually four) and monopolizes these the whole time. Here also, however, there are the unsuccessful males at the edge waiting to get in. How do they do it, and who succeeds?

Not to put too fine a point on it, it is the smart ones who make it. But what constitutes smartness? Basically, it is the ability to control and time responses—to understand the consequences of one's actions. The British ethologist Michael Chance has described the process as "equilibration"; thus, an animal caught between the desire to copulate with an oestrous female, on the one hand, and the desire to escape attack from a dominant male, on the other, must be able to inhibit his sexual response and bide his time. If he fails to do so often enough, he will, at worst, be either killed or driven out, or, at best, fail to ingratiate himself with his superiors and thus will not be tolerated by them. The stupid animal, then, one that blunders about, following without foresight the dictates of his lustful and aggressive appetites, will never make it to the top. The cunning animal, on the other hand, that can forgo present indulgence in anticipation of future reward, will be more likely to get there.

Of course, he has to have other qualities. He must be sociable and able to co-operate, or the big males will not accept him. He must also be acceptable to the females, it seems; hence his capacities as a baby minder (and the rank of his mother) are important. Besides possessing these charming attributes, he must also be tough and aggressive in order to assert his rights as a hierarchy member. It is easy to see the evolutionary advantages of such a process. It is a breeding system that puts at a premium those qualities in the male most advantageous to the survival of the group.

If this kind of social system was, in fact, typical of man's ancestors, then it provides some powerful clues concerning the evolution of the brain. Clearly, it was those animals with the best brains who were going to do the breeding, and each generation would see a ruthless selection of the best-brained males, with the dumbest and weakest going to the wall. And it was the *controlling* aspects of the brain that were being so strongly selected. The more the emotions of aggression and lust came under cortical control, the better chance the animal had of surviving and passing on his genes to the next generation.

But the expanding brain had to cope with other things besides sex and aggression. Predominant among these were the use of tools and the development of language. Large areas of the cerebellum are concerned with the control of the hand, and growth of this center must have been a response to the demands of toolmaking. Control over the emotions was one thing; control of the environment through tools and weapons was, however, equally important. Selection favored the controlled and *skillful* animal. It also favored the animal that could *communicate* best. Up to a point, a series of non-linguistic signals will do; but after a certain point of social complexity is reached, co-operation is impossible without a more flexible code. Large areas of the brain, then, are devoted to speech.

Many commentators have stressed these two aspects of brain evolution, but few have taken the breeding problem seriously. Yet without this component the major puzzle in brain evolution remains unanswered: How did the hominid brain manage to evolve so quickly? About a million years ago, the brain of one of the earliest recognizable hominids (the family that includes man and his extinct relatives and ancestors) was little larger than that of the chimpanzee. Within that million years it trebled in size—an almost unprecedented rate of evolution.

Now, whatever the pressures in favor of a larger, "thinking" brain exerted by the demands for better technicians and speakers, the question still remains: By what kind of breeding system were these newly acquired traits so quickly developed? Given that the prespeech and pretools system had, built into it, the breeding mechanisms we have described, we only have to add that the successful breeders needed to be eloquent and skillful, as well as controlled. The system would then ensure that these were the males who passed on the essential genes, and the rapid (in evolutionary terms) development of the large forebrain would be a certainty.

This suggests that throughout the evolution of the hominid lines that eventually led to *Homo sapiens,* the social system was one in which the majority of the breeding was done by a minority of the males, with the least successful males being largely shut out of the breeding system—in other words, a system based on the polygyny of the powerful. And note that this polygyny has not to do primarily with sexual appetite. It has to do with dominance and the relation of males to males. The survival value of the system is obvious.

And now comes the most controversial and difficult of the three kinds of evidence: the fossil record. It is possible to know that the model of the society of the ground-dwelling primates is applicable to human evolution only if it can be shown that the model plausibly fits the earliest of man's ancestors. It has been established that the hominid line evolved from monkeylike forms that moved from forest to savanna, and hence must have been in some ways like contemporary savanna-dwelling primates. Those earlier hominids of a million years ago on the East African savanna were elementary hunters, and this trait increased in complexity and importance as time went by. Hence, to the qualities that went into being a dominant male must be added skill in hunting. Indeed, it may have been the pressures of the chase that accelerated the demand for more advanced tools and speech.

Some writers have seized upon the fact that man's earliest manlike ancestors were hunters, in order to "prove" many things about the changes from the apelike to the human in sexual behavior. But it must be remembered that the changes did not occur overnight, and that there was much in the old vegetarian ape that was useful to his omnivorous successor.

Some things certainly changed. The female presumably came to be less and less under the control of the oestrous cycle, and the "permanent sexual receptivity" phenomenon emerged.

It has been suggested that this happened as a result of the pressures exerted by the need for co-operative hunting. Hunters need a fixed home base. The females stay in this base with the young; the males return and provision them— a practice unheard of among vegetarian primates, but common, for example, among hunting carnivores, such as wolves. It has been argued that with such a system the old primate dominance hierarchy could not operate, since this depended on females coming in and out of heat and being monopolized by the top males during ovulation; if the males had to be away a good deal of the time, this would not work.

What is more, if the male needed a female to work for him—cooking, skinning, gathering vegetable food, et cetera —he would want her "attached" for more of the time than just when she was feeling sexy. Similarly, she would want the constant attention of the male for provisioning herself and her young. If she were constantly available for sexual intercourse, this would be more likely to happen. The high level of sexuality would make the relationship more rewarding to the partners and hence keep them bonded. Thus many features of human sexuality would emerge as responses to the demands of the hunting situation.

This is fine until it is pushed one step further, as it usually is, and the evolving hominid is credited with instinctive tendencies to form monogamous nuclear families. I never cease to be amazed by the ingenuity of speculative writers in their efforts to prove that deep in man's nature is a *Saturday Evening Post* family: Dad, Mom, and the kids. Their assertiveness on this point has often a rather frantic air to it, and what they never do is ask what the consequences would have been if our earliest protohuman ancestors had allowed fair shares for all in the mating game. It seems unimaginative, to say the least, to pin these enterprising creatures down to dreary monogamy.

The point here is that none of the features of human sexuality that have developed are incompatible with a breeding system based on the relative dominance of a few males. If a male can attach one female to him for the reasons advanced, he can attach several just as easily, provided he can maintain his harem against all comers. Insofar as only a minor part of the food intake of hunters is protein and something approaching 80 per cent is vegetable, then a small army of root diggers and berry pickers may well have been an advantage to a male.

It can never be known exactly what kind of mating institutions characterized the transitional ape man. But it is possible to ask: In order for the critical developments in the evolution of the brain to take place so quickly, what kind of breeding system must have been in operation? The answer is: one that would rapidly select out the animals with the better brains and pass on their genes to the next generation. And, concomitantly, one that would push to the peripheries of the breeding system animals lacking the qualities of intelligence and control. Some kind of hierarchical system with differential access to females would solve this problem, and seems to me to be the only candidate. If every male had been allowed the chance to contribute equally to the gene pool— as would be the case in a monogamous system—man might never have made the *sapiens* bit and been forever stuck as *Homo stupidus:* promising, with his speechlike grunts and crude tools, but not really in the top league.

I have considered only the male contribution to brain development here because it is the most obvious. But, lest I be accused of prejudice, we should look at the female's role.

Was she simply a passive mechanism for passing on the genes of the big-brained, dominant males?

It could well be, but there is a chance that she actively helped the process along. I have mentioned that the rank of a male's mother may affect his chances of getting into the hierarchy. The son of a high-ranking female can be kept near the center of the group by his mother, where the big males will learn to tolerate him—a help when he comes to make his bid for membership. If this is a crucial criterion for membership in the hierarchy—and we are not sure that it is—then the qualities that go into being a high-ranking female, insofar as they involve cortical control of sex, may well contribute to the development we have envisaged.

They may also help to account for the gradual loss of hormonal influence over sexual receptivity in the female that led to the loss of the oestrous cycle. The female was no longer subject to periodic sexual mania during which she solicited any male in sight; she had gradually come to control her own responses in the same way as the male. It may well be, in fact, that this permanent sexual receptivity in the female was a by-product of the general processes mentioned earlier, rather than a result of the pressures introduced by hunting. To answer this question more thoroughly it would be necessary to know what qualities went into being a dominant female. All that can be said is that they were not necessarily the same qualities that went into being a dominant male.

But it is not desirable to take only one primate system as the model. Those polygamous primates that live on the arid savannas form "harems," in which several females are permanently attached to a male who monopolizes them throughout the year, despite oestrus and seasonal breeding. Some observers have claimed that the hominids passed through a similar stage of development, since, during the forging time of their existence—the Pliocene—there was extreme drought, and they must have adapted to these dry conditions in much the same way as contemporary desert-dwelling baboons. Of course, the creatures discussed here were not baboons but ape men; still, the baboons do rather knock on the head the idea that there could not have been stable family groups within the protohominid band as long as the females were subject to periodic sex mania and breeding was seasonal. There is no doubt, however, that permanent mating of a human kind is facilitated by the fact that the human female, in a sense, comes into heat at puberty and stays there—at a moderate level of sexual excitement—for most of her life.

There are several forms of breeding hierarchy possible, given an animal that lacks the oestrous cycle, and we cannot know which of these prevailed. Indeed, various groups of evolving hominids may have tried them all. Some may even have tried monogamy. What matters is not the actual institutional form, but the differential access to the females.

The fact that permanently receptive females were more or less permanently attached to dominant males would simply make life harder for the young males who wanted to get into the hierarchy, and would increase the demands for better equilibration—for greater control and inhibition. It would be unlikely under these conditions that some males would be absolutely barred from breeding (although it could well happen), but some would be *less likely* than others to contribute significantly to the genetic endowment of the group.

The criteria of dominance would, of course, differ as the creature became progressively more "human," but they would be basically much the same as among the primates. Hence the successful male would have to be controlled, cunning, co-operative, attractive to the ladies, good with the children, relaxed, tough, eloquent, skillful, knowledgeable, and proficient in self-defense and hunting. Depending on the nature of the group, some of these qualities might have been emphasized more than others.

With the advent of agriculture and the frighteningly rapid growth of population densities over the past ten thousand years, things have changed. But the animal coping with these changed conditions is the end product of hundreds of thousands of years of intensive selection in which, if this hypothesis is correct, differential access to mates was of crucial importance. And this *must* have left its mark on our behavior.

A brief look at the incest taboo will complete the roster of current sexual facts and their evolution. Many observers have put the taboo on incest at the heart of human social development. Animals are incestuous; man is not. This, then, is the great breakthrough. Many reasons have been given for this, and all assume that the taboo is *imposed*. But it is highly probable that it is, in fact, a natural development.

As far as we can tell from nonhuman evidence, there is, for example, little incest between mother and son. The mother is to her son a dominant animal, and mating requires that the female partner be subdominant. If a young male manages to get into the hierarchy, he may or may not mate with his sisters. On the other hand, the possibility of fathers mating with daughters is quite high. The frequency of occurrence of incest in human society is exactly parallel. This fits our picture of sexual relations evolving in a dominance framework.

It follows that with the stabilization of mating relationships, equilibration would have been more in demand. Particularly in the case of the growing "boy," it would have been important to control any sexual approaches toward mothers and sisters who were under the control of a dominant male or males; he also would have had to inhibit aggressive advances toward the latter. Hence neural mechanisms evolved to this end.

The young hominid met his first and most intensive trial of controls in the immediate family circle, but he was learning them as they applied to *all* dominant males and their females. Freud, although perhaps right about some of the evolutionary processes that led to incest taboos, was wrong about locating them exclusively in the nuclear family. The Oedipus complex has to do with the relationship of young subordinate males to older dominant males—not just sons to fathers.

The sum total of all these processes was a creature capable of control and of guilt—the mechanism that lets the individual know it has broken the rules. As the controlling elements of the brain came to dominate the appetitive elements, the evolving hominid could depend less on instinct as a guide to action. D. H. Lawrence, it seems, was wrong: sex really is in the head.

If differential access to mates is the secret of it all, how does this help us to understand our own behavior? It has been argued that man is tenaciously monogamous; but this monogamy, if we are honest, is more apparent than real. It is very rare for men of power, wealth, and influence to confine their sexual activities to one woman. Although the majority of males in a population are confined to one woman at a time, those in a position to accumulate more seem to do so. These may be straight wives, as in overtly polygamous societies, or they may go under other names. A "big man" is one who has access to many females, or is credited with such access, or who controls a large number. They may not be mates, but we know that only a high-prestige man can run even a chaste harem. How far up the pecking order is a man with one wife, two full-time secretaries, twenty typists, and the girl who comes in to do his manicuring? I can think of professors with a modest haul of, say, one wife, one secretary, one research assistant, two teaching assistants, several members of a research team, and four part-time typists. The gathering unto males of females as a sign of status must surely emanate from deep down there in the cunning brain.

Another factor that must be an end product of the processes discussed is the difference between male and female sexual behavior in *Homo sapiens*. Because the equilibration process was predominantly directed toward the male, we might expect that he is more readily conditionable in matters of sex than the female—that most males are more easily made to feel guilty about sexual matters.

Men are caught between their inherited tendencies to promiscuity and dominance, and the necessities of regularized mating; women, between the same promiscuous tendencies and the pulls toward security for self and offspring that can usually be obtained only by at least a show of fidelity. This is another product of the dominance process wherein the status of the male is measured by his control over females.

If this control is challenged, then the "owner's" self-esteem suffers. It is noticeable that it is usually women who are *punished* for unfaithfulness. Thus the other curiosity of male behavior—sexual jealousy—is part and parcel of the scheme.

In any event, the doctrine that male and female differences in sexual behavior are simply the result of the learning of different sex roles needs careful examination in the light of the evolutionary evidence. Also, the notion that male-female relationships can be totally explained by pair-bonding tendencies that never quite evolved properly (Desmond Morris again) should be treated skeptically.

The point here is that human sexual behavior is the product of enormously complex evolutionary processes. It is no good taking fragments of this behavior and trying to explain them by *ad hoc* hypotheses, however entertaining. The only theory worth aiming at is one that will account for *all* the basic emotions—dominance, love, guilt, tenderness, parental affection, jealousy, security, lust, fidelity, novelty, and many others. Such a theory must take account of the difficult evolutionary problems that we have raised.

There are obviously many confused issues here. I have been able to outline only a fraction of the complexities, have glossed over many extremely complicated issues, and missed others completely. So, if nothing else, perhaps I have put the interested reader on guard against those who seek to exploit the obvious interest of this topic by offering intellectual short cuts to solutions. As I have said, some things we can never know, and it is dishonest to pretend that answers are possible; but other things can be settled with a fair degree of approximation to the truth—given time, patience, and hard work.

The Abolition of Race

WHAT IS THERE left to say about race? The anthropologist certainly feels weary at the prospect of repeating over and over again the known truths that should have been assimilated generally years ago. But it seems that the old truths must be constantly restated; there are still too many Bourbons in the world who have learned nothing and forgotten nothing. Prejudice is tenacious and thrives on ignorance. It was once beautifully defined as "being down on what you are not up on." Hence there is no substitute for persistent repetition of the clichés.

And here I am talking of prejudice, not simply dislike. People are at liberty to dislike and avoid any identifiable social group whose culture offends them. They are not at liberty to attribute the offending characteristics to genetic "inferiority," in contrast to their own "racial purity." It is at this point that the anthropologist must step in and say, at least, "not proven" and, certainly, "not probable." People may hold what opinions of their fellows they wish, but no one should take liberties with the facts.

There are, however, many unsolved and perplexing questions about the genetic diversity of human populations, and the only honest attitude toward many of these questions is open-mindedness. But to some liberals it is heresy to suggest that there is *any* genetic diversity of a significant kind within the human species. They regard it as tantamount to fascism even to raise the issue. One can appreciate their concern: once one admits diversity, it is all too easy to start *ranking* the diverse features, and since it is usually the Caucasoid imperialists who are doing the ranking, it is not surprising they come out on top. Therefore, the argument goes, breath should not be expended on the question, because this may fan the flames.

But I am afraid this is not an argument in favor of ignoring diversity. The diversity must be examined and gloried in. It must be pointed out that genetic diversity is an evolutionary asset to a species and should be capitalized on. It should also be emphasized that any kind of ranking of attributes is not "given" in nature, but depends on the values of the rankers. Even if it should be proved that the New York Chinese have, on average, bigger brains than the New York whites (which they undoubtedly have), I would not accept this as an argument for handing over the city government automatically to the Chinese.

I often make the following point to people who insist that blacks should stay underprivileged because their intelligence is genetically inferior to that of whites: suppose it were proved beyond doubt that the opposite were true, that black intelligence was inherently higher than white. Should whites then immediately hand over all their wealth, power, housing, et cetera, to the blacks, and move their own families into the ghettos? If I can get my opponents, purely for the sake of argument, to admit the premise—which is curiously difficult —they usually conclude that the answer is no. It would not be fair or just to effect such a reversal. It is even harder to get them to see the inevitable conclusion; namely, that the present situation is just as unfair and has nothing to do with "inherent" intelligence, but with many years of cumulative human action.

It is thus difficult to see quite what, for example, should be concluded from the arguments of Dr. William Shockley— the Nobel Prize winner in physics from Stanford—whose views on race once caused a conference to be canceled for fear of "disturbances." He contends that black intelligence is inferior because of "evolutionary adolescence" (whatever that may mean). An objective diagnosis of this phenomenon, he says, would be "the greatest relief to the frustrated agony of black Americans." Presumably, black Americans would, once convinced about their adolescent intelligences, simply give up and admit that there was nothing for it but the ghetto, poverty, and an eternity of discrimination. However, even if Shockley's contention *were* true, it is nonsense to assume these things would follow.

If Shockley confined himself to examining the differences between black and white performances and the possible genetic bases for these differences, one could not quarrel. But, like so many naïve sages (and he did give the world the transistor radio), he wants to make the leap to social policy, a leap which by definition involves the *non sequitur* I have already mentioned. Social and political justice has nothing to do with the chemistry of the chromosomes; it has to do with the interests and values of human groups and the distribution of power among them. Given Dr. Shockley's terms of reference, it could be argued that Caucasoids have inferior brains to Mongoloids. Should Caucasoids then relieve their "frustrated agony" by backing out of world influence and humbly letting the Chinese, Vietnamese, and what have you dictate to them whatever terms they choose?

Here I should stress that the role of the anthropologist lies in this area of "inherent" inferiorities. If these are resorted to in racist arguments, the anthropologist can contribute. But there are many other aspects of the problem that he must respectfully hand over to the sociologist, the psychologist, and the historian. What, then, has the anthropologist to say about race?

First of all, it must be admitted that many anthropologists have stopped using the term as a scientific concept, because they feel that it is meaningless for any useful analysis of human differences. Those broad categories of white, black, yellow, red, and various other bands of the spectrum are so full of internal diversity that they cannot be used as units of analysis at all. Between the two ends of the black band, for example, there may be nothing in common other than dark pigmentation, and in some cases even this may be less dark than the pigmentation of some Caucasoids—Hindus, for instance. And here again there are problems, for Hindus are not a race, but a religion; the British are not a race, but a nation; the word "Aryan" does not signify a race, but at best a language family. All these varying categories, however, have at one time or another been dubbed "races." The catalogue of races varies from a list of three to several hundreds, and there are no settled criteria of discrimination.

Perhaps the broadest and least controversial of all definitions is the one proposed by M. F. Ashley Montagu and Loring Brace. They define a race simply as "a group of mankind, members of which can be identified by the possession of distinctive physical characteristics." But even this is a cultural rather than a biological definition. It depends on the *perception* of differences that are distinctive, rather than on the actual genetic differences between the groups. Groups that look alike may have radically different genetic make-ups, in, for example, blood chemistry. And in "race relations" it is, of course, the *perceived* differences that matter.

In the study of human variation there has been an attempt to substitute the idea of the "breeding population" for race. In zoology this concept has enormous importance, and many would regard the population, rather than the individual, as the unit of evolution. A breeding population is that group of animals that regularly mates within itself; that is, the members of the population breed with each other much more frequently than with outsiders. In time, certain genetic characteristics will become fixed in the population because of the inbreeding; eventually these may become so different from the characteristics of other populations that interbreeding between populations will be impossible and new species will have developed.

In this view, human races are incipient species. But the breeding-population approach has its own difficulties, even though it is scientifically more useful than the rather slap-happy "racial" approach. The problem is that many of the crucial features that divide mankind into identifiable groups cut across breeding populations. Natural selection does not recognize breeding-group boundaries; it produces dark pigmentation or crinkly hair or mesomorphic body form in many different groups that have no breeding relationships with one another. Thus these "racial" traits are not characteristic of particular populations, and so the breeding structure of the populations is by no means the only clue to human variation.

What is left to explain is this variation. Races, or populations, do not seem adequate units to explain it. We have to take each trait separately and try to account for it and its distribufion. Here and there "clusters" of traits will be found that seem to hang together, and these provide those broad divisions of mankind with distinctive physical characteristics whose nature can be explored.

Why should there be variations at all within the species *Homo sapiens sapiens?* (The extra *sapiens* does not indicate increased wisdom but serves to distinguish man, the only surviving member of the genus *Homo,* from his close ancestors, *Homo sapiens neanderthalensis.*) Why shouldn't people all look alike? To this there are two answers, which probably amount to the same thing, although much heat has been generated by their opposition. One says, roughly, that modern man became totally distinct about fifty thousand years ago, and then proceeded to differentiate as a result of adaptations to widely different environments. From as far back as thirty thousand years, distinctively white and Mongoloid types of skulls are in evidence; from about twenty thousand years ago, the earliest known American remains are distinctively Amerindian.

It can be assumed, therefore, that the original small stock of the ancestors of *Homo sapiens* gradually spread out over the globe (from where is not known), changing and adapting as they moved into different ecological niches. The great factor that prevented them from speciating too far was culture. Man (as he can confidently be called by this time) did not have to wait upon the process of genetic change in order to adapt. A combination of genetic changes and cultural adaptations enabled him to exploit almost all known environments (exceptions being underwater and the highest mountains). He did not have to redevelop his hairy coat in order to survive in Arctic climes—he could invent clothes. But, in any case, on this theory the races of man have diverged from the common stock in response to environmental pressures.

Another theory would put these racial differences further back. It says that the major divisions of mankind are derived from distinct stocks that had a much more remote common ancestor than is postulated by the first theory. This might not seem to make much difference, but it does. The proponents of the second theory maintain that the divergent stocks were formed before they reached the *sapiens* level, and that they crossed this Rubicon at different times. Thus the present races of man are not post-*sapiens* but pre-*sapiens* developments.

The chief argument against this theory is its lack of economy, and the unlikelihood of at least four different paths of evolution all ending up with the same result. The fossils from which the various races are supposed to be derived show more differences among themselves than the present races do! Such a remarkable convergence in evolution is not known to have taken place and would be almost impossible to explain if it had. But even if the second theory were true, the end result is one species that interbreeds and produces viable offspring. And further, if it were true, it would simply increase the depth and range of diversity, which, as we have already said, is an advantage to the species as a whole.

However arrived at, then, the picture of our ancestors of, say, thirty thousand years ago is one of small groups of hunters and collectors spread over a considerable part of the globe in a variety of environments and displaying recognizable differences in physical features. Some of these differences may have been largely due to chance. The relative isolation of the various breeding populations at this stage may have helped to fix certain characteristics, such as nose shape or head size, which had no particular advantage but which were not selected *against*. The accumulation of such differences may account for some distinctive features that are hard to account for on the grounds of adaptation.

And, of course, despite relative isolation, there would have been considerable interbreeding as populations migrated, and this in itself would have produced new and distinctive traits. The Polynesians, for example, are probably a result of one of these great intermixings. But, ultimately, the test of all these traits was usually selection. Did they give some advantage to their bearers that enabled them to produce more offspring who themselves were successful in breeding, and so on?

With some of the traits we are more happy than with others. Take the most obvious and seemingly the easiest— skin pigmentation. Why do some groups have very dark skins and some very light? By discounting the effects of sun tanning on groups who wear few or no clothes (for example, the Australian aborigines, who in fact look blacker than they are), the readiest answer can be explored: that dark skin is a protection against ultraviolet radiation. The color of the skin is determined by an organic molecule called "melanin," of which a person has either a lot or a little. Melanin in the outer layers of the skin absorbs ultraviolet radiation, which mitigates its effect. A lack of melanin leaves the individual prone to skin cancer if he is exposed to excessive amounts of radiation. Hence dark skins are an advantage in the tropics.

But this had to be qualified. Dark skins absorb 30 per cent more heat than light skins, thus increasing the heat load of the body. In a hot, dry climate, a black-skinned man would collapse from heat stroke much more readily than a light-skinned man. Conversely, there is some evidence that in a hot, *wet* climate, the darker skin would have a small advantage. In colder regions, however, it might appear that a dark skin would have an even greater advantage in that it absorbs heat, but this is offset by the awkward fact that the heavy pigmentation shuts out the vitamin D that would otherwise be taken from sunlight. In the temperate zones a light skin would have a slight advantage on this score. A gradation then could be expected of black skins in the hot, wet climes, brown in the hot-dry, and white in the cold-wet. And, *very* roughly, this follows for the distribution of man before the age of discovery reshuffled so many populations.

But this is indeed rough, since populations have shifted about a good deal. Many of the Negroes in the hot, wet areas are not native to them; many of the peoples living near the equator are not particularly dark at all, as in Indonesia and South America. These migrations make a good deal of the speculation on the survival value of skin color very tentative. Many of these so-called advantages are marginal and it seems difficult to see how they could have seriously affected survival and reproductive success. Cancer of the skin takes many years to develop; people don't tend to die of it, and anyway they have had their children by the time it becomes virulent. Vitamin D can be obtained from sources other than sunlight, and clothes can protect against sunburn.

One physiologist, Harold F. Blum, concludes that a really black skin could only reap all its advantages (from an adaptational point of view) on one of the snow-capped mountains near the equator. The "natural" color of the human skin—one that would be most advantageous in most circumstances, and from which the others are probably evolutionary divergences—is probably a pleasant medium brown, tending toward *café au lait* rather than cocoa. But I can't help thinking that some elements of chance are at work in this matter of skin color. As one of my students said at the end of a particularly frustrating seminar on the subject, "For Christ's sake, skin has to be some color!"

The same may be said of hair: it has to be some form. A mild clustering occurs in which tight, curly hair is associated with dark skins, and lighter, wavy hair with white. But this is a vague correlation. The classic Negroid features of curly hair and full lips are usually thought of as "progressive" features—in an evolutionary sense—in contrast to the more apelike straight hair and thin lips of other groups, such as Caucasoids and Mongoloids.

Teeth make obvious the difficulty of taking races, however defined, as units of explanation. Teeth come in various sizes and shapes, and no one can doubt their significance for survival. Let's take the simple dimension of size. The smallest teeth in the world are found in the peoples of Central and Eastern Europe and the Middle East, and the largest among the Australian aborigines. These large teeth also show a good deal of wear. Were they any smaller they would soon be worn down to the gums. Since the Australians use their teeth virtually as tools, the adaptive advantage of ultralarge teeth is obvious. And this seems to be the pattern. Where teeth are very much used, either as tools or in the consumption of tough food—among many hunters, for example—they are large, and the masticatory apparatus and the lower face and jaw are large in proportion. Where this is less true, the teeth are small.

But if the world distribution of teeth size and that of skin color were plotted, there would be no correspondence. This is a perfect example of natural selection (or random genetic drift) being no respecter of races or breeding populations. The explanation of variation within the species of these particular traits cannot start with races as units, because the variations cut across them in different ways. Teeth size and shape varies among the Negro peoples (Negroid race?) as much as it varies among the species as a whole.

The results of adaptation are perhaps better seen in noses. A high-bridged, long, narrow nose is of advantage in two environments—very cold and very dry. In the former it helps to warm the air as it passes on its relatively long journey up the fine nasal passages; in the latter it helps to moisten the dry air during inspiration. On the other hand, it does not seem to have any particular disadvantage in hot, humid climates; a flatter, shorter nose is marginally preferable. (I write this in hot and humid southern New Jersey, amidst a sharp-nosed family devastated by various respiratory malfunctions, so perhaps I should be cautious.) A good deal of nasal form, however, is clearly related to the size and shape of the rest of the face, so this is a tricky subject.

In eye form there is at least one fairly clear example of adaptation at work. I allude to the epicanthic or Mongoloid eye fold. This is an example of adaptation to extreme cold. It goes along with shortness of stature, very flat nose, and fat-padded cheeks. Some groups of Mongoloids (late developers from an archaic "white" stock, probably) were trapped during the last glacial period—about twenty-five thousand years ago—in northern Asia, and either adapted or froze to death. The eye fold is a brilliant protection against the effects of cold on the eye.

Adaptational response to extreme cold (up to $-100°$ F.) may also explain the relative hairlessness of this group, since moisture would freeze in a beard and hence freeze the face under it—as bearded Caucasoid arctic explorers have discovered to their distress. Beards are fine for subarctic winters, where they warm the face but do not freeze. The classic Mongoloid face is best seen in the Eskimos, the Tungus of northern Asia, and some American Indians. Other American Indians, the Malays and Polynesians, and the Southern Chinese are results of mixtures between Mongoloid and other stocks—for example, the archaic whites of east Asia from whom the hairy Ainu of Japan and the Australian aborigines sprang. (Crosses between Mongoloids and Australian aborigines produce Polynesian-looking offspring. The dark skin of the Australoids is probably, in evolutionary terms, a recent adaptation.)

Another example of a variation that cuts across races is body build. Roughly speaking, human bulk decreases in the hotter and increases in the cooler parts of the globe. At one extreme are the Eskimos—short, squat, and heavy; at the other are the Nilotes of East Africa—tall, slender, and light. It is easy to imagine the effects of reversing these body builds. Eskimos would melt in the dry heat of East Africa, while the Nilotes would perish in temperatures of $-100°$ F. This all has to do with the loss and preservation of body heat, which involves the ratio of body surface to body weight. Heat is lost from the surface of the body, so in a hot climate as much surface relative to bulk as possible should be presented; in a cold climate, the opposite is true. While again this is not an absolute correlation, it holds pretty well, and variations among, say, the Mongoloids are almost as great as variations within the whole species. The same is true for that old favorite of the taxonomists, the cephalic index—the classic measure of head shape. Except for narrowly defined populations, head shape varies widely and does not correlate highly with other features. It is difficult to see any adaptational advantages accruing from any particular head shape.

Variations in color and morphology, then, have some adaptive significance, but this is not "racial." To understand these adaptations, each trait has to be taken on its merits, and the traits cut across the conventionally accepted racial classifications in different ways. Color, teeth size, nose shape, body build, hair form, eye form, et cetera do not come in neat racial packages clearly distinct from one another. What we get is simply a sequence of clines, or graded series of differences, from one population to another.

But what about blood? Next to color, this has the most emotional significance, it seems. "Mixed blood" is looked on in some circles with horror, while "true blood"—or even, for some reason, "blue blood"—is the metaphor for a person's worth, and "red blood" for his relative virility. But, despite man's love of ranking, one thing remains true: no blood is better than any other in an absolute sense; it is just different. As with all these evaluations, the question is: Better for what? There is no intrinsically "bad blood"; but if a person is group A he had better not have a transfusion from group B, and a rhesus-negative mother had best avoid having a child by a rhesus-positive father.

Most people know about blood groups and how they are inherited, and they know that all groups are represented in the American population. Most groups, in fact, are represented in most populations—with some interesting exceptions; what differs is their distribution within the populations. Thus they are like other physical features, and, like these, their distribution is not "racial." A high incidence of group O, for example, is characteristic of both Celts and most American Indians, while group A, which is high among Western Europeans (non-Celtic), reaches its highest incidence (83.7 per cent) among the Blackfoot Indians. The Rh (rhesus) negative group has a high incidence in northwestern Europe (40 percent) but is also present in some Negroid populations and is rare or nonexistent in other parts of the world. Similarly, Negroes and Europeans share subgroup A2, which doesn't exist in East Asia, Oceania, or America. It is perfectly possible that a white American and a black American should have much the same blood-group series, but it is unlikely that the parent populations would present the same distribution of blood types.

Some types are found exclusively in certain populations, which is not surprising; blood groups are inherited and therefore relatively isolated breeding populations may develop characteristic differences. Indeed, blood groups give very important indications of population movements and the relationships between populations in the remote past. But again it must be stressed that these distributions are characteristic of breeding populations and that they *define* the populations. One cannot prejudge the issue of where one population starts and another stops; one must simply plot the distributions of the groups and see what happens. There is no neat correlation with shape of nose or color of skin or size of skull. For sorting out the dense networks of genetic material that are breeding populations, however, blood groups promise something more definitive than morphological features. One thing is certain: there is no "white" blood that is incompatible with "black" blood. White blood of group A is compatible with black blood of group A, but incompatible with white blood of group B. And there it is.

But what is the significance of these differences in blood chemistry? If they are just another example of human variation, they should be explicable on evolutionary principles in terms of their adaptive value. A start in this direction has been made, but the findings are tentative. Clearly, blood is affected by disease; therefore the most plausible explanation for the differences lies in differential resistance to disease. Given the typical distributions within whole populations, it also follows that epidemic diseases are the most likely to be involved; that is, diseases that affect whole populations at a time.

It has been suggested, for example, that the relatively high incidence of group A in Western Europe and B in India might have been caused by selection owing to plague and smallpox epidemics. B, in fact, is probably a relatively new group and may have developed late in human history. It is high among the Mongoloids—one of the last stocks to become differentiated. Persons with the ancient blood groups—O and A—seem more prone to peptic ulcers than those with B, and it has been suggested that this is due to their inability to take stress resulting from overcrowding. These blood groups evolved, as it were, to cope with the diseases of relatively free-ranging animals, and their bearers break down under more civilized conditions. This hypothesis is strengthened by the association of the A-B-O system with diet. The various blood-group types may well differ in their capacity to cope with varying amounts of fat, protein, and carbohydrate. This research is in its infancy but is suggestive. It makes blood into something quite unmysterious and puts it in the same class as nose shape and skin color.

Thus far, then, it is clear that human variation is the response of the species over time to a variety of habitats and ways of life. A number of small genetic adjustments plus a great deal of cultural ingenuity have enabled *Homo sapiens* to people the globe and dominate all other forms of animal life. What has been discussed here are morphological rather than behavioral characteristics (not that the two are separable), but surely the same arguments should apply to features of human behavior. Factors such as motor ability, temperament, and intelligence are "adaptive" in the same way as skin color; so shouldn't they also show characteristic distributions?

But these, however, are not quite the same kinds of units. Intelligence is not a concept of the same order as teeth size. It may, for example, be quite obvious why the Australian aborigines have large teeth and white Americans small ones, but it is not clear that it takes more intelligence to survive in America than it does in the Australian desert—probably the reverse. It may be true that hairlessnesss is an advantage in arctic and hairiness an advantage in subarctic climes, but again it is not clear that greater intelligence is needed to survive as a Viking than as an Eskimo. Different skills are involved in each case, and there may well have been some evolution of different abilities in different directions, but much the same intelligence is needed to perform one lot of skills as the other. Similarly, it is highly likely that differences in temperament might well have evolved in different populations to cope with different conditions. But much the same range of temperaments has been found in all human societies, and it is almost impossibly difficult to sort out the genetic "givens" of temperament from the results of training. The problem with differences in intelligence and temperament is that they are not discrete and measurable, as are those between blood groups, and that they depend heavily on evaluation of what is basic in any skilled performance. Tests, for example, test only what the testers want to test, and there is no way of knowing whether the skills tested are basic or highly specialized. It is entirely plausible, as I have said, that differences exist between various populations with regard to their capacity to execute certain skills, just as differences in stature and blood chemistry exist. But the same amount and kind of mental energy is being exerted in each case: the human brain is uniformly of the same structure throughout the species.

To start ranking these abilities is like saying that, although exactly the same type of engine may be powering an automobile and a motorboat, the automobile is better than the the motorboat. The particular adaptations of the boat engine make it suitable for the water, and those of the automobile for the land. If all the land were submerged, where would the automobile be? Each race, in fact, has demonstrated its capacity to learn anything produced by the other races, and this, like the ability of any one race to breed with any other, is the crucial factor because it demonstrates that learning ability is universally characteristic of the species. This is the brilliance —if you will forgive the nonscientific word—of the process of raciation in *Homo sapiens:* it has allowed genetic diversity without speciation, which means that the developed differences can be pooled and repooled. Common breeding and common learning can take advantage of these undoubted differences in genetically based abilities, whether mechanical, aesthetic, verbal, or whatever, and recombine them both physically and culturally.

Thus it seems to me that the so-called differences in intelligence are a total red herring. Certain differences in capacity for solving certain kinds of problems exist between individuals and between populations. What a group lacks in one kind of ability it always compensates for in another, and the same kinds of mental processes are involved in the execution of different skills. There is no race (however defined) that is not capable of developing high civilization, even if it has not bothered to do so. This is more a matter of motivation than ability. Harsh or lush environments may inhibit tendencies to create elaborate civilizations. Lack of easy communications or dense settlement prevents the diffusion of new techniques and ideas, the cumulation of which is the basis for civilization. Many of the so-called lower races of today are themselves the descendants of groups that produced high civilizations. And the same was true of them as it is of us. It was not the qualities of the race that produced these advances, but the exertions of a few geniuses —who crop up in all groups. What is meant by the great advances of the "white" race? The cumulative efforts of a handful of outstanding men and women on whom the dim multitudes are totally parasitical.

When was the last time you, white reader, made a significant breakthrough in science or art? And, if you did, how much of it was attributable to the cumulative efforts of past generations? If, for a variety of reasons, various ethnic groups have not produced the same kind of technological civilization that you have, this pales into insignificance beside their ability to take over and operate successfully whatever you produce. You may, in fact, have exhausted yourself producing material for them to take over painlessly and use against you. This is perhaps the biggest practical joke that an unkind God has played on his chosen people.

Yet we must again stress that even if these differences in specific ability exist (and we have no reason to suppose that they do not), they are very difficult to correlate with morphologically defined races. To take the simple case of motor performance: this is as variable among, say, Negroes as it is among whites, and the variations between these two groups significantly overlap. The same is true of so-called intelligence, even when measured by tests almost totally oriented toward white western European values of what constitutes basic skills in problem-solving—skills that often fare badly in the desert or tundra. While, not surprisingly, white averages tend to be higher than black, there is considerable overlap in the total range of performances. You, white reader, certainly do worse than some blacks even at your own rigged tests. On the other, more neutral tests, you undoubtedly fare worse than most members of various ethnic groups. Once it is known how to estimate human abilities, distributions similar to those found in blood groups will undoubtedly crop up. Like blood groups, some kinds of abilities will have slight advantages over others in specified circumstances. But every population has practically the full range of abilities in it, just as it has most of the range of blood groups. There may be some marginal exceptions to this, as there are with the rarer blood groups. The leaping ability of the Watutsi of Rwanda, for example, is probably unique.

So, as with the distribution of blood groups within populations, the distribution of genetically based abilities will differ, and some populations will be high on some things and low on others.

But in the same way that all populations have blood, all populations have intelligence; and as blood is blood, whatever its group, so intelligence is intelligence, however manifested.

Just as there is no absolute ranking of blood groups—although some may have marginal advantages in some circumstances —there is no absolute ranking of different manifestations of intelligence. Just as blood types can be shuffled by inter-breeding them, so can any other inherited features be shuffled, to the benefit of all concerned. To do this *within* populations, as is done all the time, is no different in principle from doing it *between* populations.

Race is an evolutionary episode. It should be seen against the time scale of human evolution. During the earlier and more precarious years, it was necessary for the basic stock to differentiate genetically in order to spread and survive. This has taken, in evolutionary terms, a relatively brief time and has got the species to where it is now. At present, the differentiation is not so necessary—unless man spreads out into the solar system, where genetic specialization might well be useful to him again. But, because the specialization has not produced new species, and because a common capacity to learn extensively is shared by all members, there exists a magnificent pool of genetic diversity on which the species as a whole can draw.

Genetic diversity within a species is a fine instrument for meeting the varying challenges of the environment. (And those who think the human species is not constantly being challenged to make the necessary adaptations are living in a fool's paradise, which could be dangerous.) What should be done now, therefore, is to take maximum advantage of the diversity and crossbreed the various specializations to produce new combinations. Doing so would still produce diversity, but it would be a more meaningful diversity for the species' future evolution than that produced by specialized adaptation to natural habitats. The advantages may be only marginal, but they are worth exploring.

The process of raciation is no longer of much use to the

human species, now that it dominates the earth. Raciation should therefore be eliminated by vigorous interbreeding so that man can reap the benefits of this remarkable evolutionary episode and move on. Even if all that was achieved was abolition of peptic ulcers and a permanent sun tan for everyone, it would be worth trying.

Family and Kinship

THE THREE ESSAYS here represent what I consider my major contribution to anthropology. But they are indubitably linked to what has gone before, and the first essay, "Comparative Family Patterns," should provide the link. In it I try to show how human kinship systems divide labor between the asexual brother-sister bond and the sexual husband-wife bond. That these two can be separated —that different functions can be assigned the consanguineous, as opposed to the conjugal, bond—is, along with the important recognition of the body of males as a separate interest group, one of the basic clues to human kinship systems.

In "Kinship and Alliance" I try to synthesize in as brief

a statement as possible my thoughts on the rudiments of kinship analysis. This essay draws heavily on the work of the French anthropologist Claude Lévi-Strauss, whose basic position I accept, but from whom I differ in detail. Most of my recent work has been directed toward integrating his ideas into my own evolutionary framework. There is a direct line from the concerns of "The Evolution of Sexual Behavior" to the essays here. An amazing revolution took place as the hominids were evolving—the invention of exogamy: the idea that people belong to specific kinship groups and that they should not marry within them. The more kinship among our primate relatives is looked at the more obvious it becomes that human kinship is rooted in primate patterns (common baboons, macaques, and chimpanzees have matrilineages); what is also clear is that exogamy is a human phenomenon. Those primates that have permanent mates (for example, the Hamadryas baboons and Geladas) do not have kinship systems; those that have kinship systems do not have assigned mates. Somewhere along the line man's ancestors put this all together. They began to assign mates—spouses—but only in terms of the kinship system. Kinship came to determine not only who was related to whom, but who could marry whom. And thus the basis, the root, of kinship systems lies in their function of combining the principle of descent, or relationship, and the principle of exogamy—marriage out of the descent group. Lévi-Strauss had this insight before much primate evidence was available (he maintained that primate life was basically unordered), and without an evolutionary perspective—which, in a sense, serves only to strengthen his case. Once these functions of kinship systems are compared with such data as is available on the evolution of the brain and the importance of polygyny and dominance in breeding systems, a breakthrough in the knowledge of the relation between evolution and truly human behavior may be possible. Most of my efforts now are devoted to this end.

The final essay "Marriage, Mobility, and Modern Literature" is a favorite lecture of mine. It takes the alliance theme and brings it up to date. Who gets to marry whom really *is* still important.

THREE

Comparative Family Patterns

I AM INTERESTED in putting the family into an evolutionary and comparative perspective, a perspective that focuses on the human species as a whole. The species as it stands today is the end product of a complex evolutionary process that has produced a creature who, on the one hand, is moved to form certain bonds and pursue certain ends, and on the other hand, is intelligent and flexible enough to seek a variety of means to those ends. The range of variation cannot be understood without first understanding the themes on which the variations are played. These, in turn, can be understood only if we know what the creature is about in the first place, and this can be understood only from the knowledge of how it got to be that way.

But first I must try to jeopardize the entire argument by asking whether or not there is a subject matter. In dealing with, say, contemporary industrial societies, there is a distinguishable social unit called the "family," consisting of parents and dependent children. This is so clearly a basic social, legal, domestic, and economic unit that it has come to be regarded as in some way inevitable. Both sociologists and laymen treat this unit as the basic building block of social systems and, when they are being moralistic, as the basic building block of social order and stability. Sophisticated social scientists, recognizing that other arrangements are possible, nevertheless insist that extended families are based on nuclear family units combined into various patterns. (Note how the very term "nuclear family" begs the question.) Some observers, realizing that such a position needs justification, have claimed that the nuclear family is universal because it is a basic biological unit; somehow the forming of nuclear families is in the beast. (It is ironic that many of those who claim this position in one breath deny in the next that man has any biological propensities to social behavior, and insist that all his institutions are cultural.)

It seems to me that anthropologists should be more open-minded about this issue, and ask themselves, like good zoologists, just what the species does about matters such as the raising of children, and observe the patterns that occur. After all, the family is a complex arrangement with at least four basic dyads—father-child, mother-child, sibling-sibling, husband-wife—and it develops through time. Failure to see the family as essentially a dynamic unit composed of subunits has vitiated, for example, discussions of incest and the incest taboo. Incest involves three other dyads—father-daughter, mother-son, and brother-sister. Each of these represents a totally different kind of sexual relationship, and blanket remarks about the incest taboo, directed as they are to the family, miss the point.

On the whole, it seems to me wise to consider the family less as an institution or unit and more as a field of action. In this field, various bonds operate for various purposes and it is the purposes that determine which bonds will be forged, which strengthened, which ignored. The biology of the species gives not the family unit, but the potentiality for bonding, which can be the basis of a nuclear family. It is quite possible that the bonds between family members are simply intensifications of more general bonds. Thus the father could be simply a special kind of older dominant male, the mother a special category of older nurturant female, and so on. This is important inasmuch as many psychologists see the personality of the adult essentially as playing out family roles. The difficulties young males experience with older males are often put down to an "unresolved Oedipus complex," in which all older males become the disliked father. This may well be putting the cart before the horse, because the father may simply be the first adult male with whom the growing boy tries his combination of threat and bonding, which he will try with all adult males anyway. In other words, the young-male-old-male bond shows up most strongly in the nuclear family but the problems inherent in it do not originate there.

I think that the relationship between a mother and her children is different from the relationship between a father and his children. A mother is not simply an available older female to whom we react as such; she is essential to the mental and physical well-being of the child. The accumulation of facts on this issue is overwhelming. It is a basic ground rule for any primate species that, if the object is healthy and effective adults, the mother and child have to be associated safely and securely through the critical period of birth and at least to the point where the children become independently mobile. In humans, with their extremely long dependency period, this is even more important, so that, in a very real sense, the mother-child tie is the basic bond in our system of social relationships (see Diagram 1) and one that is really taken over from nature. (In the diagrams that follow a triangle stands for male, a circle for female; 1, 2, 3 . . . n means indefinite other wives or husbands, as the case may be.) Thus, whatever else happens, any society needs to protect and provision its mother-child units. The impregnation of the mother is a relatively simple and brief matter. There is no logical reason—although there may be many practical ones—for the putative genitor to pay further attention to his sex partner. Why he so often does must be explained, not just taken for granted. The approach I am taking treats the institution of marriage and the family as problematic rather than given.

One obvious way of protecting and provisioning the mother-child unit is to attach to it the mother's mate (Diagram 2). To attach one male to one female for these purposes can have advantages. For one thing, with equal sex ratios and simultaneous maturity in the sexes, this is statistically the most convenient. In many primates where there are more females in the group than males (on average 4 to 1), the

rates of maturity are different, with females maturing twice as fast. Thus there are always more fertile females than males. To achieve such an imbalance in man, the position would have to be falsified by, for example, raising the marriage age of males and lowering that of females. Other reasons for the one-to-one attachment are the sexual division of labor, which requires contributions from both sexes, and the bonding effects of repeated sexual activity. None of these, however, requires a one-to-one assignment of mates, and even such an assignment does not necessarily lead to the setting up of family units in our sense. Here the existence of rights over females must be distinguished from the existence of actual domestic units. One thing clear in all human societies is that there is a regular assignment of mates—regulated sexual access. Random mating is rare or nonexistent. But this simply establishes that all people have recognized spouses; it says nothing about the social units that emerge. Those who argue for the universality of the nuclear family are often saying only that most societies recognize and name the roles of husband-father, wife-mother. The point seems to be that if the woman's contribution to the economy is important (and they provide 80 per cent of the food in some hunting societies), then rights over this contribution are important. Equally, the mother-child unit's claim on animal protein is important. This is still not a family in the popular magazine sense. It is up one stage from the primate pattern where the defense and coherence of the troop was in the hands of the males, but where food-sharing did not exist. With hunting and food-sharing, the assignment of mates becomes more important, and because women at this point become objects of exchange, rights over female offspring take on importance.

Even so, the arrangements between males and females can work out in various nonfamilial ways. In some primitive hunting groups, the total pattern is still very like that of primates: the females and young stay pretty much together as a group; the adult (initiated) males follow their own pursuits; the adolescent (uninitiated) males form a peripheral set. Here the unit is the total group divided into these subunits. Ecological pressures can force a different kind of organization. Sparse resources plus an extensive territory can force the group to split up. It may split into units of mother-child plus an adult male, or two or more mother-child units plus an adult male (Diagram 3). To call the latter "nuclear families with a husband-father in common," as G. P. Mur-

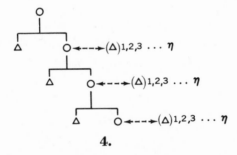

3.

dock does, is to make of it an almost ludicrous caricature. The advent of agriculture can settle these various types of units, thus perpetuating them; it also gives rise to other possibilities.

One possibility is that the males attached to the mother-child unit can be consanguineous rather than affinal (thus anthropologists sometimes distinguish consanguineous families from conjugal families). The commonest of these schemes makes the brother(s) of a woman her protector and provisioner (Diagram 4). The incest taboo prevents him

4.

from becoming the father of her children, but this can easily be taken care of by using other women's brothers for the task. This relatively logical solution is adopted in varying degrees, although the reasons for the variation are not clear. At one extreme the brother-sister unit is the domestic, commensal, and legal unit, and the sisters are impregnated by males having no legal and certainly no domestic status in the household. The classic example of this scheme is that of the Nayar of Malabar. Here the bond that is activated for protection and provision is the brother-sister bond. The husband is reduced to genitor, with some rights of sexual access to a woman who is shared among several men. The brother-sister bond in other systems can remain the dominant legal tie, while domestic rights are granted to the genitor. The classic example of this, in the Trobriand Islanders, has as its domestic unit the nuclear family, while the legal unit is the brother, sister, and sister's children (Diagram 5). Provisioning here again is partly the brother's responsibility. Among the Nayar the sisters are totally retained in the consanguineous family; the Trobriand woman is lent to a husband, but rights over her children are retained by consanguines. Also, in the latter case, her children are claimed back at puberty, making the nuclear family a phase in the dynamics of the domestic cycle.

It is possible to work out other solutions that only minimally activate the husband-wife tie. In the Western Pueblos, for example, the traditional domestic unit was the group of consanguineous women with their dependent offspring (Diagram 5). To this group (a grandmother, her daughter and daughter's daughter, for example) two lots of males were attached: sons/brothers and husbands/fathers, that is, consanguineous males and affinal males. The economic provisioning of the household was primarily the business of the affinal males, the ritual provisioning that of the consanguine males.

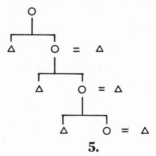

5.

Some affinal males became permanently attached but it was quite common for men to bring an affinal relationship to an end and move on to another household. This has been described as a high divorce rate, which begs the question. I prefer to describe it as a high turnover of husbands. The female unit stayed intact and did not need any permanent males so long as some male help was provided from time to time. What we have in this example, then, is female households with males circulating among them. The mother-daughter tie is activated and others ignored. This is similar to patterns described for some ex-slave societies and urban industrial populations where constellations of related mother-child units form a domestic group, with both consanguineous and other males as a highly variable quantity (Diagram 6). Interestingly, in these circumstances the men seem to form their own all-male groups (Damon Runyon's permanent floating crap game) and the adolescents theirs. This corresponds, for example, to the Pueblo situation, where the men traditionally congregated in the kivas and society houses. This tendency of societies to strain toward the hunting pat-

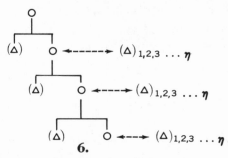

6.

tern of adult males together, relatively separate from females with young, and with adolescent males as a third unit seems to be universal. The problem of the females, roughly speaking, is apparently to divert the attention of the males to themselves; the problem for the adult males is to claim the young males by detaching them from their mothers. Many institutions, such as initiation ceremonies, for example, seem to be aimed at solving the problems inherent in this basic division of the sexes.

A male is most likely to attach himself to the mother-child group when it is in his interest to do so. Some socio-ecological situations demand the co-operative efforts of closely attached males, and in these instances fathers want to keep their sons with them (Diagram 7). This arrangement is more con-

$$\triangle \ = \ \bigcirc_{1,2,3} \ldots \eta$$

$$\eta \ldots_{1,2,3} \bigcirc \ = \ \triangle \qquad (\bigcirc)$$

$$(\bigcirc) \qquad \triangle \ = \ \bigcirc_{1,2,3} \ldots \eta$$

$$\triangle \qquad (\bigcirc)$$

7.

venient in many ways than that of uncles trying to recover nephews at puberty. The father-son tie is thus made the spinal cord of this system—but usually, as in China and Japan, it results also in a strong mother-son attachment because the mother gives up her place in a consanguineous group and attaches herself to her husband's unit. For various reasons, she often sees her security as vested in her sons. The brother-sister tie here is ignored at the expense of the husband-wife, father-son, and mother-daughter ties. Polygamy is common under such circumstances for obvious reasons, and so several mother-child units may be incorporated in the male groups by attachments to individual males. Such patriarchal extended families are common (China, Africa, Indo-Europe, et cetera).

Insofar as the total group (for example, the nation-in-welfare states like Sweden) can support the mother-child groups, no males need be attached to it. Societies, however, are rarely that generous. In most subhuman primate societies, the group as a whole is, in some sense, responsible for its members, and individual responsibilities are not assigned. These are part of the humanization breakthrough following hunting and food-sharing.

In all these family arrangements the basic unit is that of mother-child and the basic problem that of its provisioning and protection in the context of the socio-ecological conditions of the society. Various other bonds—brother-sister, father-son, husband-wife—will be either exclusively or partially activated to meet the problem. The nuclear family is simply one of the more common of these solutions. Here the husband-wife tie is utilized to the exclusion of others, with all the attendant problems of a bond formed not during socialization, but later in life between relative strangers who have to make a new and often difficult adjustment.

Also, the whole argument of this essay illustrates how such seemingly related factors as marriage, household, domestic services, sexual access, and legal authority must be seen as independent variables. An example from my own work might serve to make this point. A common custom on a small Irish island of about three hundred people was for a couple who married to stay in their natal homes, sometimes for life, sometimes for a shorter period. Children stayed with the mother, and the father-husband had visiting rights and contributed to the wife's support. Typically a household consisted of a widow, her married and unmarried sons and daughters, and the children of the daughters (legitimate and illegitimate). Even in 1965, 20 per cent of the marriages adhered to this pattern. Here again, the consanguineous ties of mother-child and brother-sister are emphasized at the expense of a reduced husband-wife tie, and the household is basically consanguine-ous.

In our own system (and those like it), all the above-mentioned variables coincide. Why this has happened must be explained by social historians. But in a sense this adaptation occurs for much the same reason it does in some primitive systems: there is a premium on mobility, and domestic units larger than the nuclear family are cumbersome; consanguineous units are impractical.

The consequence, however, of dumping all the functions involved onto the nuclear family can be disastrous, and this is why the nuclear family should be seen as simply one kind of solution, rather than as a basic biological premise. Perhaps then too much will not be asked of it. So much that is written about the breakdown of the family—about family failures, conflicts, neuroses, and the like—is inspired by a kind of mystical functionalism, which sees the nuclear family as a God-given system that would work if only things didn't happen to spoil it. On the contrary, what is remarkable about so fragile an institution is that it works at all. Families that fail are probably simply those that refuse to ignore the natural conflicts in the situation; while those that survive are families with the greatest capacity for collective self-delusion.

As regards the future of the family in industrial society, this comparative and evolutionary approach suggests that instead of trying to prop up an institution of a supposedly given kind, human society should explore the possibility of other combinations and permutations. If the family were indeed a given, man might rightly be perturbed if it were threatened. But since the mother-child tie is the only given, man is free to ring a number of changes around the security of this unit: rotating spouses, consanguineous households, temporary unions, communal establishments, and even legalized (as opposed to informal) polygamy, for those who can afford it, may all be possible in the automated world of the future. Rather than trying to preserve the family as it is now known, man should perhaps be thinking of how it might be transformed. All that is given in human nature is the mother-child bond—and considerable imagination.

FOUR

Kinship and Alliance

THE BONDS between kin are potentially the most fundamental of all social bonds because they are based on irreducible biological facts. The relationships between parents and children, siblings, grandparents and grandchildren, uncles and nephews are all, in a sense, biologically given. Whether or not a society will make much use of this is another matter —which is why I said the bonds are *potentially* the most basic. The use to which they are put in building up social relationships depends on another given human capability: the urge to classify and categorize objects in nature, including persons. All animals, for example, have their uncles and their cousins and their aunts, but, with perhaps the rare exception of the chimpanzee, they do not recognize these relationships and utilize them in building their societies. Human societies vary from those that, like our own, make a minimal use of kinship ties to those, like the tribes of aboriginal Australia, where the whole society is a large kin group in which everyone is a relative of everyone else. The contrast is not simply between advanced and primitive societies; nevertheless, it is true that technologically simple societies tend to make more extensive use of kinship ties than those that are technologically advanced. In the latter, the roles of citizen, employee, manager, et cetera tend to usurp the kinship roles, and nonkin relationships tend to be more important in the social structure than those between kin.

It is possible to imagine a society that ignored kinship ties altogether and built its social system completely out of other sets of relationships. And yet no such society has ever existed, for the simple reason that women bear and suckle children and it is usually the most economical strategy for a society to allow them to rear their own offspring. Even in those societies where extensive fosterage is practiced (in Samoa and ancient Ireland, for instance) and children are farmed out to foster parents, the basic processes of suckling and training have to be carried out by someone playing the role of mother. This, however, underlines a point often made by anthropologists: that kinship is about social relationships rather than biological relationships, even though in most instances they overlap. Thus the existence of a kin relationship depends on how the society defines kinship. For example, a true blood tie—such as that between an illegitimate child and its father—may not be recognized by the society as a kinship relationship; while a nonblood relationship, such as that between an adopted son and his adoptive father, may well be so defined. It is not simply the existence of consanguinity, or "common blood," that makes for a kinship bond, but the use to which the society puts—or does not put—the fact of biological relatedness. Relationships that to us are obviously biological may not be regarded as such by other peoples. The Trobriand Islanders of Melanesia and the Australian aborigines are notorious for denying that the father has any part in the creation of his children other than to "open the way" for them. Similarly, but with a reverse ideology, the Kachin of Burma and the Albanian hill tribes deny that the mother has any role other than that of providing temporary housing for the father-created fetus. Perhaps the most famous debate in literature on this topic is that between Apollo and the Furies in Aeschylus' tragedy *Eumenides*. The Furies, avengers of murdered kin, demand the life of Orestes, who has killed his mother. Apollo denies their claim on the grounds that a mother is not kin to her son, who is created solely by the father. Apollo won the day through the casting vote of Athena—a prejudiced judge, inasmuch as she sprang from the head of Zeus without any maternal intervention.

Theories aside, all societies capitalize on the mother-child relationship as a basic unit in the social system. Built into this relationship is the tie between siblings—children of the same mother. (Children of the same father, even when by different mothers, are of course also siblings—or at least half-siblings—but I want here to concentrate on the basic mother-child unit.) This unit has to be protected, provisioned, and controlled, and it is the men of the society who have the primary responsibility for performing these functions. A common strategy, therefore, is to let the mother's mate act in the role of protector and provider, and allow him to exercise control over his wives, sons, and daughters. When this happens, the result is the institution of the nuclear, or conjugal, family: a man and his wife and dependent children. Often, circumstances allow a man more than one wife, thus producing the polygynous family. While this is a common pair of solutions to the problems of begetting and rearing children, there are alternatives. But to look at these properly let's go back to some first principles.

Two of these have been implicit in what has been discussed: the obvious biological fact that women have the children and men beget them—whatever the local theories may say to the contrary—and the fact that men exercise control over resources, including women and children. The most elementary form of kinship system derivable from these facts is, of course, the one in which a man gains control over a woman and thence over her products—his children. But to do this he has in a sense to detach the woman from a previous relationship to her own father, mother, and brothers. Thus the questions arise: Why is this process of detachment necessary? Why shouldn't the siblings, for example, form a breeding unit? Well, on rare occasions this has been done, but by and large *Homo sapiens* as a species tries to avoid such a solution and frowns on mating relationships between parents and offspring and between siblings. The former prohibition is not unusual in nature, where various species disperse their young and send them off to mate elsewhere; the avoidance of mating between siblings is less common, and some human societies have even sanctioned brother-sister marriages. The Swedish parliament has debated whether or not to lift the ban on this form of marriage. But by and large it is frowned on and forbidden. A vast literature exists on this subject, and man is obsessed with the dilemma it poses: that those one loves the most one is forbidden to love. This theme recurs in myth and literature and in the products of fantasy as revealed to analysts. The most poignant and beautiful expression of the agony of those who cannot accept the prohibition can be found in the brother-sister love affair in John Ford's *'Tis Pity She's a Whore*.

To many anthropologists the avoidance of mating between

siblings is *the* basic fact of life because it forces men to look outside the narrow circle of consanguineous women in order to find mates. A man must, in a sense, release his sisters and daughters to other men, who, in turn, release their women to him. In this game he has two alternatives: he can release them entirely, in return for control over the women he receives, or he can release them partially and retain control over them in some respects, concurrently sacrificing some of his control over the women he obtains to their consanguineous males. The elemental situation created by the first principles can be envisaged as in the figure, taking a male ego as the focal point. The women need men to get

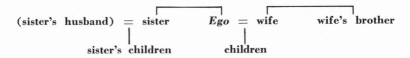

impregnated; these men cannot be their brothers; the brothers therefore have to release them; the brothers, in turn, receive women from other men; the products of these unions complete the mother-child units; two sets of men have an interest in the unit—the brothers, or consanguineous males, and the husbands, or affinal males. (Affines are relatives by marriage, as opposed to blood relatives; but of course any one person can be both to ego—for example, if he marries a cousin.)

This is a different starting point for kinship analysis than the nuclear family, although the latter is traditionally where anthropologists start. The essential roles are brother, sister, sister's husband, sister's children. But other relationships are obviously built into the scheme; the most important is the relationship between cousins who are the children of a brother and a sister, or, in anthropological parlance, cross-cousins (as opposed to parallel cousins, who are the children of siblings of the *same* sex; for instance, two people whose fathers were brothers would be parallel cousins). Also built in is the relationship between the brothers-in-law and between the mother's brother and his sister's children; as we shall see, these are crucial relationships in many systems and it is important to recognize that they are part of the elemental scheme.

The next move in the kinship game depends on the degree of control retained or relaxed by the brothers and gained or relinquished by the husband. Why should the brothers wish to retain control over the sisters? The answer is simple. One of the great problems in any society is how to achieve continuity over the generations. Property, rights, obligations, offices—all have to be passed on in some orderly way. When a man dies, his position and property have to be reassigned, and one of the neatest and most logical ways to do this is to give them to his heirs—his genetic successors who, in turn, become his social successors. To us the definition of "heir" as genetic successor is obvious, since the focus of our kinship system is the nuclear family. A man's heirs are his children—or at least his legitimate children. But this focus, as has been shown, is not any more natural as a starting point than the mother-child group and, in particular, the pair of siblings: the brother and sister. After all, the sister does not have to be obtained; she exists. So why shouldn't her children be her brother's heirs, thus keeping things literally in the family? There is no reason at all, except for the awkward fact that the brother-sister mating unit is not possible. The sister, therefore, has to be impregnated by another man—and this leads to problems. Of course, the brother could allow the sister to be impregnated and still retain absolute control over her, surrendering nothing to her mate. Some systems have come close to achieving this, but the arrangement is precarious. It is more usual for the sister to be "lent" to another man, who gains rights to her sexual and economic services, but not to her reproductive services. Her children thus belong to her brother or brothers; they are his heirs and successors—not the heirs and successors of their father, who will be concerned with *his* sister's children.

This solution to the continuity problem is called "matriliny" and such a kinship system is called "matrilineal": for the purposes of inheritance and succession, the important kinship links are those traced through the mother and females, not through the father and males.

The polar opposite of this would be a situation in which a man gained absolute control over his wife at the expense of her brothers. If a man wants to generate his own heirs, he has to obtain a woman to bear his children, and he has to obtain control of, and all rights over, that woman. As might be imagined, marriage and legitimacy will usually be more important and surrounded by more sanctions in such a system than in a matrilineal system, where, theoretically at least, marriage is unnecessary and illegitimacy impossible.

The system in which a man produces with the aid of a wife his own male heirs, who, in turn, produce theirs, is called "patriliny," and is described as "patrilineal." For all crucial purposes of continuity, the relations traced through the father and males, and not through the mother and females, are the important ones.

These are examples of two uses to which specific kinship ties can be put. In all societies people have relatives through their mothers and fathers who are recognized as such; but for certain purposes—in cases, for instance, of inheritance and succession—certain ties will be selected as crucial. Now problems arise out of the imposition of the selection on the elemental situation. The problem in matrineal systems is largely one of keeping control over the sister in order to control her sons; in patrilineal systems, the sister is irrelevant and the aim is to gain control over the wife in order to have absolute rights over her sons. In the elemental situation, the relationship between a mother's brother and his sister's son was built in; but this relationship will work out differently in matrilineal and patrilineal systems. In the matrilineal system, the mother's brother will tend to be a figure of authority and respect. In the patrilineal system, he has no authority over his sister's sons; yet he is closely linked to them: it was his release of his sister that provided their father with a wife and them with a mother, and so ensured their position in the line of patrilineal continuity. Often in patrilineal societies, a ritualized "joking relationship" pertains between men and their sisters' sons. The latter are allowed a privileged familiarity with the former—thus expressing ritually their privileged relationship.

The matrilineal and patrilineal principles have been examined as modes of regulating inheritance and succession, but they can also be used as methods of recruitment to groups. The commonest kind of corporate grouping found in most of the societies of the world is the kinship group, and a common form of this is the "descent group," so called because it is based on a relationship between people who share a common ancestor. A popular form of descent group is the clan, which is a group of people descended in the male or female line from either an actual or a putative ancestor. The ancestor may be a historical human being from whom all the members can trace descent, or a mythological person or animal from whom descent is claimed, even if it is not demonstrable.

Often the operational unit of the kinship system is a group smaller than the clan called the "lineage," which consists of people who can trace actual descent from a known ancestor. If the descent is traced in the male line, it is called a "patrilineage," if in the female, a "matrilineage."

Lineages, like clans, are often corporate groups, in the sense that they act as a body by owning impartible land, by being collectively responsible in law for their members, and by worshiping common ancestors. It is easy to see in these cases how the two principles are used for recruitment. Matrilineages and patrilineages grow from a founding ancestor or ancestress (as shown in the figure).

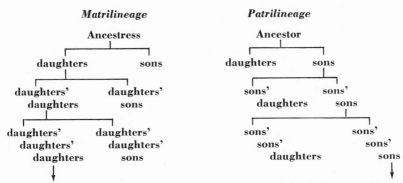

Because descent from the founder is traced in one line only—the male or the female—such groups are called "unilineal" descent groups. As social units, they have certain advantages, the major one being that they are discrete and nonoverlapping; hence membership is unambiguous, and ownership, rights and duties, and legal position are neatly defined for any individual. The lineages and clans can have many functions that will depend on factors in the social system other than principles of recruitment. They may be exclusively religious groups or political units; they may exist simply to regulate marriage; they may be primarily productive units—or any combination of these.

Since these functions can vary, any society can have both types of descent groups operating. Thus it can have matriclans that are ritual units and patriclans that are productive units. In such a double descent system one is a member of both a patriclan, through his father, and a matriclan, through his mother. The analysis does not differ in this case from the simple unilineal case, but it does imply that any individual will play more roles: if a male, he will be both a father and husband in his patriclan, and a brother and maternal uncle in his matriclan. In the latter role he will be concerned with his rights over his sister and her sons, and in the former with his rights over his wife and his own sons. Such systems can theoretically run smoothly if the complementary functions are well arranged and there are no clashes of interest between the two groups.

These descent groups usually regulate marriage. Sometimes this is positive and the release or obtaining of a woman is a matter for the whole group. More frequently it is simply negative and there is a rule forbidding members of the same lineage and/or clan to marry each other. It is sometimes said in anthropology that this is an "extension" of the incest prohibition, and occasionally it works that way, as when members of the same descent group are forbidden to have intercourse with each other—which, of course, rules out marriage. Often, however, it is possible for them to have intercourse without penalty, yet they are strictly forbidden to marry. It is not quite correct, therefore, to regard the rule of outmarriage, or exogamy, as simply the familial incest taboo writ large.

The functional effect of the exogamic restriction is to force men to look for wives not only outside the family circle, but outside the descent group as well. Thus, relations of affinity are set up between groups, which, insofar as they are corporate, have an interest in the marriage of each member. After all, the continuity of the lineage as a group is at stake and is what the marriage of a member ensures. Products of the marriage, then, are in some sense the property of the descent group at large. Often, for example, when bride price is paid for a woman, it is paid by the descent group as a whole rather than just the husband. If the husband dies or the wife leaves, the children still belong to the lineage or clan. This is usually described as the obtaining of rights over the reproductive capacity of the woman—even if not over her person. What the lineage is interested in primarily is her offspring (we are here dealing with a patrilineal case; in the matrilineal opposite, the woman's lineage must ensure that it retains rights over her reproductive capacity by some device such as claiming her offspring back when they reach puberty or when they marry).

The rule of exogamy thus has the same effect on descent groups as the rule of incest avoidance does on families: the groups are forced into relations of affinity with each other to ensure continuity. Marriage both links groups to each other through mutual dependence and ensures the continuity of the groups through time. However, there are also rules that have the effect of making relations of affinity perpetual between groups. These are positive rules of marriage. The negative rule of exogamy simply states: Thou shalt not marry members of thine own descent group. If one added a positive rule to the effect that one must marry only members of certain other descent groups, then between the descent groups concerned there would be reciprocal relationships of affinity that would continue over the generations. The groups would be in the relationship of suppliers and consumers of women to each other on a regular basis. This is quite common in many tribal societies, and it will be examined further; first it is necessary to go back to the elemental situation to see what happens when descent groups and rules of marriage are imposed on it.

The relationship between cross-cousins was a part of the elemental kinship structure. The brother and sister are separated by marriage, but it is possible for them to be reunited if the children of the brother and the children of the sister—the cross-cousins—marry each other. Such marriages have many practical consequences regarding property, residence, et cetera; but here attention should be given to their structural effects, which are perhaps better seen from another perspective than simply that of the marriage of cousins. By their marriages, the brother and sister constitute two separate families. By marrying each other, the children of these families reunite the two; thus we can see this marriage as the families exchanging—in a direct, reciprocal way —their children. Or we can see it in terms of a custom, which does exist, of exchanging sisters: I give my sister to another man, who, in turn, gives his sister to me. The children of these marriages exchange sisters. Whichever way this is looked at—as an exchange of children between families or as the marriage of cross-cousins or as the exchange of sisters between men—the outcome is the perpetuation of an exchange relationship over the generations, a constant feeding back of spouses in a closed system of perpetual affinal relationships. The simplest starting point, that of sister exchange, is shown in the figure.

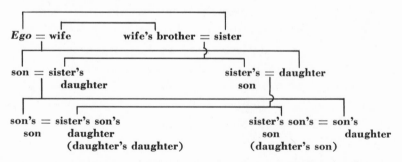

This model is based on the assumption that all the children of one family marry all the children of the other, and this cannot always be the case because of the imbalance of sex ratios. Thus such arrangements will be set up between ego's family and several others, and ego's children will have the choice of marrying their father's sister's daughter or their mother's brother's daughter—their two cross-cousins (refer back to the elemental situation).

It is possible to achieve even greater elaborations of the exchange system by banning marriage with one or the other of these cousins; by insisting, for example, that a man marry his mother's brother's daughter rather than his father's sister's. What this does is to preclude any direct exchange of spouses: if I give my sister to you, I cannot take your sister in return (see figure).

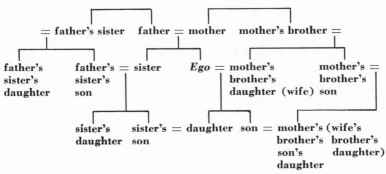

Here ego marries his mother's brother's daughter, and by extrapolation, his sister's son marries his (ego's) daughter, while his son marries his wife's brother's daughter, and so on. By precluding a direct exchange between the families, this rule forces them to engage in a wider network of ties: rather than exchanging sisters with another man, ego gives his sisters to him, the other man gives his to someone else, and so on through chains of alliance. These alliances can be perpetuated as in the direct case so that families will be bound to each other as wife givers and wife takers in perpetuity. The chains can also become closed. It can be seen from the figure that ego's mother's brother could have married someone whose brother could have married his father's sister; then, by following the rule in the next generation, ego's mother's brother's son could marry ego's father's sister's daughter, and again in the next generation the circle could be completed. Any number of families could play this game—there is theoretically no limit to the number of "players"—but the model is simple: A gives wives to B which gives wives to C which gives wives to A again—A→B→C→(A). This differs from the ideal model for the "direct" system which is simply A←—→B.

In each case we have been regarding A, B, and C as families, but we can see what the situation would be if they were units like descent groups, with rules of exogamy plus rules of preferred marriage.

The simplest situation—in which the units involved are corporate groups—is the tribe divided into two moieties. These can be matrimoieties, where recruitment is through females, or patrimoieties, where recruitment is through males. All that is necessary here is a simple rule of exogamy for the A←—→B situation to come up. Men of A would marry women of B and vice versa. Between the moieties, then, the same relationship exists as between two exchanging families; indeed, people in one moiety often refer to their potential spouses in the other by the word for cross-cousin. It is important to see both direct exchange at the family level and the same type of exchange at the corporate-group level as expressions of the same basic tendency: between any two units A and B (whether these be individuals, descent groups, families, or moieties) a symmetrical relationship of reciprocity exists whereby women are directly exchanged. Similarly, the equivalent at the corporate-group level of the "mother's brother's daughter" marriage between individuals is an asymmetrical, or indirect, exchange of women between descent groups. For example, clan A would be a wife giver to clan B, which could not reciprocate in kind but would give wives to clan C, and so on.

Anthropologists have argued about the meaning and function of these systems—which do not seem to appear at higher levels of technological development—but their underlying rationale seems clear enough: given the elemental situation in which social units have to look elsewhere than in their own ranks for wives and husbands, these more or less systematic forms of exchange ensure regular supplies. A descent group, for example, does not just cast its bread upon the waters and hope for a return; its alliance with other, similar groups similarly placed *ensures* a return. This forces the groups into a position of dependence on each other, and out of this dependence society is built. It is a little like the situation created by the division of labor, where each group performs a specialized task but not the whole range of tasks needed for survival. Hence, every group is dependent on every other group for an exchange of goods and services. In the systems discussed up to now, every unit "produces" women it cannot "consume" and so has to exchange; thus the system of dependence is created. Why exchange women rather than goods and services? The answer is that in these technologically simple societies the division of labor had not proceeded very far and one unit was pretty much like another in what it produced. Thus the integration of society could not proceed from the interdependence brought about by specialization. It is significant that the alliances referred to were often between enemies; there is a proverb that crops up here and there to the effect that "we marry those we fight." Thus, potentially separate, hostile, and self-sufficient groups are welded together into a wider society. It has been claimed that the indirect, or circulating or asymmetrical, method is more likely to produce this situation—which explains its existence in large populations; the direct, or symmetrical, method seems to be confined to fairly small populations.

Following the usage of Claude Lévi-Strauss, the systems discussed here can be called "elementary structures of kinship" (*structures élémentaires de la parenté*), which he opposes to "complex" structures. Descent groups can occur in either kind of structure; what differentiates the types is the way relations between the descent groups—or other units —are mediated through the marriage system. Very briefly, in complex structures—such as our own—the exogamic units do indeed cast their bread upon the proverbial waters. Women are shipped out, but there is no reciprocal agreement on the part of any other unit to ship other women back in. I cannot marry my own sister, mother, or daughter, but I have no claim on anyone else's. A complex system, then, to follow Lévi-Strauss's terminology, has only a negative rule of marriage; it lacks any positive regulation that would lay down not only the range of kin within which I could *not* marry, but also the range of kin within which I *must* marry. (Elementary systems do not usually specify an individual but, rather, a category of individuals from which a spouse must be drawn.) Thus a society composed of unilineal descent groups like patriclans might have a simple rule that a man cannot marry in his own descent group; it would leave completely open the question of the descent group in which he might find a wife. Theoretically, it could be any other descent group in the society. Therefore, any patriclan might be both giving wives to and taking wives from all the other patriclans in the society.

Occasionally, the negative rule of exogamy is made more complex by banning marriage not only in ego's own clan, but in the clan of his other parent, and even in that of one or all of his grandparents. Sometimes the rule is simply that he cannot marry anyone with whom he can trace a kinship tie. The effect is always the same: to send ego further and further away from the circle of close kinsmen in search of a mate. At its most extreme, it is the opposite of the elementary tendency to marry as close a kinsman as possible —a first cousin, for example. The complex tendency strains toward making kinship and affinity domains exclusive of each other, while the elementary strains toward making them synonymous with each other.

It is clear that the subject here is *tendencies* rather than absolute categories. There is a continuum from the most complex system to the most elementary along which societies fall. In complex systems, such as our own, there can be elementary tendencies, as in small populations with a high incidence of marriages between cousins. By and large, however, our own system is about as complex as can be imagined. The only rule regulating marriage choice is the negative one that covers a limited set of relatives—and this varies from country to country in Europe, and from state to state in the United States, for example, with regard to the legality of marriage between first cousins. Religious rules affect marriage between cousins negatively and also the marriage of uncles and aunts with nephews and nieces. Such oddities as the English ban on marriage with a deceased wife's sister have cropped up and been passionately defended as cornerstones of Christian morality. In our own society there are no descent groups, and, while an attenuated form of patrilineal succession operates in some areas of the legal system, it has never led to the formation of corporate groups. It is important to recognize that a complex system like ours, lacking formal kinship groups above the family level and having no positive rule of marriage, is not a monopoly of advanced technological societies. In fact, in formal terms, anthropologists usually class us with the Eskimo. What this amounts to is that complex systems are found at all levels of technological development, while elementary systems are not found above a fairly low threshold of development. This makes

sense. The Eskimo can manage quite well without an elaborate elementary system (if that paradoxical expression may
be allowed), but one could not envisage the bureaucratic,
industrialized, highly mobile population of the United States
divided into two moieties with rules of intermarriage, or into
matriclans with a "mother's brother's daughter" rule as the
operator of a circulating system of alliances. The mobile
nuclear family is the effective unit in our kinship system, and
the whole tendency in the history of kinship in all the
Indo-European peoples has been to shrink effective kinship to
the level of the nuclear family as the industrialization of
society progressed. The situation is much like that in many
hunter-gatherer societies where the effective unit is the small
family, which has to be independent and mobile in order to
survive.

Since a system like ours lacks corporate descent groups,
such kinship groups as exist are said to be "ego-centered,"
or "ego-focused"; that is, they are congeries of persons who
are related to ego in various ways and degrees. This is
contrasted with descent-group organization, which is said to
be "ancestor-focused"; that is, the members of the group
have an ancestor in common who is the fixed founder of
the group. So far in this discussion, the concentration has
been on unilineal descent groups where descent from the
apical ancestor is traced exclusively through either males or
females. There is another form of descent group, however,
in which *all* the descendants of the ultimate ancestor are
members; this obviously involves tracing links through both
males and females and therefore is not unilineal. It is usually
called a "cognatic" descent group—cognates being relatives
through either males or females. In the light of the first principles it can be seen that this form of organization takes advantage of the reproductive abilities of both the brother and
the sister, and proliferates downward through both sexes.

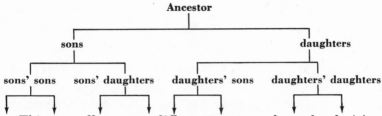

This is really a very different outcome from the decision to employ both forms of unilineal recruitment (double descent). The distinction is a pons asinorum that must be crossed early in the understanding of kinship systems. Cognatic descent groups differ most sharply from their unilineal counterparts in not being discrete units. It is easy to see that they will overlap endlessly and that any person can have multiple membership. I can be a member of the group of each of my four grandparents, each of my eight great-grandparents, and so on. This theoretical multiplication of membership can be reduced by secondary rules of recruitment, however, which effectively produce discrete units. It may be the case, for example, that a group owns land— perhaps the land that belonged to the original ancestor. There might then be a rule that only the members of the descent group—all the descendants of the ancestor—who lived on the land were entitled to full membership and rights. To be exclusive and discrete groups, cognatic lineages have to make such secondary rules. They cannot easily be exogamic units, and sometimes it pays them to have a rule of endogamy (marriage within the group). But mostly the marriage rule in such systems applies to an ego-centered group of relatives rather than to any corporate groups. The result is certainly a complex structure, according to our earlier taxonomy.

Again it must be stressed that a society can use more than one mode of reckoning. It can have cognatic descent groups for some purpose—like landholding—but use unilineal rules in reckoning succession to office, for example.

At the same time, its exogamic unit can be an ego-centered group of kin—say, all ego's kin within the range of third cousins. If such an ego-centered group acquires formal recognition and some legal duties, it is called a "kindred." Most commonly, it is an exogamic unit and little more; but it can be important as a legal entity in such matters as bride price and dowry payments, and the payment of indemnities or the exacting of revenge. The Anglo-Saxon sib (whence the term "sibling") was an ego-centered group whose members were responsible for, among other things, paying compensation to the sib of anyone whom ego killed, the father's side of the family paying more than the mother's side.

Such groups cannot of course act as ongoing corporate units in a kinship system the way unilineal descent groups do, but they can coexist and perform complementary functions. In our system, the kindred has no formal recognition; however, it is probably true that both our fathers' and our mothers' relatives are ideally considered to be in some sense equally kin to us, and in law "next of kin" can come indiscriminately from either side.

This bilateralism of the system is reflected in the way we classify and name our relatives. The basic terms are familiar and are set out below.

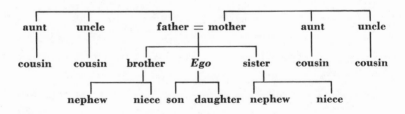

Siblings of the father and mother are equated, as are their children, and the children of ego's brother are not differentiated from the children of his (or her, if ego is female) sister. Terms for affines are constructed by adding "-in-law" to the terms used by the wife for her relatives.

In order to point up the contrast with a radically different system, the English terms will be used, with the strong proviso that they do not *mean* the same thing in another system and language: it is simply a matter here of making the differences in the classifying system as graphic as possible. An alternative system of nomenclature is shown below.

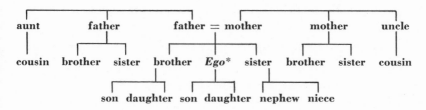

* *Ego*'s wife must be "cousin."

The equations made here are father = father's brother; mother = mother's sister; parallel cousins = siblings; own children = brother's children. Note the differentiations: mother's brother is differentiated from father's brother; parallel cousins from cross-cousins; brother's children from sister's children. The wife is "cousin," that is (if ego is male), either father's sister's daughter or mother's brother's daughter—a cross-cousin. In addition, if the father-in-law was called "uncle" and the mother-in-law "aunt," it would be clear that both sister exchange and its long-term consequence cross-cousin marriage were involved. This would be indicated by the terminology, with its lack of affinal terms and its specification of in-laws as certain types of consanguineous relatives. What at first looks to be a rather bizarre classification makes perfect sense, given the kinship/marriage system involved. To someone in such a direct-exchange system, the failure to make crucial distinctions—such as between father's brother and mother's brother, and cross- and parallel cousins—would seem equally bizarre.

It is clear how, given the elemental situation, systems of

considerable elaboration can be built if, speaking anthropomorphically, the society decides to make use of the situation and the tendencies inherent in it. Different societies capitalize on different elements in the situation and weave their patterns of marital alliance, inheritance and succession, and group membership out of them. In consequence, different ways are found of moving women around the system and linking one generation to the next. Anthropologists are well on the way to understanding the mechanics of these systems and their structural consequences; what they do not fully understand is why societies adopt one strategy rather than another, or why in time they move from one strategy to another—for kinship systems are not immutable, and elementary systems change into complex, unilineal descent groups die out, and so on. The next step in the analysis of kinship systems, then, lies in the study of the adaptational advantages of different systems. And this is a study that involves the understanding of more than just the mechanics of the systems themselves.

FIVE

Marriage, Mobility, and Modern Literature

IN THIS ESSAY, I am going to discuss the role played by marriage in facilitating social mobility in modern Britain. The "evidence" I have is literary—from plays and novels—and that is bad enough. But worse still, I have to poach on the preserve of the sociologist: modern industrial society.

Faced with the disappearance of their subject matter, the primitive society, social anthropologists have had to trespass more on the traditional domain of the sociologists. For it is one of the strange paradoxes of a strange discipline that as its subject matter progressively disappears, the number of its practitioners dramatically increases. This is true, however, only if one accepts that the sole province of social anthropology is the little community. If this is so, then there is not much left for the poor anthropologist but pottering about in North Wales or the West of Ireland, in the hope of finding something whimsical and sociologically offbeat. This role of the paradox-hunting rural sociologist is not a happy one, and although my own vested interest would lead me to defend it as legitimate, I would like to argue that it is not the only possible role for the displaced anthropologist. The differences between him and the sociologist lie not so much in the scale of the subject matter as in the different questions asked about the same phenomena. After all, huge areas of the world, such as India and China and the whole continent of Africa, have until recently been in the hands of anthropologists rather than sociologists. India is a particularly good example. Anthropologists don't balk at handling something as complex as caste; why then should social class be thought beyond them? It is surely the *kind* of approach to social class that distinguishes the anthropologist from the sociologist, and not the fact that the sociologist approaches social class while his colleague shuffles off to the nearest village to study the function of poaching or the politics of the local football club. Sociologists have been interested in communities, too, so, again, it is the kinds of questions asked, and the research tools used, that mark the dividing line between the two disciplines. This dividing line, in any case, is pretty hazy, and I think the time has come to stop being obsessed by it, lest the anthropologists and sociologists, like other closely related but fiercely divided workers, become entangled in petty demarcation disputes.

Because the anthropologist has been traditionally concerned with custom rather than with behavior, he has approached the whole question of the place of marriage in society in a different manner from the sociologist. However, running through all the complex anthropological literature on the subject is a common theme: marriage customs make more sense when marriage is considered not so much as the adjustment of relations between two individuals, but as the mediation of relations between two groups. Not only marriage customs, but the actual marriage patterns might also be more profitably considered in this way. The "flow of women round the system," or the "circulation of spouses," as it is sometimes rather brutally put, is a good indication of how a social system works. This can be either formal, with specified relatives marked out as marriage partners, or informal, with a number of pressures combining to produce "flows" of spouses in particular directions. The exact nature of this mediating process will depend on the nature of the groups involved. One of the simplest differences here involves exchange of women between groups of equal status on the one hand, and a similar exchange between groups of unequal status on the other. There may not be any exchange at all, of course, and the traffic may be all one-way, with, for example, higher-status groups taking women from lower-status but not giving any in return. Sometimes goods are given in lieu of women, and customs of bride price and the like are set up. Women are seen as scarce goods, or as media of exchange, or as prestations and counterprestations in the complex series of transactions in the conjugal market place. Thus, in some societies, the alliances set up by marriage are the only relations that hold between groups, and all economic and political action flows along the channels created by marriage.

The anthropologist has been fascinated by the ambivalence built into these marital relationships. One group must depend on other groups for women and must release its women to other groups. The individual is dependent and hostile, grateful and antagonistic; his relations with wife givers and wife takers are bound to be strained—particularly if considera-

[handwritten margin note: more in E.T. trad. than western societies, lesser extent nowadays than in Fox's]

tions of status are involved. The mother-in-law joke *is* the oldest in the world. And I am not sure that that other curious custom, the honeymoon, might not be interpreted with advantage in this light: the relationship with in-laws is so potentially hostile that the marriage has to be consummated at a distance.

It might be objected that this is all very well in some systems, but in ours marriage is left to the free choice of individuals, and all these anthropological considerations are irrelevant. Needless to say, I do not believe this. Free choice simply means that custom has not crystallized into law and that law and custom intervene less effectively to prevent chaos. In any case, free choice—in the sense of every male in the society having absolute freedom to choose any female outside the bounds of the ecclesiastically disapproved categories—is a myth. Marriage in our own society has always been subordinate to economic or political considerations, and particularly to considerations of status, where these have been at all important. And even where they would not seem to be important, innumerable social pressures have intervened to define, if not the exact spouse, at least the category of persons from whom the mate will be drawn. This can be very formal, as in some primitive societies where a specified person or class of persons is marked out by custom. One does not just marry anybody.

Ours is a highly stratified society, and strata are not usually the tightly knit corporate, well-organized groups that, say, lineages are. Consequently, it should not be expected that the patterns of marriage between them be well defined. This depends on the kind of stratification, of course. India's caste system, for example, is the ultimate in interstratum separateness as expressed through marriage. The essence of caste is the denial of women to other groups. With well-organized subcastes and religious sanctions, the endogamy of the group

124

[handwritten marginalia:]
Marriage
Disagree
This is false because many marriages in western societies are love marriages of them
Only upper class societys are stratified
Both societies this has decreased
Selection
Disagree Not the point
Point of castes is to segregate what is considered upper-class from lower class.
However this caste system has been abolished by some societies esp. individuals who want to marry regardless of caste
eg. Actress Hema (Hindu) married a...
large opposition from society. Strong need within 'caste'

can be preserved. This serves the function of keeping the lines of division between the groups clear and unmistakable. I would maintain that this is why, in any stable stratified society, there are tendencies toward endogamy. If the strata begin to intermarry too much, the lines of division become blurred and the statuses confused. There *can* be intermarriage of strata with the distinctions retained, as long as the persons who marry in, be they male or female, are cut off from their origins and thoroughly absorbed. This would be necessary, for instance, if a high stratum was running short of women and had to take them in from a lower stratum. There are many theoretical possibilities, but the three most interesting are (1) the situation of complete endogamy, in which strata do not intermarry at all; (2) the situation in which marriage is allowed but the mobile spouse is absorbed into the receiving group and cut off from the group of origin; (3) the situation of free intermarriage, which, in all likelihood, will blur and break down the distinctions between strata. These three possibilities could, besides being discrete strategies, also be stages of development in interstratum marital relations.

Social classes are rarely so well organized as castes, estates, or ethnic groups, insofar as marriage is concerned. And in any case, there are many other relationships between them that seem to loom larger than the marital, and it is these that have been the concern of the sociologist. However, in our own society there is, and has been throughout modern history, a complex body of customs and usages, conventions and quasi-legal considerations that governs interstratum marriage. In relatively stable times, cross-stratum marriage would be rarer than in times of rapid social change; the conventions would be firmer and more widely accepted. (Peasants marry princesses only in fairy tales.) Insofar as the society changed, so would the pattern of marriage between the classes. And this is where mobility comes in.

125

Times of rapid social change are usually times in which there is a shift in the power between the strata. The top lot loose their grip to some extent and the barriers come down. The effect of this is usually felt mostly in the political and economic spheres, but in many ways its most important expression is in the changes in interstratum marriage; for it is on the management of this that the group's distinctiveness depends. Of course, in the case of social classes, unlike castes, the "group" is not usually managing marriage at all. No; it is the accumulation of myriad individual decisions, rather than the ruling of a caste court, that will determine these changes. But that does not mean that the pattern of mobility will be haphazard. On the contrary, all the individuals of a class share the same values and fear their dilution and loss. In protecting their daughters they are protecting their group, even if there is no Society for the Preservation of Middle-Class Purity to deal with this in an organized way. This is a case where circumstances conspire to affect a pattern of intergroup relations.

Social change will increase interstratum mobility via marriage, but it is important to determine the kind of mobility and its direction, and all the circumstances attendant upon them. The question can be simply put: Who moves which way and why? And why this type of move? This brings me to the crux of my argument. I would maintain that it is rare, if not impossible, for an increase in interstratum mobility that is a result of rapid social change to be random, to be simply free-for-all. In other words, either males or females move, and only in one direction. (I am speaking of the dominant, socially important movement, of course.) The content and direction will depend on the circumstances and, in particular, on what advantages the groups concerned wish to maximize, to borrow the language of the economists. Another correlate of this situation is that some groups will feel threatened by this increase in mobility and react accordingly.

Marriage, then, is an important way of mediating relatic between groups and is best understood as a part of these relations, along with political, economic, and status considerations. There is an element of ambivalence and hostility endemic in the affinal relationship. In stratified societies, strata can either not intermarry at all, and so maintain their distinctiveness, or intermarry, in which case it is the dominant stratum that controls the process. In times of considerable structural change, interstratum mobility via marriage will increase according to definite patterns that will involve the movement of one sex in one direction, according to the circumstances that lie behind the social change as a whole.

In English society there have been several significant changes in patterns of marital mobility, each linked to the state of society and the nature and rapidity of social change. Even when, in relatively stable times, marriage lies *within* the broadly defined strata, people can become obsessed with the slightest gradations in status. The novels of Jane Austen testify to this. Most of the marriages made in her novels are strategic, political, and blatantly economic. The laws of supply and demand are at work, as in any other market. "Good" husbands are scarce and have to be paid for with a handsome settlement. Slight increases in status and connection thereby are often dearly bought. (Anthropologists often talk of bride price when discussing savages, but our own custom of groom price is dignified with the euphemistic "dowry.") Aristocratic marriages, and certainly royal marriages, have always been political. Among the *bourgeoisie* it was the alliance of two businesses that accounted for many marriages, just as the alliance of two great houses did at a higher level. Among the lower orders, things were perhaps easier—but peasant marriages have been traditionally hard-driven bargains. Of all classes, the town proletariat was perhaps the freest from these considerations. So much for marriages within the strata.

mainly depended
on individuals
marrying.

English society has been remarkable for its openness in interstratum marriage. Classes have always intermarried there has never been any legal bar to their doing so—a marriage and mobility have been variously linked. Unlike the nobility of the rest of Europe, English nobility has never been a closed caste or even an approximation of one. Younger sons and daughters have always married down into the gentry and the *bourgeoisie.* However, until the nineteenth century, interstratum marriage was not common. In the eighteenth century the most prominent type of interstratum marriage was probably that between nobility and lesser gentry—with some dipping into the professions. The way men and women moved was probably similar. In the nineteenth century, the successful *bourgeoisie,* wishing to buy as much status as possible with its growing wealth, managed to marry into the nobility. Here, I imagine, the pattern was largely that of daughters of rich merchants marrying the younger sons of the nobility in order to restore or shore up the fortunes of the latter. Second-generation rich merchants might very well have looked for upper-class wives in order to fix their status, too, but the predominant pattern of access to noble status was through their daughters. The literature of the time gives abundant indication of the conditions and rules. The twentieth century has seen a *de facto* merger of the top rich and the top titled. Also, it has seen an emancipation of the workers previously left altogether out of this reckoning. A new pattern of movement is in evidence—that of lower-stratum males marrying middle-stratum females. To some extent, this will always be the pattern in a relatively open society, where it is the male who is likely to be independently mobile. He is therefore likely to seek out a wife from the stratum to which he aspires. In more rigid societies, it is often the women who are used as passive instruments of mobility by their fathers so that grandchildren may inherit status. In our society, a man can achieve it in his own lifetime if he plays the game properly—a man, but a woman not yet so easily.

Women can move up the scale because they still tend to take their status from their husbands, although rapid movement is most likely only on the part of models. This is the reason why education now seems to be the chief escalator for lower-stratum males. It is not a case of the middle classes' handing over their females to the workers. (This they never did and would never do.) It is a case of workers'—or sons of workers—gaining that indubitable stamp of respectability, the university education, and then clinching their changed status by marrying a middle-class wife. The middle-class parents cannot, on status grounds, deny their daughter to an export manager or research chemist, even though his parents may be a miner and a charwoman. Indeed, despite his background, his status may even appear to be higher than that of the middle-class parents.

The motivations and mechanisms of this new form of marital mobility are different from those of previous eras, and I think that it is education that makes for this difference. There is not much statistical evidence yet, however; so it is necessary to turn to literature for clues.

Two mobile early-twentieth-century characters in literature furnish some contrasts. Mellors in D. H. Lawrence's *Lady Chatterley's Lover* is a self-made intellectual. Lawrence is at pains to point out that he is no peasant, but an educated man. He has books on the shelf in his gamekeeper's cottage of a kind that even "our wives and servants" could read without blushing. He can discuss art and literature and politics. He rose from the ranks to be an officer—a considerable achievement in those days. He can talk standard English if he wants to, but lapses into the vernacular to annoy Constance's friends—in particular a lady friend whom he dislikes intensely. He seems to get on well with Lady Chatterley's father, whom he does not dislike—they have a kind of distant man-to-man relationship. But he rejects upper-class values and even despises them. He becomes a gamekeeper and, despite his talents, hides away in the woods. Yet he aspires to a woman of the upper classes and abandons one of his own class. The woman he aspires to is somewhat weak. She has an affair with an artist whose person and painting Mellors hates—for lacking the "bowels of compassion." She is attracted to Mellors and hopes to marry him, although the book ends on a doubtful note. Lady Chatterley's husband is hurt, not so much by her infidelity, but by the fact that her lover is a gamekeeper. This class theme crops up continually. (The book loses artistically by making Lady Chatterley's husband impotent and by not making Mellors a true gamekeeper, but rather a disaffected intellectual. In some of his short stories, Lawrence toys with the peasant-and-the-lady, or back-to-the-haystack, idea, but in his novels it seems he cannot bear the sexy peasant to be all sex; he has to educate him up a bit —to Lawrence's own level, that is. We must not forget that Lawrence, the miner's son, ran away with a professor's wife, herself a German countess.)

Denry Machin, in Arnold Bennett's *The Card*, is no ordinary yokel, either. He is determined to rise in the world and succeeds by a series of ruses and entrepreneurial dodges. He engineers himself a grammar-school education by cheating on his examinations, and gets a job with a solicitor by subterfuge. He ingratiates himself with the local aristocracy and *bourgeoisie*, escapes from an entanglement with a "common" dancing teacher, and ends up marrying the daughter of a respectable bourgeois—although in fairness to Denry we should note that her father had gone bankrupt. The fact remains that he does not marry, or even contemplate marrying, a working-class wife. He ends up solidly in the rich *bourgeoisie* as Lord Mayor, and president of the football club.

But there is a difference between him and Mellors. Denry is an old-fashioned social climber. He wants to *belong* to the middle class. He wants to *be* middle-class, and a middle-class wife is part of the scheme. He actively acculturates. He accepts their values and culture. Mellors rejects all these possibilities and retires to his gamekeeper's cottage and his animals and birds. But he is attracted to a woman of the upper class. And he takes her—not without encountering hostility and opposition. He is not a simple peasant in love with the king's daughter; he is an intelligent, educated, and articulate critic of the class whose woman he is taking. Both Denry and Mellors take women from a class above them, but only Denry joins it and is approved; Mellors rejects it and is hated.

In contemporary literature there are not many examples of the Machin syndrome, but the modified-Mellors syndrome is prevalent. In fact, the modern, socially mobile heroes are spread on a continuum from Machin to Mellors, skewed toward the Mellors end. Jimmy Porter in John Osborne's *Look Back in Anger* is the nearest parallel to Mellors. Again, despite his working-class background, he is no yokel. He has been to university, although it was not even red brick but rather "white tile." (Osborne must have meant the London School of Economics.) He aspires to a woman of higher social class and gets her. He hates her mother and her domineering female friend, but in the end dominates and seduces the friend. He has a half-admiring relationship with his wife's father—"a plant left over from Edwardian wilderness." (The freemasonry of men again.) He has a lot of potential but prefers to live in an attic playing his trumpet and selling sweets in a market. Like Mellors, he finds solace in animals, but his are imaginary bears and squirrels. They help to make life tolerable for himself and his wife, between whom the only contact seems to be childlike, through the animals, or physical. He has rejected a girl of his own class in order to take the girl from a higher class, and yet he is nostalgic for his lost love. He is violently and articulately critical of his wife's class, particularly as represented by her mummy, who seems, along with the posh Sunday papers, to sum up all that he hates about it.

He is a kind of Mellors, mobile up to a point; but when it comes to joining the class that, by education and marriage, he now has a right to enter, he backs out and retreats. But he cannot go back to the workers from whence he came; he has to contract out of the whole effort.

Closer to Denry, but not really like him, is Joe Lampton in John Braine's *Room at the Top*. Joe's motives are Denry's, all right—to get at all costs out of the working and into the middle class, largely because of the luxury the latter would afford him. His method is even more direct: get the daughter of a rich man with child and so force his way in via marriage. He, like Mellors, was self-educated in the army, although Joe used his time in a POW camp to continue his accountancy studies, hating the "gallant" middle-class escapees who had, unlike him, something to escape to. He has to abandon a middle-class woman who would have held him back in his ambition. There is another girl—of his class—with whom he toys but ruthlessly puts to one side. He has a violent conflict with the lover of the middle-class woman he abandons and with her husband, and shows the dislike of art and artists that all these heroes seem to share. With the girl he marries, his relationship is purely physical. She also is weak and ineffectual; a nice girl like Lady Chatterley, Denry's wife, and Jimmy Porter's Alison. He hates her mother, reasonably, one might venture, and has the inevitable ambivalent relationship with her father, whom he half likes and who, in turn, half likes him. (The father himself in this case is a Denry who has risen and married a middle-class wife, and from whom one might expect empathy, if not sympathy, for his unbidden son-in-law.) But once in the class to which he aspires and goes to such lengths to enter, he is not happy. Basically, he despises it, although he covets the material advantages it affords him. In his motives he is a Machin, in his judgment a bit of a Mellors. He assimilates reluctantly, unhappily, and critically. He is in it only for the cash.

An unexpected candidate, perhaps, and one who treads a middle path between the Lamptons and the Porters of this world, is Kingsley Amis's *Lucky Jim*. Jim Dixon comes from the same sort of background—local grammar school, provincial university. Like Machin, he wants the good life and an easy job. He aspires to a girl of a higher class who has a rich uncle to ensure these things for him. Here is the father figure again, and also the tolerable relationship between the two. He hates the mother figure of Mrs. Welch and carries on a one-man class war against her on the Jimmy Porter pattern, only less articulately. He is better at pulling faces and writing rude words on mirrors than at anything else— although the phrases he uses are more true to type than the well-rounded sentences of Jimmy Porter. Almost uncannily, his girl has an artist lover whose person and art Jim hates. All in all, Jim Dixon hates the culture and values of the class into which he would like to move. He hates the pretensions of fashionable art, recorder-playing, and the ceremonial lunacies of provincial university life. Here, too, the girl is colorless, but Jim abandons a girl of his own class for her. In this case it is a merciful release; whatever class his Margaret belonged to, she would be insufferable, but her whole manner and behavior stamp her as uncompromisingly lower-middle (minus), and it is from this that Jim wants to escape. In the end he gets the girl he wants and the job—but, as in *Lady Chatterley*, it is not clear whether the relationship will work out.

What all these characters have in common is that they marry women from a higher class. In each case this involves rejecting a woman of their own class (with the slight exception of Joe Lampton). They all have an ambivalent relationship with the father of the girl, and hate the mother, or mother figure, and females of the class. They also hate the young males, whether they be chinless wonders from Sandhurst, ex-RAF officers, or artists (these in particular are despised). They differ in their views of marriage as a deliberate instrument of policy. Joe Lampton and Jim Dixon are consciously and deliberately mobile—Jim less so than Joe—and the girls are part of the design. In the case of Jimmy Porter and Mellors, however, the taking of the girls is part of a refusal to be mobile; this is the crucial difference. *They take the women of the upper stratum but refuse to join it.* The relationship of hostility and hatred is greatest here. Inasmuch as Joe Lampton and Jim Dixon are willing, like Denry Machin before them, to accept, even superficially, the rules of the middle class, they are tolerated—if uncomfortably. But Mellors and Porter refuse to play. Porter, in fact, regards the marriage as an act of plunder.

To take the women of the group and yet stay outside its conventions—even attack them—is under any circumstances upsetting for the group, especially when an exchange of women is precluded. The highly patterned movement I spoke of is in evidence here. There is no two-way movement of both men and women; it is a movement of males up. The males achieve some status on their own and then clinch this with a marriage. (Even Joe Lampton was a qualified accountant.) Like the peasants of old, they have to perform tasks to prove themselves worthy of the king's daughter and half the kingdom. The task in this modern fairy tale is to get a university degree or, in the words of academic registrars, an "equivalent qualification."

But note the crucial difference between the modern characters and Denry Machin—a difference that skews the distribution toward Mellors. None of them really yearns to be assimilated into the class he marries. At best he will play along, at worst he will attack it in some way—or he will retreat from the whole business. They can none of them accept uncritically the mores of the middle class; they all resist absorption. Their education has perhaps given them standards that lie outside middle-class morality, by which they judge, and judge unfavorably, the worlds of their respective wives.

If these interstratum marriages, which seem to obsess modern novelists and playwrights, are on the increase, and if the universities are the market places for them, what can universities today tell us about the prospects for the future? My concern, naturally, is central to anthropology: the circulation of women in the system as culture bearers, which makes their distribution by marriage extremely important. In the cases discussed here it is the movement of spouses *between* strata that is important. In the old days, what chance was there for a working-class boy to meet, much less to be in a position to marry, a middle-class girl? None. A girl might rise by virtue of beauty via the chorus line, but that was rare. Even up to and including World War II, this move of working-class boy to middle-class wife was rare. But a distinct pattern has since emerged that goes something like this. Middle-class boys still go mostly to Oxford and Cambridge, where there are not many places for middle-class girls. So, as the number of middle-class girls wanting to go to university increases, they are squeezed out to the provincial universities, whose populations are largely lower-middle- and lower-class males. Not many girls of the latter class go to universities; if they go anywhere, it is to training colleges, where they meet boys of their own class. Thus, even if only the marriages made in the universities and not elsewhere are considered, the statistics could be expected to show a high proportion of lower-middle class and/or working-class males marrying the nice girls from respectable homes and good schools who are in the provincial universities. The Oxbridge middle-class boys will probably marry girls of their class who didn't go to university anyway.

Let's suppose that all this conjecture is true and that this marriage pattern *is* on the increase. To what will it lead? The absorption of these people into the already existing class system? In other words, will the sons-in-law play the game in the Machin fashion, or string along like lucky Jim? Or will this marriage pattern lead to the existence of new status groups of disaffected intellectuals who feel they have no place in the class system as we know it? Will they withdraw? Only those, I suspect, who take to attics or cottages in Cornwall. By and large, they will have to accommodate, if only to please the wife's relatives.

In terms of the theory of interstratum marital mobility advanced earlier, the situation is one in which the females of a higher stratum who had not been available to males of a lower are being made available because of changes in the educational system. This is a one-way movement of males into the higher stratum. An exchange is precluded for status reasons—middle-class boys cannot marry lower-class girls. The problem is whether the higher-stratum members (other than the girls concerned in the marriages) who are hostile to the newcomers can absorb them effectively, and thus preserve their own distinctiveness; or whether they will lose their women to a new class of disaffected intellectuals who will not accept their values.

The paradox of the situation is that the mechanism that allows the males to rise and claim these females—the educational escalator—is also what leads to the disaffection. The escalator picks out the most intelligent to be mobile; hence, if they do reject the middle class it is likely to be an intelligent, well-directed, and articulate rejection. I think more will be willing to assimilate than to reject, but those who reject remain a problem for our still important status system.

The focus of the interstratum relationship will, of course, be the two familes concerned: the working-class parents of the boy and the middle-class parents of the girl. In these stories this is not dealt with. The males seem to have been born in a vacuum; they have no parents as far as these writers are concerned (Joe Lampton's are killed off), and so the problem is dodged. But the boy's parents and their class are not under threat anyway. It is in the relation of the boy to his wife's parents that the real strain, ambivalence, and hostility will lie, and this is the stuff of drama. It is also the stuff of the anthropological theory of marriage.

An Irish Island

I FIRST VISITED Tory by accident almost. I was on the Donegal mainland, opposite Tory Island, learning Gaelic as part of my interest in bilingualism. One day someone announced that a boat was leaving for Tory. Out of curiosity I hopped aboard the small open yawl for the nine-mile journey out to the towering rock I had seen from the shore, but never quite believed was real. The boat was to come back that night or, at worst, in the morning. But a storm blew up—not uncommon on that most northerly part of the Irish coast—and it was a week before I got back. During that time I was totally dependent on the islanders; I hadn't even brought a toothbrush with me. Luckily, I had borrowed some boots and a raincoat from the official Donegal folklore collector, Seán Ọh-Eochaidh, friend of many incompetent visiting scholars. Otherwise, I was without any means of survival. That was one of the most hilarious and fascinating weeks of my life, and I went back to Tory every year after that for at least the next five. I hesitate to call this "field work," although I did the standard things. Somehow the time spent on the last outpost of true Gaeldom shouldn't be counted as work, field or otherwise.

I have complained about field work as an end in itself, but there is no question of its personal appeal. The delight in trying to unravel the complexities of another culture has to be savored to be believed. The tourist never has to do it, and those who go native, like T. E. Lawrence, are usually too involved in their own egos to understand the culture they are using. The anthropologist treads an uneasy tightrope between distance and absorption. Distance usually wins out because the people he is "studying" are really so different from him that absorption would be impossible (although empathy certainly is not). And yet I had trouble avoiding absorption on Tory. For a start, I am part Irish, and once the stout is flowing and the singing begins, the genes take over. Another anthropologist visited the island one summer. It was nearly a week before he realized that I was not an islander. But why should total identification be a problem? Nowadays many a "native" is writing about his people, and the sensitivity and "objectivity" of, for example, Alfonzo Ortiz writing about his own Tewa Indians should make us forget the problems of objectivity altogether. The sermons about it that we used to get from those teaching us field work were part of a puritan plot to stop people from having any fun. Work and play had to be separated or God would strike us all dead. How did H. L. Mencken define puritanism? "The haunting fear that someone, somewhere, might be happy." To admit that you were enjoying something for which you were getting a grant was regarded, in my initiation school, as frivolous. You had to stress how much you had suffered. Well, the sand fleas, the unrelieved diet of potatoes and salt fish that gave me scurvy, the constant drizzle, and the truly awesome gales were a sort of suffering, I suppose. But I count them as nothing compared with the excruciating boredom of university administration and the harassments of "civilization" generally.

There is a sadness to all I have written about Tory, because it is, like the Pueblos, a dying culture. And I am unashamedly romantic about this. I like the Celtic fringe and Celtic twilight, and it is distressing and painful to me that the most beautiful language in Europe should be dying on the lips of those who are still capable of speaking it. There is no language like it, and unlike Latin, it will never be the same once it is a dead language. It is so alive, so full of that peculiarly Irish mixture of cynicism and sentimentality, of ironic humor and bitter stoicism, that it needs the strange Irish culture to sustain it. And that culture, with all its sadness and privation, but with all its heroic refusal to be crushed by mere circumstances (that is, the English), is going down fast under the weight of television and a helicopter service. Tory is a last outpost, but the sad irony that authentic Gaeldom flourishes now only where there is also authentic poverty spells the doom of both. Doom is inevitable; but, at least for a while yet, the outsider who wants to catch the last sparks of that culture can do so—and be stunned by the beauty of a Bronze Age epic from the lips of an old man, or a flash of poetry in the love song of a young girl:

> *Tá mo chroidhe-se brúighte briste*
> *Mar leac-oidhre air uachtar uisce;*

> *Mar bheidh cnuasach cnó tr'éis a mbriste,*
> *Ná maighdean óg tr'éis a pósta.*

"My heart is bruised and broken / like ice on top of water; / like a bunch of nuts after breaking, / or a young maiden after marrying"—a Connaught song, this, that found its way north. Or a young man might disarm you completely with a piece of irreverence like this:

> *Chuaidh mé 'un aonaigh is dhíol mé mo bhó*
> *Ar chúig phunnta airgid is ar ghiní bhuidhe óir;*
> *Má ólaim an t-airgead is má phronnaim an t-ór,*
> *Caidé sin do'n té sin nach mbaineann sin dó?*

"I will go to the fair and I'll sell my cow / for five pounds in silver and a guinea of yellow gold; / and if I drink up the silver and eat up the gold, / what's that to those who mind their own business?" My translation of the last line is rather free, to get the spirit of it.

The three essays here cannot convey the spirit of it, though. I've included the one on myths and fighting, even though it might offend, because the spirit does come through—some of the life, some of the zany quality. The essay on names gives some of the island flavor while having, I hope, a broad appeal by virtue of its universal implications. It illustrates very nicely the principles of cognatic descent that I discussed in "Kinship and Alliance."

But it will all go. *"Tá na focail briste i'mo bhéal,"* a man complained to me of the loss of Gaelic: "The words are broken in my mouth." This is a phrase sometimes used to describe how one was interrupted, cut off while saying something, left speechless. And no culture can survive without its natural speech.

SIX

The Vanishing Gael

THE PHENOMENON called "acculturation"—the gradual re-
placement of a traditional way of life by new customs and
institutions—is a constant preoccupation of social anthropologists. Usually they have turned their attention to exotic
societies of the Pacific, Africa, and the Americas. But the
breakdown of traditional cultures is taking place under our
noses—in rural districts, in city slums, and in the remoter
areas of the British Isles. The Celtic fringe of Western Ireland and Scotland provides us with examples of what are
probably the last remaining primitive societies on England's
doorstep. In particular, some of the islands retain the characteristics of homogeneity, simple technology, and a kin-
ship-based social structure that delineate the anthropologist's
"simple" society.

How long will they last and in what form? They are under constant pressure to change—a pressure sometimes overt, stemming from government and official intervention, and sometimes covert, a result of subtle changes in economy or social life neither sought after nor imposed. In Western Ireland, an official determination to preserve the Gaelic culture and language produces strains toward conservatism, but this has not prevented a cultural decline, and even an evacuation of some islands that were mainsprings of the Gaelic way of life (the Blaskets, for example). The farthest offshore island, Tory in County Donegal, is the remotest of the Irish-speaking areas, one of the most traditional, and one of the most flourishing. What is it like? How has it survived? How will it continue to survive, if at all?

The island is one hour's journey, on a good day, from the Donegal coast. It stands spectacularly on the horizon like a huge aircraft carrier, the cliffs at the east end rising to more than three hundred feet. In legend it was the home of sea pirates who were there before the Gaels, including the mighty Balor of the Evil Eye, who ravaged the mainland for cattle and sport before dying at his grandson's hand. Colmcille (Saint Columba) Christianized the island and, together with Balor, figures prominently in Tory mythology and history. The remoteness of the island, making it belong rather to the Atlantic Ocean than to Ireland, has preserved for its two hundred and fifty inhabitants a unique way of life. Although it is only three miles long and a mile at its widest, it contains two distinct settlements—four, counting the lighthouse and its buildings at the extreme west and the prehistoric hill fort, Balor's Castle, at the extreme east. The two towns, West Town and East Town, although only a quarter of a mile distant, are socially worlds apart. West Town is the urban center. It has the harbor and slipways, the church and school, the dance hall and graveyard, the three shops, and the nurse's surgery. East Town is simply a collection of houses on a ridge. But there is a fierce communal loyalty. Some West Towners have never been to East Town, and most East Towners affirm a strong preference for the "country," for its quiet and friendliness, as opposed to the bustle and relative impersonality of the "metropolis." Thus even within the island we have a center where change is possible and likely because of shops and the growth of debtor-creditor relationships, and a traditional, rural enclave that resists change.

The islanders' fields are spread out around the two towns, those in the East radiating like the spokes of a wheel. The fields are divided into strips and present a complex pattern of both design and ownership. Most families own about one and a half acres—"enough for a donkey and some potatoes." A few cows and horses, sheep and donkeys, and vast numbers of chickens are the only livestock. Most families own a small rowing currach for inshore fishing, and there are several larger, motor-powered boats for travel to the mainland and for more adventurous fishing. The boats are almost all constructed, with great skill, on the island.

For most of Tory's history the problem of sheer physical survival has been uppermost. A population of up to six hundred crowded onto this shelf of rock, supporting itself at subsistence level from sea, shore, and farmland. There was room for all to fish, but the little canoes, which were the only vessels, were dangerous in heavy seas. The cost in human life was high and the returns negligible. The shore line was limited and its harvest valuable. Every year it was re-divided and the kelp and sea rod, winkles and other shell-fish were eagerly gathered, as was valuable driftwood (there are no trees on the island) and occasional contraband. The small amount of peat was meticulously divided also, but this was gradually to run out; today it has almost totally disappeared. The land was the main problem. Throughout the eighteenth century, under landlord supervision, a system of common ownership and field rotation was practiced that ensured a fair distribution of good soil among the households. This broke down, and in the early nineteenth century the land was divided and individual ownership of fields recognized. Subsequently, the system of inheritance led to progressive fragmentation of holdings and the scattering of strips. Heirs shared land equally, as a rule, so that plots had to be divided again and again, generation by generation. A man might find himself with several tiny holdings in half a dozen different places. The complications of inheritance and ownership gradually became more intricate, with sometimes three or four people sharing the work and produce of one small strip of land. Such a system was obviously subject to recurrent crises of a classic Malthusian kind. The complications of increasing population pressure on a fixed area of land, married to bilateral inheritance, could be resolved only by reducing the population and rationalizing the system of land tenure. Several natural factors—disease, death at sea, a high infant mortality rate, imbalance in the sex raito, nonmarriage, and emigration—helped to ease the pressure. In the mid-nineteenth century the landlord of the island "removed" about one hundred of the inhabitants and reallocated the fields, bringing them together into large units and forbidding sales or inheritances that would reintroduce fragmentation. The removals were a success, but still the fragmentation did not stop. Emigration on any scale did not occur until the late nineteenth century, and even then Tory was not depopulated at anywhere near the rate of the mainland.

Thus the ninteenth- and early-twentieth-century picture is of an overcrowded island whose inhabitants struggled for bare subsistence against the hostile environment. The social structure, too, developed its own problems. The island was largely endogamous, few marriages were to mainlanders. The complications of kinship consequent on this can be imagined. While presenting a united face to the outside world, the island was, like all such communities, given to interfamilial feuding. Family loyalties were (and are) tremendously strong, and the usual cure for quarrels between families— intermarriage—did not always take. A significant custom, still present though declining, decreed that even after marriage the spouses should remain in their natal homes if they still had families to support. Thus a woman would stay with her elderly parents or her brothers and look after them while her husband stayed in his home and visited her. Children stayed with their mothers. The shortage of houses at the height of overcrowding may have encouraged this custom, but in times of low population, and even today, it is practiced. (In 1962, ten marriages out of a total of fifty followed this pattern.) The pull of the intimate family ties, the strength of the group around the same hearth, was thus stronger than bonds of matrimony. The husband-wife roles were sacrificed at the expense of those of child-parent and brother-sister. A woman's first loyalty was unquestionably to her own family, not to her husband. Men also were unwilling to move in with a wife if she still had relatives living with her. Many men moved in late in life, after the wife's parents had died and her brothers had emigrated.

Over the generations, a wider kin group than the household developed, often embracing quite distant relatives. This group acted together for some purposes but was in no sense "corporate." In the event of a quarrel the members of the group would stick together; they would help one another in sickness and mourn one another's death.

A crisis could often arise because of Catholic marriage rules. Persistent intermarriage tended to bring most people into the prohibited range of cousinship. In this century the authorities have encouraged adoptions of mainland orphans to ease this problem. In the past, dispensations had often to be sought.

These problems were met in various ways—practical, magical, and fantastical. Religion was (and is) a great strength to a people facing a seemingly relentless universe. The island is sacred to Colmcille, who made it his home and a center of learning. His name (coupled with that of the Blessed Virgin) is foremost in all prayers. Along with the religion, there developed an attitude of fatalism, a feeling that the ways of the sea and of man and of God are incomprehensible and uncontrollable. An effort can be made in the practical sphere, but after a certain point all is chance or the will of God. Even in the days of powerful motorboats there is great caution and respect for the sea.

Law and order, such as was necessary, were maintained by the priest, while the "king" of the island functioned mainly as an arbiter of shore disputes—and as chief magician. The office of "king" has lapsed.

The terrible winters were whiled away with story, song, and dancing. Aside from the practical arts of weaving, knitting, and boatbuilding, there were no plastic arts on Tory. The voice and the imagination were all that this impoverished people had as material for a folk art. But a serious gaiety in the performance of songs and dances and in the telling of stories lightened even the dreariest existence. In these relatively affluent days, the old ones look back to the time when the island was "jolly!" In this jollity there was a grim recklessness—a laughing defiance of the inevitability of suffering—that went with the ingrained fatalism. In the winter, when the island was cut off by storms and food almost nonexistent, the men would gather in a house and spend a whole night gambling for one of the few cows still alive.

The problem of sheer physical survival has passed with the

advent of the large motorboats and the building of tall, strong houses; with the erection of piers and slipways; with the removal of landlordism and the advent of official patronage; with the checks from abroad and the work in Scotland. No longer is a large population fighting to maintain itself at subsistence level; rather, a dwindling, largely elderly population is coasting along in reasonable comfort, with the problems of survival lodged in other hands. The problem now is not how to live with the sea and each other and not starve. It is how to persuade enough young people to stay and make their homes on the island.

A pattern of migrant laboring has taken firm hold. Earlier in the century, emigration was the rule. One just left for America or Australia. But once the wave of emigration subsided, it was discovered that there was work in Scotland, on roads and farms: casual well-paid work. At first the men would leave for several years at a time, but then it was discovered that a man could earn enough in the winter to keep him and his parents and he could return in the summer to the pleasant, free life of the island. So each September most of the men leave (a few stay behind and go on fishing trips), and in May and June they return. A changed pattern of fishing has emerged. The herring industry (there was once a curing station on Tory) has declined, and lobsters and crayfish have become the center of new industry. Their season coincides with the summer homecomings, and the young men combine lobster-fishing in the summer with laboring in the winter and make a good all-round income. Usually a number of brothers and paternal cousins man a boat and share the profits, part of which goes to keep the old ones. Often one brother is a permanent islander, using and maintaining the boat in the winter. Some brothers take turns at staying away for two years at a time.

After World War I, it was common for girls, too, to work

away, often for years at a time, and many decided to marry and settle outside. However, enough stayed at home to provide marriage partners for the men who, after an intensive period of migrating between eighteen and thirty, were ready to marry and settle down. Recently, however, the young girls began following the migratory pattern, and it has snowballed; in 1962, for instance, all the marriageable girls left for "winter" jobs. What is more, these jobs are usually of longer duration than the casual work of the men, who still average three to four months a year on the island. The girls average three to four weeks. The chances of these girls marrying on the island are reckoned to be pretty slim. (What is more, women from outside have seldom, if ever, moved to the island when they married Tory men.) For the girls at least, Tory is no longer a base for expeditions to the outside world but a childhood home they return to in the holidays.

For the present generation of schoolchildren, the future pattern of life is established. With very few exceptions they will go away to work. This is a conscious ambition on the part of most of the older ones, and indeed there is no practical alternative. Working away has become part of the life cycle, a *rite de passage* as firmly established as baptism and confirmation. It is the initiation into adulthood.

However, the pull of the hearth, of the family, of the free and easy life of the island is still strong and attractive to these young people. Tory is home; its ways and values are understood. Within the small world of the island one can have status and friendship. These are hard to achieve in a world of laboring and domestic service, where one's ability to sing or step dance is not a qualification for promotion. Even when they are in Scotland, kinship ties are still all-important. The migrants are "fed" along a kinship network. It is always to members of their extended kinship group fully resident outside the island that they go for help in finding work and hospitality. This serves both to cushion the impact of the out-side world and to keep them within the Tory orbit.

This new pattern of life has profoundly changed the island culture. Farming is no longer important, and many fields are left idle. Food can be bought at the shops with wages and government pensions. So can clothes and other necessaries. Spinning and weaving have died out, although some women are still expert knitters. The shops have introduced an element of economic competition and a new type of motivation and social relationship, but the owners are firmly enmeshed in the web of kinship and this motivation is not disruptive. Shore gathering has practically vanished, except for sea rod, which the children collect and dry for sale to nylon manufacturers. There is a school and a nurse and, weather permitting, a regular postal service.

All these features have eased the pressure on land and people. There is no overcrowding, no land shortage and dispute, no loss of life at sea, no possibility of starvation. But gone with these is the distinctive way of life that rose to meet them. The absence of the young people for most of the year makes life dull for the old ones. Instead of a whole round of activities throughout the year, there is only a short burst in the summer. The old sports and entertainments are forgotten. The old songs are known to an ever diminishing circle. The stories die as the old men die. The language gets corrupted. Only the belief in ghosts retains a hold on every islander: the magic, the curses and spells, the beautiful old prayers, the cures and miracles are all vanishing. At the summer dances the young people are now asking for quick-steps and jazz, and are complaining about having to listen to the "mournful" old Gaelic songs and their seemingly pointless preoccupation with shipwreck, dowries, cows, and death. Although Gaelic is still undoubtedly first language to all Tory people and the language of all ordinary conversation, the last man who knew no English is now dead.

Emigration has not seriously affected the island society; it has simply taken away some people. The culture has been left intact. Migrant labor takes and returns people each year—the same people—and they return changed and the culture changes with them. New ideas, needs, values, and artifacts are fed back into the culture yearly, and yearly the culture changes. The very factor that preserves the island as a social unit—the desire of the young to return—will probably destroy it as a last stronghold of Gaelic life in these islands. It is only the twilight of the once bright life that can still be seen when, in winter, the old ones gather round the fires with nothing to do but reminisce and gamble for beef.

SEVEN

Myths and Fighting

The Living Past

WE ARE LOSING CONTACT with old British national myths, apart from the Arthurian cycle, which continues to exert its fascination. Guy Fawkes is rapidly becoming a mythological figure; yet he is almost mythless. There are few who can weave a symbolic story around him today, or who would care to. Father Christmas is a foreign import. Even Hereward and Robin Hood have been rendered anemic by television. The feeling of continuity is gone, especially with the older myths. How many Cockneys could tell about the Lud of Ludgate Hill? Or who among the inhabitants of Colchester could trot out the exploits of Coel—or would even know

153

there was a connection with the old king of the nursery rhyme? We are too mobile, too literate, too urban, too little concerned with our connection to a place to care much.

It comes as a shock, therefore, to find in the West of Ireland communities still in intimate contact with their mythological past. Here a place name is not something of interest only to etymologists; it is itself a mythological record. The names of the people themselves are the end product of a genealogy that often stretches back to the time before the coming of the Gaels and links them with the deeds and misdeeds of ancient god-kings. Many Celtic scholars have been amazed to hear from the mouths of illiterate peasants versions of the great myth cycles of the *Tuatha Dé Danánn,* of *Cuchulainn,* and of *Finn Mac Cumhail;* tales that are recorded only in the earliest known Celtic manuscripts, and which, it was thought, were known only to scholars.

The scholars, of course, with their overvaluation of literacy, were astonished at this evidence of the tenacity of oral tradition. An anthropologist, on the other hand, is used to dealing with illiterate societies and to asking about the function of myth. He should be less astonished than the literary scholar to find such traditions perpetuated. But here at least one anthropologist records his amazement at the strength of some of these traditions.

My initiation into the legends of Donegal was through an old man in the village of Gortahork, who told me a tale of the gory beheading of one MacKineely or MacNeely (in Gaelic: Mac Ceann Fhaolaidh). He was a chieftain who ruled over the locality still known as Cloghaneely (Cloch Chinn Fhaolaidh), which you can still find on any map of Donegal. This chieftain was the son of one Gabhan (Gowan), and, like his father, a smith. His sworn enemy was Balor of the Mighty Blows, who lived in a castle of high towers on Tory Island, nine miles off the coast of Donegal. Indeed, the

map showed that on this island was a hill, Dún Balor—
"Balor's Fort"—and that the highest point of the island was
Tór Mór—"the great tower." There was also marked a
cleft, or defile, known as "Balor's Prison"—but more of that
later. Like most Irish mythological chieftains, Kineely was
engaged in either great deeds or cattle-stealing, mostly the
latter. He envied Balor his magic cow, which gave twenty
gallons at a milking, so he stole it. He brought the cow back
from Tory and tethered it on Inishboffin, a small island just
off the coast. This is not, as has been suggested to me, an
island for space-age rocket scientists; the Gaelic name is
Inis Bó Finne, which means "island of the beautiful cow."
Now Balor, incensed by this theft, pursued Kineely back
to the smithy. He seized the thief and took him to a large
white stone on which he cut off his head. (One can see this
red-veined white stone on the outskirts of the town of Fal-
carragh.) Retribution followed swiftly, for the punishment
was out of all proportion to the crime, and Kineely's son,
called Lugh (pronounced "Loo"), followed after Balor. Now
Balor had an evil eye in the middle of his forehead (in this
version), which was covered by a shield of metal; if he
opened this shield, the eye destroyed all within its gaze. Lugh
pursued him to a lonely glen. Balor turned and opened the
shield, but Lugh thrust home a spear and all the evil spewed
forth from the eye and ran down the glen, destroying every
living plant. To this day nothing will grow in the Poisoned
Glen (map again). Balor, needless to say, was dead.

My narrator was quick to tell me that Balor had been a
plunderer and a monster who terrorized the mainland. He
had got his due. There was also, he added hurriedly, "something about MacKineely and Balor's daughter," but we didn't
go into that.

It was only later that I discovered that what I had heard
told as just "one of the old men's stories" was in fact a ver-

sion of the great Celtic Solar Myth. In the manuscript versions that survive, Balor is a leader of the Fomors, the race that inhabited Ireland before the coming of the Gods of the Gaels (*Tuatha Dé Danánn*). The latter were the creatures of light and the sky who came, naturally, from the East, and battled with the Fomors, who were amphibious monsters (*fó-mára*—"undersea") and represented the powers of darkness, evil, and infertility. Lugh was the Apollo of the Celtic pantheon—the god of light. Towns still bear his name (Lyons, Laon, Luton, Leyden), which he gave also to a month and to the great midsummer festival, *Lughnasa*, still celebrated in Ireland by the lighting of fires on Saint John's Eve. In Welsh mythology he was Llue or Llew (in English Lewis; French, Louis), and he found his way into the Arthurian cycle as Gawain/Galahad. Gabhan the Smith is the inevitable armorer god, the Vulcan of the Celts. But where does MacKineely come in? In one version of the legend there is an accomplice of Gabhan known as "Cian." Cian had heard the story about Balor's daughter, and how he had imprisoned her because he was afraid of the prophecy that she would bear a child who would kill him. With the help of the sea god Manannán (after whom the Isle of Man is named), Cian managed to get to her, and, as the story runs, "there was a child." Balor threw the boy into the sea, but Manannán saved him and took him to Gabhan for him to rear. It was, of course, Lugh, who later killed his grandfather with a hot coal through the eye. In the high version of this same story, Lugh was the great hero-warrior of the gods, who engineered their victory over the Fomors. His father's liaison with Balor's daughter was strictly legal and a result of an alliance between the Celtic gods and their primeval enemies in which brides were exchanged. Bress of the Fomors took to wife Bríghid (who was later canonized as Saint Bridgit and is now the most popular female saint in Ireland), while Cian married Ethniú, the daughter of Balor. When the alliance broke down, owing to various bits of dirty work, Lugh led his father's people to victory over the Fomors, and in the process killed his maternal grandfather with a sling bolt made of the brains of slain enemies mixed with lime. There are other versions, and the genealogies get somewhat muddled, but Cian and Kineely are obviously connected. It is possible that Donegal tradition has assimilated a historical chieftain to the father of the Celtic sun god.

If this Aryan solar myth could linger into the folk tales of Cloghaneely, how much more must it mean to the island of Tory—Balor's sea fortress? While waiting for the boat to take me over to the island, I was treated to a number of more or less scurrilous stories about its inhabitants (all two hundred fifty of them) that served largely to show that for the mainlanders of Donegal this incredible tower of rock out in the Atlantic was simply a massive ink blot for their own projected fantasies. But one thing did become clear: Balor did not have all his own legendary way out there, because the island was sacred to Colmcille (Saint Columba). This early missionary (A.D. 521–597), like many apostles of peace, caused so much trouble and bloodshed by meddling in politics that he finally suffered the horrible fate of being exiled to Scotland. There, on Iona, he wrote wistful poems about his "little cell on Tory," where he had been happy. This the mainlanders regarded as an inexplicable lapse in an otherwise sage and holy man. It seems that when Columba was in the district, Tory was still in the grip of the Danes. He decided to go over and rescue the Gaels and convert them, and, while he was at it, to turn the Danes into stone—an unexplained proclivity of early saints. He had one of those contests with other saints in which they failed and he succeeded in opening the waters to the island. At least this is one version. Another is that he tried three times to land from a currach, and no one would help him. Then a man called "Duggan" (Dubhgan) helped him ashore. He later granted his helper some privilege or other, which devolved upon his male heirs in perpetuity. As I was hearing this story the boat came in from Tory. Among the young men on board to whom I was introduced was an Anton Duggan.

As we made the rough crossing in the little boat I talked to an old man who asked, between puffs on his blackened pipe, what I might be doing going to Tory. "Is it the Gaelic you're after?" I said it was, and perhaps some stories—"Oh yes," he interrupted me, "you'll be wanting to hear about Balor then?"

I heard a lot about Balor. He was spoken of as though he had been there last year—or maybe was even there still, up in Balor's Fort. This was an old Iron Age hill fort, guarded by a huge earth wall and a ditch, and several smaller walls. It must have been nearly impregnable in its time, and it defended a number of well-preserved hut circles with their hearths intact. Balor's Prison was a sinister cleft some forty feet deep. Here, I was told, he used to put his prisoners and let them rot. "He even put his daughter in there, so they say, because she got a baby and not a husband. He was a right auld divil." Daughters, it seems, still had the same threat held over them if they misbehaved. Yes, Balor was still very much with them. "Shall we go up where Balor was?" I was asked by an old man who wanted to tell me *his* version. So up we went while he related how Balor lived in his castle and terrorized the islanders. There were trees on the island then, but Balor cut them all down to build ships and there haven't been any since. He used the ships to rob merchants who were taking gold to America, and he planted the gold up on Tór Mór. Many people had tried to find Balor's gold and failed. A young woman read in an old book about Balor (did I know that he was in a book?) and she found out where to dig. She had to line up on two landmarks on the mainland. She started digging, but the government stopped her because she had no permit.

In fact, the young lady in question was a professional archaeologist, and her findings concerning the Iron Age fort on Tory Island can be found in a very respectable learned journal. But I liked the bit about Balor's gold. This was typical of the private versions of the myth—those that people made up to satisfy themselves. The older and more skilled of the storytellers stuck more closely to the "classical" version of the tale, but with many embellishments. Several of these concerned massacres of islanders or of Balor's men or both. In the ancient versions of the myth there are no massacres, but in Tory history—according to the various *Annals*—there have been several. Perhaps these have become tacked onto, or woven into, the mainstream legend—like the lack of trees.

What was striking about all the Balor tales was the lack of interest in the doings of Cian, Lugh, and all the other high gods of Gaeldom. The concentration was on Balor himself; on his wickedness, his cunning, his tyranny, his success, and, above all, on his exploitation of the mainlanders—Lugh and the rest. Now Tory has been described as being more of the Atlantic Ocean than of Ireland—which might very well describe the sea-born Fomors. And there is no doubt that in some ways this is how the islanders see themselves. That Balor provides them with a perfect vehicle to express their own relationship with the outside world is obvious; he also provides a means of self-assessment—his wickedness is never played down. He is an object of ambivalence—loved and hated; the trickster and the monster; the fierce father and the ruthless exploiter of the world outside. He is all vice and all virtue magnified.

But he has to hold the field with the official patron. The

church is Saint Colmcille's Church and the school Saint Colmcille's School. There is Saint Colmcille's Chapel now in
ruins, and a host of prayers, stories, and magical formulas
surrounding the saint. The islanders gave me the proper version of the Duggan story. It was indeed a Duggan that had
helped the saint ashore. But more than this, the saint had
granted that Duggan and his heirs a special privilege. Seven
nuns were buried in a grave on the island—victims of shipwreck. The clay from this grave had magical properties: it
could calm waves, prevent potato blight, and, above all, it
could kill rats. The eldest Duggan had the privilege of "lifting" the clay, which he would do if he were asked humbly.
Many of the older men carry some of the clay in their waist-
coat pockets, and it is tied in little bags to the prows of fishing boats, along with Saint Christophers and other medal-
lions. There have been skeptics who have doubted the power
of the clay; many visitors to Tory have heard stories of rats
brought to the island to test its powers. The rats always died.
When Tory boats pull up at harbors around the Donegal
coast, the rats flee—and so on. But a more important function
of the clay is the protection it affords against the potato
blight. It must have been divine wisdom that inspired Colmcille to put in this clause, because there were no potatoes on
Tory in his time. But in truth Tory was spared during the
devastations of the 1840's; a fact the islanders refer to with
pride.

Thus both traditions—that of the pagan sea god Balor, and
that of the Christian saint Colmcille—serve as ongoing ingre-
dients in the ideological warfare between Tory and the hostile
world outside. The island is special; through Colmcille it is
sacred. But in Balor it also has something less prissy, something vigorous and "cussed." Colmcille is spoken of with
pride. He made Tory the center of Christian learning in Ireland ("in direct contact with the Holy Father in Rome we
were then"). But Balor is spoken of with something more

like affection. "He was an auld divil," they say, with a smile and a shake of the head.

This intimate contact with a pre- and early-Christian past is all the more remarkable because there are no events between the death of Colmcille and 1884 that have achieved legendary status. It was in 1884 that the gunboat *Wasp* left Westport in County Mayo with a crew of fifty, bent on collecting rent and rates from the islanders, who were more than two thousand pounds in arrears and refused to pay. The gunboat sank with great loss of life—according to admiralty records, on account of a "navigational error." But every Tory child knows it was the king who called out the islanders and who, uttering an ancient spell, "turned" the cursing stone, brewed up a storm, and sank the ship. There have been no landlords since, and no one has ever attempted to collect rent or taxes from the island. The wreck of the *Wasp* is history, but it is ripe for legend; it is in the same legendary tradition as the Balor tales. Colmcille gives a veneer of sanctity and respectability, but the Cyclopean Fomor and the curse-chanting king (the succession is now in dispute) more truly reflect how the islanders see their national character.

The name of the island may have intrigued the reader. It is pronounced to rhyme with "sorry" and is written "Torry" on old maps. It is obscure in its etymology. In the favored version, it is a derivation of *toraidhe*, which means "robber" or "brigand," and was indeed the insult hurled at the king's party by the Whigs in the eighteenth century. However, if the name is a genitive form, its nominative should be *torach*. The Irish post office favors this, but seems to be alone in its choice. *Torach* means "towery," and this makes sense in terms of the island's appearance. Yet again, Tór Rí—"the tower of the king" (Balor)—has been suggested, and one scholar ingeniously traced the name to a Scandinavian source as Thor Eye—"the island of Thor." Another possible source is Tór Inis—"the island of the tower." This was the home of a legendary hero, Conann. The islanders believe his tower (*Tór Conainn*) gave its name to the "conning tower" of the modern submarine. Like much else about the island, the name is a mystery, but the brigandish overtones seem the most satisfying.

The legend of Balor is not confined to Tory, and scholars have spilled much ink in showing that the story stretches from Dingle to the Isle of Skye; ultimately they link him to the ancient Celtic god of death—Bel or Béli—a relative of Baal, one of Jehovah's rivals, and the root of words like "baleful." But Donegal has made the story its own, and Tory is its natural home. Thus does a piece of pre-Christian Celtic cosmology—the myth of the rise of the sun god—come to play its part in the everyday lives of fishermen, crofters, and gangers in the twentieth century.

The sense of continuity, of attachment to place, that this achieves is awe-inspiring. If the Duggans are really descendants of Colmcille's henchman, then they have held their ritual office for fifteen centuries, while the Celts brought Balor and the rest to Ireland in about 300 B.C. And even if this continuity is itself mythological, they believe in it; and this belief gives a sureness and fixity to their place in the scheme of things.

These stories, then, have been kept alive in the oral peasant tradition because they served a purpose; they had a symbolic value. They were the means of preserving and communicating attitudes, ideas, and feelings not only about the great questions of life and death, which are behind all myth, but about the little questions of community and social relations; about "us" and "them." It will probably not be long before this lively continuity with the past is lost, and Dún Balor, sharing the fate of Ludgate and Colchester, becomes a dead name for the philologist to conjure with.

Agonistic Encounters

It would be wrong to give the impression that Tory Islanders spend most of their time fighting. But on those infrequent occasions when fights do occur, they become matters of intense interest, and the cleavages and tensions of the whole community are brought resoundingly to the surface. Here I will be concerned mostly with Tory men fighting among themselves; but of course when they are on the mainland, they close ranks against men from other parts of Donegal, such as Gweedore, or from the other islands. At a wider level of conflict, when in Glasgow, for example, they all join together as Donegal men against other Irish, such as those from Connemara. It goes without saying that all the Irish, regardless of local feuds, unite as Catholic nationalists against the Protestant Scots. Long ago, these two sides would have come together as oppressed Gaels against the English, although even then, the Lowland Scot was more likely to be pro-English than his Highland Catholic neighbor.

Anthropologists have often pointed out how this Chinese box system of higher and higher orders of allegiance works to allow communities to have their violent cake and eat it, too. There is an anthropological paradox that violence can integrate communities as well as rend them—as long as there is someone "out there" against whom the factions can make common cause. If this level of externalized violence falls off, internal violence will increase, becoming more and more dangerous. So, as English kings have always known, when faced with trouble and division at home, it pays to start a foreign war—either against a superior civilization like that of the Saracens (who suffered successive waves of barbarian invasions called "crusades"), or against the more handy French or Irish or Scots. Even more subtle than starting wars against them was the policy of using the Gaels, once conquered, as front-line troops in foreign wars. "There is no one like the Highlander," Queen Victoria is reputed to have said after the news of the thin red line at Balaklava. And while no one wasted much praise on the fighting Irish, they took the brunt of Napoleon's pounding at Waterloo; Wellington, being a kind of Irishman himself, was not insensitive to their qualities.

I will leave aside the question of why the Irish have a reputation for bellicosity, as well as the question of why they are so bellicose. Certainly communities differ, and so may national characters, in the amount of violence they tolerate or encourage. There are several ways they can handle violence. They can forbid it altogether and punish those who resort to it, which is really a matter of reserving "legitimate" violence to the governors of the community or the state. They can bring up their children to avoid violence except as a last resort. Or they can allow violence only under certain restricted conditions—such as in sports, or in "legal" manhunts or pogroms. But there is no one way of dealing with the potentially disruptive effects of violence. It is sometimes said that there are communities that are totally nonviolent, but this statement can easily be refuted. Pueblo Indians, Eskimos, Bushmen have all been cited as examples of nonviolent people, and all turn out to have high rates of personal violence. The Bushmen have a higher homicide rate than Chicago! A book was written about them called *The Harmless People*, which only goes to show that while anthropologists might be nice folks who like to think well of their fellow men, they can be poor guides to reality.

Violence can be channeled, suppressed, repressed, and variously kept in corners, where it can fester largely unobserved by those not looking for it or not wanting to see it.

But it is a rare community of human beings that does not have its quota of violent activity. It is interesting not to try to explain this away somehow, but to see how it is handled. Our own futures will, in all likelihood, depend on facing the potential for violence shared by all men in all societies and asking what we might do about it, not in pretending that it isn't there or that it crops up only because of bad conditions. Men have different interests and they are passionate about these interests, especially when resources are scarce or pride is threatened. It is not difficult to provoke anger; to consistently turn it inward can be as dangerous as letting it run wild; pent-up anger can burst out in fits of going berserk, witch-hunting, child-beating, or suicide. And another fact must be faced. Violence is pleasurable. This sticks in many a gullet. One response is to blame bad training or a warped personality for the pleasure and excitement many feel when watching or participating in acts of violence. That may be; but this pleasure and excitement seem to be very easily learned—and why not? They are taught to a creature ready to learn them.

I don't think that Tory men are "by nature" more violent than other men. In most of their dealings they are gentle and considerate. But they have a threshold of anger and, once it is reached, they are quick to respond with aggressive acts— always, however, in defense of what they conceive of as their legitimate interests. The tensions possible on a densely populated little island with few resources are without number. There is no authority other than the priest—and how much influence he has is open to question. When alcohol is brought to the island, as it is from time to time, and rapidly consumed, there is a consequent lowering of inhibitions. Quarrels at the verbal level are rare, and antagonists will usually just avoid each other. A visitor to the island will be surprised when, suddenly, a fight starts for seemingly no reason and with few preliminaries. At first sight, it seems to be an unstructured scuffle. But this is the main point I want to make about Tory fights: they are never unstructured. This may seem strange, for it appears that fighting is something below the level of culture and rules; that it takes men back to something primeval—nature red in tooth and claw. Perhaps. But equally primeval is the principle of ritualization, and I think this is the clue to the islanders' ability to manage their aggression. The principle of ritualization can be stated in a general form: usually, in any community of animals, there exist forms of combat that allow antagonists to settle their differences with violent exertion and yet with a minimum of serious damage. Sometimes the exertion itself can become ritualized—as when an exchange of shots at a distance in a duel or the drawing of blood in a fencing match satisfies the "honor" of the antagonists. And honor is very often important. The ideal outcome of an agonistic encounter (let's give it its ethological name) is one in which the parties feel that honor has been satisfied.

In this respect, the Irish attitude is quite Mediterranean. What is usually considered to be at stake when one man challenges another is honor or reputation or pride. (The whole thing is a peculiarly male affair. Women fight, but not over honor.) When a man makes a challenge, he puts his pride on the line; he can't back down without suffering a wounding hurt to that pride and a loss of reputation. It is an old story, perhaps older than history. It seems to tap something deep in men, something to do with the old interplay of dominance and virility that we see so effectively at work in nature. It is the stuff of literature, the story line of many movies. It is something the sociologically unsophisticated respond to with immediate empathy and excitement. But, then, the sociologist has been defined—along with the psychiatrist—as a man who goes to the strip-tease show to watch the audience. The obvious is the last thing he tends to see.

How is this universal theme treated on Tory? I have recorded details of some thirty fights on the island, and four off the island involving Tory men. I have details of fights from other parts of Ireland and between Irishmen in London; while they have some things in common with the Tory pattern, there are differences.

On Tory there is rarely an obvious cause for a fight. The principals are usually traditional antagonists in that often they have inherited the antagonism. Sometimes no one can remember why the feud started; sometimes there is a rambling story about some insult or piece of chicanery in the distant past. But for the most part no one cares. "He's doing it to show he's a man," they'll say. Sometimes, however, there *is* a recognizable cause—a dispute over a girl friend, usually, or a wife or a sister, and for the usual reasons.

Here is a fight sequence. The setting is the parish hall late at night where a dance is being held. The band is playing traditional Irish dances. The old ladies on the benches along the walls look on and tap their feet. The young people are dancing "The Waves of Tory"—a rather stately reel ending with a hilarious "over and under" movement that has everyone laughing and excited. Then the young men go to one end of the hall, near the door, where some of the older men have gathered to watch. In the ensuing lull, some of the men slip out to get bottles of Guinness, which they drink outside in the dark because it is illegal and the priest wouldn't like it. The priest is at the dance. He usually comes to watch for a while and, as his singing voice is much admired, is often asked to give a song. He once made an attempt to stop the dances from going on all night. He said it was bad for the children and told the hall committee to stop the dances at one o'clock at the latest. They said the people wouldn't stand for it, that "it was against the custom of the island." Several lads got drunk and went and threw bottles at the priest's house. Next day they apologized and cleared up the mess. After that, the priest just left the dances at midnight and said nothing.

This night, however, he did not go home at the accustomed time. There was a noise outside the hall during the lull. Shouting, curses. People rushed through the narrow door to see what was happening. A door off the stage at the other end of the hall was opened and people poured out, knocking over instruments in the rush. But it was all over when they got there. Old Paddy had been shouting imprecations at Wee Johnny. But Paddy had come into the hall before Wee Johnny could do anything but shout back. The crowd drifted back inside, and the band struck up again. Paddy sat at the side, muttering. Suddenly, as the dance was about over, he jumped up on the stage and started to shout and kick the big drum. Several people tried to restrain him. He yelled that he would surely do some killing before the night was out. They tried to calm him but he pushed his way outside again. Wee Johnny was out there drinking with his cronies, and as the doors opened a flood of light from both ends of the hall hit the dark roadway. Paddy, swinging wildly at Wee Johnny, caught him by surprise and grazed his mouth. As both men were more than a little drunk, it is unlikely either of them could have focused well enough on the other to make an accurate hit; but Paddy's glancing blow enraged Johnny, who roared and made for his assailant. He was grabbed and held back by several hands. By now both men were rather dazed. For a while they just looked at one another—each one firmly held by their supporters—and presently they began shouting insults again. Over and over Paddy repeated—my translation from the Gaelic is *very* rough—"You don't need to hold me, I wouldn't dirty me hands with him." Johnny replied that Paddy's hands were so dirty to start with they couldn't get any worse.

The priest came out and told everyone to go home. No

one listened and soon, still protesting, he was brushed aside.

The hall had emptied and most of the old ladies were now lining the roadside. At one end was Johnny's party—all men—milling about and arguing with him. At the other end was Paddy's group. Scattered between them were various groups of men not attached to either party; all around milled little boys imitating their elders, cursing, bluffing, swaggering, threatening. Most of the little girls stood some way off with their mothers, who had banded together to deplore the episode—quietly.

The noise from Paddy's group was getting louder. Paddy was setting off down the road. The bastard, he was shouting, was going to get it this time, he'd been asking for it long enough. Several of the men on the way tried to reason with him until the main body of his supporters caught up with him and began to restrain him again. They were close to Johnny's group now—about three or four yards away. Johnny moved forward and was restrained again by his men. "Hold me back or I'll kill him for sure," Johnny shouted again and again. The two crowds came close and even intermingled, and some minor scuffling went on. Two of Johnny's supporters began to argue and immediately attention passed to them. This seemed to disturb the principals, who began shouting again, louder now, and clawing their way through the mob to get at each other. They were pulled back, dusted off, showered with nonstop advice, and implored to cool down and go home.

Once the antagonists were separated, some of the nonpartisan older men moved about between the two, waving pipes and either talking quietly or shouting. There was a lull in the movement during which both principals again came forward yelling at each other. The insults rose in pitch and complexity until Johnny, provoked beyond words, tore off his coat and threw it on the ground.

Now this is a serious matter on Tory. "I'll take off me coat" means "I'll fight." "If he says that again, I'll take off me coat"—this is an invitation to a real fight. As long as the coat stays on, serious fighting is not intended. But even the act of peeling back the sleeves is a drastic escalation.

The coat was immediately retrieved by his group and desperate attempts were made to get it back on him again. At this point, a newcomer could have been forgiven for thinking the fight was between Johnny and those who had his coat, for he was inflicting more damage on them than he would ever get to inflict on Paddy. The coat stayed off.

Now Paddy began to disrobe. He was immediately prevented from doing so. Then began a sequence of the men taking off or trying to take off their coats and their supporters either preventing them or, failing that, trying to put the coats back on. This continued for some time and the spectators dwindled. A halfhearted attempt was made to start the band up again, but no one wanted to miss the fight. Innocent bystanders got swept into the rushes and counter-rushes, the scuffles and tramplings, the shouts and insults. Secondary squabbles flared up. But the supporters held on grimly to their men.

It may seem incredible but this episode went on for two and a half hours. By that time everyone was sobering up, and the dash and fury of the early part of the fight were over. There was a last flurry; again the principals were pulled back, and now someone was bringing Wee Johnny's weeping mother forward; the crowd parted for the old lady. With prayers and admonitions she pleaded with Wee Johnny to come home and not disgrace her like this in front of her friends and neighbors. Saints were liberally invoked and the Blessed Virgin implored often. People hung their heads. Johnny, looking dazed, told her to quiet herself—she didn't —and hurled at Paddy and his group: "I'd have had yer blood if me mother hadn't come. Ye can thank her that you're not in pieces on the road, ye scum." Paddy spat and said nothing, and Johnny and a few of his crowd went off to his house, turning occasionally to shout back something indistinct.

"Well," said one of the old men, turning to me with a chuckle, "and wasn't that the great fight, for sure." "Right enough," I said.

The Great Fight was the subject of discussion for days afterward. The priest said that he would ban dances if this kind of thing ever happened again, but he was told that the hall was built by Tory men and that they would settle their affairs in their own way, according to "the custom of the island." The details of the fight were discussed endlessly. What position was taken depended on where one stood in relation to the combatants. Either Johnny was justified and Paddy a troublemaker or vice versa, or they were both troublemakers. But the excitement and interest, despite the clucking and disapproval in some quarters, were very real. When either of the principals walked through the village, everyone stopped to look respectfully. Each of them had a little more swagger than before, talked a little more aggressively; each had shown he was a man; each had been the center of attention. "A man when he has the great anger on him is a wonderful thing, is he not?" I was asked. He was surely, I said, but weren't people disturbed by this kind of thing? A nine-day wonder, I was told; it never comes to anything, anyway. The women were particularly skeptical, passing many a sharp comment about men who were quick enough to fight but ran at the sight of hard work. And one young woman laughed, "Oh, those lads—always heroes when there's a crowd."

The significance of this remark, and of the whole episode, was brought home to me by an extraordinary (to me) oc-

currence a few days later. I was up on the hillside outside
the town taking photographs when I saw Johnny walking
down the road alone. From the opposite direction came
Paddy, also alone. Waiting for the clash, I wondered how
neutral I could be, and whether I should intervene or, more
likely, run for help. But Paddy passed on one side of the
road, looking out to sea, and Johnny on the other, looking at
the hills. Neither acknowledged my presence or the other's,
and each went his own way without a word.

This was my first fight, and I had no reason to think that
it was anything but a random one. But some fifteen fights
later, I was beginning to get bored with the predictability of
the performance. First, there was always some drink flowing. Then, there were insults and a few rushes. There also
had to be plenty of people about, the right people—that is,
supporters, invariably kin—of both sides: there had to be
enough close kin of each principal, on the one hand, and
enough related to both, on the other. The close kin of each
were the "holders," while the kin of both were the "negotia-
tors." Always the "hold me back or I'll kill him" pattern
predominated—often to the extent that, when even the supporters had become bored, the antagonist would go around
begging to be held back. The removal of the coats, the attempts to calm the men down, the pushing and scuffling—all
fell into a predictable pattern. And, when she was available,
the mother of one of the parties was paraded, with her lines
well rehearsed (or so it seemed), to bring the fight to an
end. Yet always the participation was intense, as though
this were the first time. And after each fight the same discussions would rage. Whatever other purposes they may have
had, the fights served as great entertainment. But after a
while they took on, for me, the punch-drunk anthropologist,
the air of a ritual ballet. It was all choreographed, seemingly

rehearsed, stereotyped. The language was always the same; the insults that at first had seemed so rich in their inventiveness turned up time after time. It began to dawn on this overtrained anthropologist that it was not mayhem and chaos, but ritual in the simplest sense. It was entirely rule-governed, even though no one could have told me what the rules were —in the same way language is rule-governed, although only grammarians know what the rules are. And in the same way that we know when the rules are broken even if we don't know what they are, so we all knew (and deplored the fact) when the rules of the fight game were broken, as they sometimes were. For example, it was unthinkable for a group of men to set on a lone antagonist who had no kin with him, or for two lone men on a road to start a fight with no audience around. When these things did happen, there was universal condemnation. A "proper fight" was a different matter. Two men with a quarrel—never mind what—had stood up to each other and had it out. They had shown they were men and willing to fight, but the situation was so structured that they never actually came to blows. No matter. Honor was salvaged by the mother's intervention—a man could not refuse a mother's prayerful pleas. Failing this, exhaustion and the pressure of kin would make each give way. But if a man actually fled, or flinched from the ordeal in any way, he lost face.

Sometimes, if there were few people around, the antagonists might actually come to blows. But if the fight were managed properly, everything would eventually come out even—although each side would declare itself the winner and claim that it was the other side that had backed down, run away, or called for help.

Outside the community, fights are a different matter. The fights involving Tory men that I have witnessed in Glasgow or London have been very nasty: broken bottles, boots, and gore. After one such episode, an islander ended up in the hospital with nine stitches in his scalp. But then that was in a Glasgow dance hall. Only the police were neutral; that is, they hit everybody just as hard, without regard to national or local origins.

I am reminded of Edward Evans-Pritchard's description of fighting among the Nuer of the Sudan. Within the local community, fights are with clubs, and killing is not acceptable. Between Nuer tribes, fighting is with spears; the men can kill each other but women and children are not to be killed or captured, and cattle are taken. When Nuer raid Dinka for cattle, however, there are no rules and women and children are fair game.

I am also reminded of the ritual fights—or agonistic encounters—of animals. It seems that men, including Tory men, try to ritualize combat between members of the same community, much as animals do. As Konrad Lorenz has pointed out, many animals that are equipped to kill have powerful inhibitions against killing their own kind. Very often combats are reduced to exhausting wrestling or butting matches, or even to simple displays of threat and counter-threat. The stags who compete for harems at rutting time lock antlers and wrestle. Stallions, playing the same game, nip each other on the neck, instead of slashing each other with their hoofs. Some animals, like the fiddler crab with his great exaggerated right claw or the marine iguana with his horny crest, have evolved special organs for this purpose alone. Man has not evolved special organs; he has that remarkable organ, culture, to do this ritual work for him. Perhaps this is an example of culture building on nature, rather than, as is usually assumed, running counter to it. As I said earlier, one could regard fighting as a relapse to the precultural, the pre-rule, state of nature. But nature has its way of coping with fighting among conspecifics: the fighting is ritualized so that the status competition can take place without anyone getting too badly hurt (although with animals, as with humans, it doesn't always work). It might well be, then, that culturally patterned, ritualized fighting is something "in our natures"; that men, left to themselves, will, within (and even between) the small communities that are their natural environment, manage to come up with elaborate bluff and threat operations that will satisfy pride while doing a minimum of damage—although not always as little as is inflicted on Tory Island. After all, the elaborate single combat of the Greeks and Trojans cut down the killing considerably. Instead of looking into the heart of violence itself, which he understands very well, perhaps man should turn his attention to the circumstances in which such ritualization does not seem possible in order to find the clue to true mayhem. And the clue is simple: with the stranger, there are no rules.

EIGHT

Personal Names

IN *The Aran Islands* J. M. Synge makes the following observation on the system of personal names then in use (1898–1902):

> When a child begins to wander about on the island, the neighbors speak of it by its Chritsian name, followed by the Christian name of its father. If this is not enough to identify it, the father's epithet—whether it is a nickname or the name of his own father—is added.
>
> Sometimes when the father's name does not lend itself, the mother's Christian name is adopted as epithet for the children. . . .
>
> Occasionally the surname is employed in its Irish form, but I have not heard them using the "Mac" prefix when speaking Irish among themselves; perhaps the idea of a surname which it gives is too modern for them, perhaps they do use it at times that I have not noticed.
>
> Sometimes a man is named from the color of his hair. There is

thus a Seaghan Ruadh (Red John), and his children are "Mourteen Seaghan Ruadh," etc. . . .

The school master tells me that when he reads out the roll in the morning the children repeat the local name all together in a whisper after each official name and then the child answers. If he calls, for instance, "Patrick O'Flaharty," the children murmur, "Patch Seaghan Dearg" or some such name, and the boy answers. . . .

If an islander's name alone is enough to distinguish him it is used by itself, and I know one man who is spoken of as Eamonn. There may be other Edmunds on the island, but if so they have probably good nicknames or epithets of their own.

While I was on Tory Island (Oileán Thoraighe) in 1962, I collected the names of all the living adults and found the system to be basically the same as that reported by Synge for the Aran Islands, and yet distinct enough to warrant a separate analysis.

Kinship terms are seldom used among the islanders except between young children and their parents and parents' siblings. Cousinship is indicated by saying of a person something like "his mother and my father were the children of two brothers" (*a mháthair agus m'athair clann na beirte dearbhráthar*), or "we are children of brother and sister" (*clann dearbhráthar agus deirbhsheathar*). But in a small community where the genealogical links between persons are common knowledge, such descriptive explanations are rarely called for. Personal names are used instead and in themselves help to indicate a person's position in the kinship structure by showing his line of descent for up to four generations.

A person will, in fact, have three sets of names: a Gaelic "ceremonial" set; an English "practical" set; and a Gaelic-English "personal" set. A man's full Gaelic name will consist of his baptismal name, followed perhaps by his epithet, such as Óg ("young"—usually means youngest of several brothers), Bán ("fair"), Mór ("big"), Beag ("small," "wee"), followed by his surname. Such a combination might yield, for example, Pádraig Og Mac Ruadhraigh. Upon marriage, a woman retains her family name and adds both the descriptive phrase "wife of" (literally, "woman of") and the names of her husband; for example, Máire Ní Dhubhghain bean Shéamuis Mhic Ruadhraigh—literally, "Mary, daughter of Doohan, wife of James the son of Rory." A number of circumstances will determine whether her husband's name will stick as a surname or whether she will go on being known by her maiden name. These names in their full forms are used on ceremonial occasions—dances, when a man or woman is called upon to sing or step dance, for prayers in church during a serious illness, for calling the roll in school, and for engraving a tombstone.

The practical names are the rough English equivalents of the Gaelic names and are used in dealing with English speakers generally, particularly when working in England and Scotland. The government is usually dealt with in English, mainly because, although Gaelic is the islanders' native tongue, the language they read and write is English—a situation brought about by the pattern of migrant laboring, which forced literacy on them when they worked in Britain. Also, they find Dublin, or "civil service," Irish difficult to follow. To the outside world, the examples given above, Pádraig Óg Mac Ruadhraigh and Máire Ní Dhubhghain bean Shéamuis Mhic Ruadhraigh, would be "Paddy Rogers" and "Mary Doohan." Sometimes these names stick and are used among the islanders rather like nicknames. Usually the English version is a rough phonetic equivalent of the Gaelic—Ó Duibhir becomes "Diver," Ó Dubhgain becomes "Doogan" or "Duggan," Mac Fhlaithbheartaigh becomes "MacClafferty," and so on. Sometimes this practice is abandoned in favor of taking an English name for its similar meaning to the Gaelic, as with Mac Ruadhraigh and Rogers (both meaning "red"). The name Fuaruisce ("cold water") is sometimes hopefully rendered "Whorriskey," but mostly the simple "Waters" is substituted. Those going to England for work are particularly inclined to pick an "English" name—that is, one the foreman will recognize.

The third, personal set of names, used for reference, consists of two or more Christian names, either Gaelic or English or both, strung together in the manner described by Synge for the Aran Islands. Some people have as many as five or six names and epithets strung together in this fashion. Second and subsequent names, if in Gaelic, will be in the genitive case. These are the names of lineal ancestors on either the mother's or father's side of the family. An individual will take as many names as is necessary to distinguish him from everyone else. The surname system is inadequate for this task because four surnames cover 80 per cent of the population. He does not, however, choose these names arbitrarily, but inherits the whole string of them. He can stop at any point in the string. If a man is called "Jimmy-Dhonnchadha-Mháiri-Mhicí," his father must have been Donnchadha-Mháiri-Mhicí, his paternal grandmother Máiri-Mhicí or maybe Máiri-Mhicí-Tom. Thus, if the man wants to add to his names, he would have to add "Tom." Usually one or at most two names in addition to his given name are enough to distinguish a person. As Synge observes, if a man's given name is unique in some way, he may be known by it alone, although on Tory he will usually have a "latent" string of names that he could use if his Christian name were to crop up again. If any of the ancestors in the string had epithets or descriptive terms, these are included. But there is a tendency to use only the epithet of the last person in the string. Sometimes, if an ancestor was firmly known by his surname (if, say, he was an immigrant and the first of his name on the island), then this is added also. Some examples of these names are:

Eóghan-John-Dooley-Mhalainne	Dooley was a man from Malin in County Donegal
Mary-John-Dooley-Mhalainne	Eóghan's sister
Cait-Dooley-Mhalainne	His paternal aunt (Kate)
Jimmy-Mháiri-Bhillí	Jimmy-Mary-Willy
Peigi-Phaidí-Shéamuis-Dhomhnaill	Peggy-Paddy-James-Donal
Pádraig-Hiúdaí-Dhuibhir	Patrick Hugh Diver
Paddy-Johnnie-Fhlaithbheartaigh	Paddy John (Mac) Clafferty
Nóra-Thomáis-John-John-Eóghain-Neilí	Nora-Thomas-John-John-Owen-Nellie

An alternate type of name—a man may have two or three types—consists of the addition of the Christian name of a parent to the surname. Thus, two paternal first cousins might be respectively Jimmy Diver Nancy and Jimmy Diver Madge.

Categories of kin can be roughly divided into objective and subjective. In the objective class come *dream* and *clann*. The islanders speak of a "crowd," or "tribe" in English, or *dream* in Gaelic, when they are referring to a surname group: the Duggans, the MacClaffertys, et cetera. These are sometimes divided according to town: the East End Duggans, the West End Whorriskeys. It is not necessary to trace the genealogical relationship between the people concerned; they are assumed to be related by virtue of the common name. Nothing much follows from this except the belief that certain qualities go with each name, and some status disputes are indulged in as to which is the oldest tribe on the island (*an dream is sine den oileáin*), an honor usually accorded the Mac Ruadhraigh (Rogers) "crowd." *Clann* is different. It means simply "children," or "offspring," but it is used to denote a group of people related by common descent to a known ancestor, even if this descent cannot always be traced with accuracy. Thus there is a group known as *Clann Neilí*, which will be discussed later, who trace their descent over seven generations to one Nellie Doohan.

Of the subjective categories, the most important are *gaolta,* *muintir,* and *tiaghlach. Mo lucht gaolta* refers to "all the people with whom I have any kinship connection," and most islanders would regard this category as conterminous with the island population itself. *Mo mhuintir* (sometimes *daoine muintire*) refers to those relatives "I know and acknowledge" —"my people," or "my friends." (The latter is used in the technical sense of close relatives.) Relatives beyond the range of *muintir* are *i bhfad amach* (far out). Finally there is *tiaghlach*—"family," or "household." On Tory these two do not necessarily coincide, because families do not necessarily break up on marriage; in fact, a considerable proportion of spouses remain in their natal homes throughout their lives. On Tory the term *tiaghlach* would usually refer to the household.

Kinship is reckoned in terms of relation to a common ancestor. Thus two first cousins are *ua* (grandchildren): *támuid i n-ua amháin*—"we are first cousins" (grandchildren only). Second cousins are *dá ua* ("second grandchildren"), third cousins are *fionn ua* ("fair grandchildren"), and fourth cousins *dubh ua* ("dark grandchildren"). The etymology of the latter two terms is puzzling, but the significant fact about this form of reckoning—which Arensberg and Kimball did not find in County Clare—is that it works in terms of degree of distance from a common ancestor, exactly as with the reckoning of membership in the *clann* group.

When I was collecting genealogies from the islanders, I found that they were decidedly uncomfortable with the standard genealogical method, that is, starting with themselves and working out from close to remote relatives. When they were asked simply to tell about their relatives, they responded spontaneously by picking some dead ancestor and describing his descendants. What is more, the most knowledgeable of them could cover the entire island in this way, eventually relating everyone to some ancestor. Thus the island is divided into something like twenty-two *clann* groups; that is, approximately this number of ultimate ancestors is recognized. The number is not easy to fix, because there is sometimes dispute as to whether or not one group is part of another. Sometimes two such groups are thought to be related, but are regarded for practical purposes as distinct. The absolute origin in time of some of the groups can be established because they are known to be descended from immigrants. For example, all the Whorriskeys (ϕ Fuaruisce) are descended from two brothers or cousins who came to the island (perhaps they were shipwrecked) at the end of the eighteenth century. Several of these groups are relatively recent—the Wards (now extinct), Dohertys, O'Donnells. Others go back to antiquity.

It is a mistake, however, to designate a *clann* by its surname, for, unlike the *dream*, it is not merely a surname group. Surnames—insofar as they are effectively used—are inherited patrilineally, but the *clann* group is not patrilineally recruited. It comprises all the descendants of a named ancestor through males and females. If one went by surnames only, the female connections would soon be lost to memory. Surnames are of the least importance in the reckoning of *clann*ship. Before the naming system is considered, however, it must be noted that these descent groups will of necessity overlap. Thus the individual is a member of at least two and sometimes several of these groups: those of his mother and father. Anthropologists have often been confronted with this feature of cognatically, as opposed to unilineally, recruited descent groups and have been puzzled about how such groups could function. If individuals are assigned to either their mother's or father's group, then discrete groups will emerge; but according to the cognatic principle, discrete groups will not be possible. If these groups all exist for the same purpose, conflict between them over the allegiance of members is inevitable. A person cannot serve both his mother's group and his father's group if these are, for example, competing for the same resources (these groups are usually concerned with the inheritance of land).

A large but typical *clann* group—the *clann Neilí*—is a good example of how this works. The following chart shows a division into three segments, or lineages, composed of descendants of Nellie's three children, Eóghan-Neilí, Liam-Neilí, and Máiri-Neilí. The Liam-Neilí are themselves subdivided into the Liam-Liaim-Neilí, the Neilí-Liaim-Neilí, and the Caitlín-Liaim-Neilí. But here it is significant that the children of Neilí-Liaim-Neilí were known exclusively by her names *only* when they were being specifically associated with her *clann* group. They were normally called after their father, Séamus Bán. This was their "natural" name, the one by which they were most readily known. This is an instance of the names of one *clann* group getting lost; the continuity of descent from Nellie was broken by the intrusion of the other *clann* group. However, it is surprising how often people have alternative strings of names and are not known exclusively by either. Often, too, the names get truncated, and for practical purposes a person will be known by the name of only one parent. This, for example, was the case with the great-grandson of Eóghan-Neilí, who was known as Tomás-John. But everyone knew that his complete string of names was Tomás-John-John-Eóghain-Neilí. Similarly, the great-grandson of Liam-Neilí was usually known just as John-William, but again his complete string was available with prompting. Sometimes a name will be left out and, as with the great-grandchildren of Máiri-Neilí, the string will start with the grandparent, not the parent.

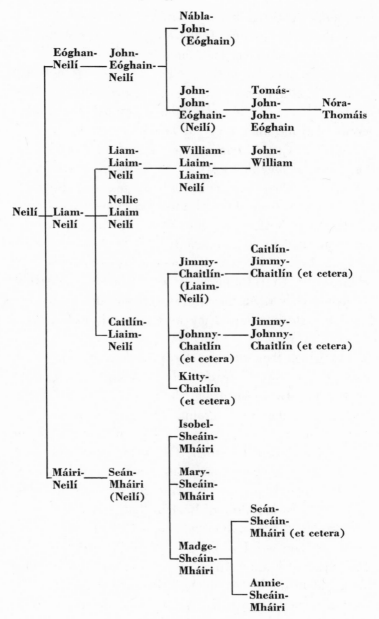

Clann Neilí

The interesting thing about this system is its relationship to the overlapping of *clann* groups. In some cases, a person's identification with one group is strong and he bears only its names. But—and this is more common—when his allegiance is not so total, he may have two sets of names, or even more. Sometimes one set will lie dormant and be brought out when the occasion demands. Thus, to some extent, the names constitute a system of reckoning membership in these descent groups, and are a measure of their relative strength. In both sexes, there is a stronger pull to the father's group, but a significant number of men take their mothers' names in preference to their fathers' as names of "first choice."

The degree to which the name continuity of such a group can be maintained, with the names converging on the founder's name as in our example, is some measure of the continuing solidarity of the group. This solidarity tends to weaken after about six generations, and the disintegration of the group is reflected in the native commentary: *"Tá na h-ainmneacha caillte"*—"The names are lost." The attempt to keep the name continuity often conflicts with the desire to distinguish person from person, hence the existence of alternative name types.

The formula on the following page shows the ideal structure of the Tory name, using these symbols: C = Christian name, S = surname, e = epithet, Fa = father's Christian name, Mo = mother's Christian name. Any item symbolized in lower case can be omitted from the progression of names. The columns represent the alternative possibilities, the rows the matrilateral and patrilateral progression of names. The formula can be expanded following the same rules.

Generation

+1   +2

		Fa	{ e es s			FaFa	{ e es s
Patrilateral				+			
						FaMo	{ e es s

Ce +

| | S | { fa
mo |

		Mo	{ e es s			MoFa	{ e es s
Matrilateral				+			
						MoMo	{ e es s

Formula for Ideal Structure of the Tory Name

To see how this basic choice between matrilateral and patrilateral progression worked out in practice, I tabulated instances of each type of first-choice name progression (see table), distinguishing by sex of nominee ("m" and "f") but ignoring the optional epithets and surnames. I collected these names separately from the two settlements on the island, East Town (*Baile Thoir*) and West Town (*Baile Thiar*). It is commonly believed that the East is more traditional than the West, but this is not reflected by the differences in the naming system.

Name type	West Town	East Town	Total
m + Fa	24	25	49
f + Fa	26	16	42
m + Mo	13	4	17
f + Mo	6	4	10

Name type	West Town	East Town	Total
m + Fa+FaFa	15	5	20
f + Fa+FaFa	13	4	17
m + Mo+MoMo	0	0	0
f + Mo+MoMo	0	0	0
m + Fa+FaMo	0	3	3
f + Fa+FaMo	2	1	3
m + Mo+MoFa	0	3	3
f + Mo+MoFa	0	1	1
m + MoMo	2	1	3
m + MoFa	3	1	4
f + MoFa	1	0	1
f + Fa+FaFa+FaFaFa	3	0	3
f + FaFa+FaFaFa	0	1	1
f + FaBro	0	1	1
m + MoMo+MoMoFa+MoMoFaMo	3	0	3
f + MoMo+MoMoFa+MoMoFaMo	1	0	1
	112	70	182

Tabulated Instances of First-Choice Name Progression

What can be seen from the table is the overwhelming preference for taking the father's name (and his father's) by both men and women, and the fact that for both sexes one possible combination does not occur: m/f + Mo + MoMo. I am told that this has occurred in the past, but infrequently. The fourth cluster consists of some miscellaneous name types. The oddity here is the girl who took her father's brother's name. (The rest skip a generation and start with the grandparental names.) Such cases usually result from an uncle or grandparents bringing up children in the absence of parents. But if these relatives are seen as *in loco parentis*, the pattern remains the same as for the majority.

The following is a summary of the laterality preference as it affects men and women respectively in their first-choice names. The figures in parentheses are percentages of the row totals.

	Patrilateral	*Matrilateral*	*Total*
male	72(70.6 per cent)	30(29.4 per cent)	102
female	67(83.75 per cent)	13(16.25 per cent)	80
total	139(76.4 per cent)	43(23.6 per cent)	182

The overall preference is patrilateral, but there is an interesting minority preference among males for matrilateral names. Practically a third of the men and less than a sixth of the women have matrilateral names.

The Welsh system of stringing ancestral names together with *"ap"* is obviously similar to the Tory system, but the Welsh use male names only. In some Scottish coastal villages, a man will be known by the boat he owns, and his children will inherit this epithet. A system similar to that on Tory operates in some working-class communities in England. A man may be known as "Mary's Tom" and his son as "Mary's Tom's Johnnie." Synge notes the use of occupations as marks of distinction in Wales (*Dai Bread*—"the baker") and comments on the lack of occupational differentiation on the Aran Islands, which makes this method impossible. In some rural communities a man is known by the name of his farm. W. M. Williams, in *The Sociology of an English Village*, gives examples of this. The contrast with the Tory system is marked, however, in that one can, in Gosforth, the village he describes, move from side to side of the family in choice of names—both surnames and Christian names being used. This naming pattern is linked to the inheritance of farms in the same way that the Tory naming system is probably linked to the inheritance of land.

Such a highly personalized naming system works only within the particularistic boundaries of a small community. The world at large is not interested in the particular antecedents of a man, and the islanders recognize this in their use of surnames with the outside world. The old family or clan names placed a man in his wider kinship group in the days when this was important; it no longer matters today. Within the community, the naming system described above distinguishes a man from other men and places him in his immediate kin group. It helps to establish his descent, and this is what is important.

In our impersonal society names are legal, fixed, bureaucratically ordained. Yet a legal name is, in fact, merely the name one chooses to be known by, and people's names, in the widest sense of labels attached to them to establish their identities, are shifting and ephemeral things. A man or woman may have several names serving very different purposes. Their function is similar to the types of names (ceremonial, practical, personal) used on Tory: they serve to distinguish different roles, different phases of the life cycle, different degrees of dignity or formality. A man may be John Arlington Jones, Esq., to his bank, but "Johnny" to his parents, "J.A." to his business associates, "Jack Jones" to his cronies, "Jones" to his schoolmaster and old schoolmates, "Dr. Jones" to his students, "Wee Johnnie" to his Scottish grandparents, "Jackie" to his mistress, and "Mr. Jones" to tradesmen. This is not counting nicknames ("Joker Jones"), terms of endearment ("sweete," "daddykins"), terms of abuse ("old Jones," "Tightwad"), or diminutives ("Jonesy"). When we ask Jones what his name is, what should he answer? With the name on his birth certificate? In that case, my name would not be Robin Fox. What's your name?

A New Mexican Pueblo

I HAVE ALREADY EXPLAINED how I came to be in Cochiti. As
an undergraduate in London I had been fascinated by the
Indians of New Mexico and Arizona—particularly the
Zuni and the Navaho. But my teachers had told me that
these were essentially "reservation" savages and not quite
in the same class as "real" black Africans, for example.
All the black Africans I saw on the newsreels seemed to
be wearing khaki shorts and listening to transistor radios.
But no matter. I had read D. H. Lawrence's *Mornings in
Mexico*, which contains the most exquisite evocation and
also the most wrongheaded interpretation of Pueblo music
and dance on record. Then, too, I recognized that although
The Plumed Serpent is set in Mexico proper, the Indians

in it were those Lawrence knew from New Mexico and Arizona. So I set off with more than field-work interest; it was a literary pilgrimage into the bargain—Lawrence was dear to my postadolescent heart. I was somewhat put off when I found that his Taos farm had been turned into a creative writing school; I was also put off by the parasites who would trade their phony memories of Frieda for a drink or two. It was like Sligo with all those "cousins" of Yeats hanging around the bars. I fled the literary vultures and made for the desert and Cochiti.

I had read everything written about the area, but despite my enthusiasm for the Lawrentian Indian, I was unprepared for the shock of coming face to face with a truly tribal society that, veneered as it was with Spanish and Anglo loan things, was Indian to the core. I suppose I really had expected reservation Indians—acculturated, assimilated, drunk. So I got my culture shock. But at the same time, I was surprised at how strikingly reminiscent their society was of small-town and village life in England and Ireland, once one got around the exotica. The gossip and scandal, the extended family with its strong supporting role for mothers and children, the teen-age gangs and gangs of small boys, the male culture and the female counterculture—all these were familiar. But for the first visit, the exotica were blinding—partly because I was struggling with the difficult language (Keres). Pueblo Indian ceremonialism is spectacular and pervasive. The intense spiritual life is exhausting; its conflicts and tensions are hard to manage. Yet it does pull the pueblo together in the face of strong forces making for factionalism and breakdown. That first summer I was too dazzled by the language, by the pleasure of actually living in and unraveling a matrilineal kinship system, to see the tensions clearly. But during my next visit I began to see the cracks

in the social fabric, and by the same token to see its unusual strength.

These themes come out in the essays that follow. There
is a running theme of conflict: between factions, between
veterans and others, between baseball teams, between individuals, between families. But there is the countervail-
ing theme of integration: through ritual, through the mediation of veterans, through authority, through the strength
of traditions such as curing. Again, as on Tory Island, I
was to be drawn to the basic Hobbesian problem of the
possibility of social order despite the war of all against all
(or some against some). I came to admire the feat of social
engineering that was the Cochiti social system. "Nations,"
Adam Ferguson said, "stumble upon establishments which
are indeed the result of human action, but not the execution of any human design." And all the better for that, one
is inclined to add. One dreads to think what the human de-
signers might have done if let loose in Cochiti; one knows
too well what a mess they make when and where they get
their chance. No one could have designed the Cochiti social system. It has sorted itself out over the centuries, and
has established itself on a good evolutionary principle: the
more variation there is, the better the chance for survival.
It is sometimes asserted that the more complex a society
is, the more vulnerable it is to change. With Cochiti, quite
the opposite seems to be true. The complexity of their society is its safeguard; if one element goes, there are others
to take over.

I am as romantic about the Indians as I am about the
Irish, but not, I fear, as romantic as some anthropologists
are. I was amazed to find that nothing had been written
about those two major obsessions of Pueblo life: baseball
and television. They weren't regarded as really "Indian"
and besides, they wouldn't look good in Ph.D. theses. Tele-

vision was relatively new—and used largely for watching baseball—but the playing of baseball and the baseball league had been around long enough to have merited some attention.

The reader might want to check back to "Kinship and Alliance" to refresh his memory on matrilineages before reading "Witches, Clans, and Curing"; then, if he is interested, follow up even further by reading *The Keresan Bridge*. The essay on witchcraft looks forward to "Religion and the North American Indian." But perhaps it also looks sideways—to medical practice in "civilized" culture, to psychosomatic medicine, to group psychotherapy, and to the encounter movement. Like all studies of witchcraft, it also exposes the paranoid streak in man that drives him to search for scapegoats and run purges and pogroms. Richard Hofstadter, in his otherwise excellent book *The Paranoid Style in American Politics*, looks as far as millenarian cults in the Middle Ages for comparative material. But he frustrates the anthropologist because he does not take the next step—he does not link the paranoia of the American right to its roots in the almost universal belief in witchcraft (or malignant spirits or ghosts or whatever). The conspiracy of the Illuminati or the Elders of Zion or the ubiquitous "Communists" or the homosexuals or whoever it is who are "out to get us" is simply the conspiracy of the witches that the Pueblo doctors work so hard to keep at bay. And God help any fellow traveler who is so identified—although Pueblo canons of evidence seem about as unreliable as Senator Joseph McCarthy's. To call Stalinism and McCarthyism "witch hunts" is to do more than just make a vivid metaphor. The witches were not wiped out at Salem. They are within us, and when we are afraid of forces in society beyond our control, we externalize them with ease, and with frightening rapidity. Any of us might be the next witches.

I have not been to Cochiti since 1959. They tell me that it is very changed now. I hear that new government houses have replaced the old adobe structures, that a dam on the river is being exploited as a resort with "concessions" and holiday homes. Perhaps I won't go back. The Indians could handle baseball and even television—but vacationers?

I don't intend to draw comparisons or contrasts between Cochiti and Tory. At this distance, I am struck more by the human elements they have in common than by their cultural differences. But that may be a reflection of a change in attitude and theory on my part, rather than simply of the passing of years. I don't know. Being dazzled by differences is adolescent in its way; the conviction that people everywhere are much the same seems to come with age. There may be a rather tedious moral in that, but I won't draw it. The reader will no doubt want to reflect on this very problem—on the interplay between common human elements and local cultural traits. In "Comparative Family Patterns" I used material from both Tory and Cochiti to point up comparisons, just as I have in "Language in Two Communities."

The passing of the truly tribal Indian is even more poignant in its way than the passing of Gaelic culture, for it is our most immediate link with precivilized man, with all that was human before civilization set up its distorting mirrors in which we see what we take to be the true human condition. Singing a Gaelic song, I am still part of a culture I know. I am in the Iron Age at least: heroic, warlike, pastoral, stratified, and soon to be literate. With a Cochiti song, I am back at the close of the Old Stone Age, in the hunting group that has just found maize and is precariously cultivating it:

Amu amu hawerena masi, amu amu hawerena masi;
Yuni yusi, tyinyi nuka, matsitch ka'chanoma;

Yuni yusi, tyinyi nuka, 'rikats ka'chanoma;
Amu amu hawerena masi;
Aiye aiye awa hawa'aya awa awehye.

"Peace, peace, all little growing things, peace, peace, all
little growing things / Over yonder, from above to below,
the huge raindrops are falling / Over yonder, from above
to below, the tiny raindrops are falling / Peace, peace all
little things . . ." The last line is a meaningless chorus.
This is roughly transcribed, freely translated, and no
doubt imperfectly remembered. But the memory it evokes
is a long one, beyond the age of metals, back to the little
bands of hunters crossing the Bering Strait more than
twenty thousand years ago and bringing with them lullabies for the children they carried, lullabies that would
later become songs to coax the newly domesticated plants
into hesitant growth. For this song is a lullaby with a
double meaning—the "growing things" are either plants
or children. The rain nurtures the plants that nurture the
children; the rain comes from the Sky Father to the Earth
Mother and brings forth living things, in the same way
that earthly parents engender life in the child who is
being rocked. One knows what Lawrence meant. In the
midst of these Indians one feels close to a mystery—to a
message that is coming through the distortions of modern
culture and asking to be heard. One feels close to the
beginning of something at the same time as one weeps
for its end.

NINE

The Enduring Indian

IN THE 1920's AND '30's anthropologists were confidently predicting the eclipse of the American Indian. His culture was to vanish and he was to become merged with the mainstream of American life. His tribalism and cultural distinctiveness could not withstand the pressures of the most advanced civilization known to man. He was an anachronism, a strange vestige of the Stone Age, and would succumb.

Never has a prediction in social science been more wrong. Far from vanishing, some Indians have increased in numbers and some tribes have gained new dignity and strength in the process of expanding. They remain tribes—proud, distinct, traditional. They remain Indian. Their values and life goals antagonize and fascinate the surrounding whites, with whom they are completely at variance. They are threatening because they arouse guilt feelings about the past, because they challenge the American to reconsider his whole system of values. Yet at the same time they are a living museum, a human zoo, a bit of cultural interest for tourists. Americans are never quite sure where they stand in relation to the Indian. He is not a black, but he is not quite white. The bartender may refuse to serve Indians but boast of his own Sioux ancestry. The Indians lost, and Americans have never forgiven failure. But they went down fighting, and Americans admire a fighter. Had they wanted to wipe out the Indian they could probably have done so. But they never made up their minds. They thought he would go of his own accord. But he's still there.

Those who fought the hardest went the fastest. The Indians who survived had two qualities. They were sufficiently resistant to the whites to remain distinct, but they were sufficiently accommodating to accept enough of white culture and domination to survive. The survivors par excellence were the Pueblo (village-dwelling) Indians of the Southwest. Living on the high, dry mesas of the Arizona desert or clustered along the banks of the Rio Grande in New Mexico, these descendants of the cliff dwellers met and survived three waves of invaders who changed, but did not destroy, their settled, peaceful, urban way of life. First, in the thirteenth or fourteenth century (no one knows quite when), came the Navaho and other Apaches, sweeping in from the north. It was probably this invasion that forced the cliff dwellers from the canyons of Colorado into the fortified towns of the mesas and river valleys. But adversity strengthened rather than destroyed, and the Navaho even adopted many Pueblo ways, especially religious practices. Then, in the sixteenth century, came the Spaniard, bringing horses, metal, and Catholicism. The Pueblos absorbed them all, including the religion, but they kept their religious rituals intact, unmixed with the alien faith. Two religions were better than one, but they were different and served different ends. The Spaniard also brought a new form of government to replace the old theocracy, but the priests continued to rule by putting their own nominees into the new positions as "governors" and *fiscales* to please and fool the Spaniard. They learned Spanish, but they never forgot their own tongues and they never let Spanish intrude into the ceremonial life that was the core of their culture.

The Pueblos made an abortive attempt at revolt in 1680, after which the Spaniards established complete dominance until the coming of the Americans who "liberated" New Mexico in 1846. The Americans brought Protestantism, education, and anthropology. It is difficult to estimate which did the most damage. Catholicism the Pueblos could take—even learn to love—with its rituals and symbols; but those Protestant pastors, who seemed to epitomize all the fanaticism and brutality of the "Anglos," were utterly foreign to them. The pastors got a hold only when dissident groups in some pueblos took them up as a form of revolt against the prevailing theocracy. Otherwise the pueblos remained intractably Catholic.

The ham-handedness of anthropologists and the vacillations of American government accentuated the now famous Pueblo clam-up. Ceremonies went underground and lies were freely told to investigators, who in turn freely published them. Only in villages so remote that they did not feel the full weight of the conquerors can one see in public the most sacred of all the dances—the dance of the masked gods, who are called *"katsinas."* Even here the rule of secrecy reigns concerning ceremonial matters, and anthropologists are not welcomed. Among the Rio Grande Pueblos it is rare for a white man to be allowed to stay overnight. Under this cloak of secrecy and stubborn resistance to intrusion, Pueblo life and religion maintains itself much as it was before Columbus; the details have changed but the essentials seem impervious to change. The Pueblos are not uniform, however, in their responses to the attacks of alien cultures. Some accommodate more easily than others, and in different ways. The small pueblo of Cochiti (less than three hundred permanent inhabitants), on the Rio Grande, is interesting in that it probably lies about halfway along the continuum from ultraconservative to ultraliberal in matters of acculturation. One of its liberal aspects is its cautious toleration of occasional anthropologists—hence my own visit there.

Cochiti, like all the other pueblos, has always been battling for physical, cultural, and social survival. Survival has meant different things at different times but there have always been three factors to contend with: the elements, the invaders, and civil strife. The major burden has been borne by the religious system, and it is to this that we must turn in order fully to understand the survival of Cochiti. Religion in this little community is not something apart from "ordinary" life, not a Sunday hobby, not even a matter of churches and creeds. A Cochiti does not so much believe certain tenets of faith as live an organized ritual life. There is no comprehensive theology of Pueblo religion; it is a well-organized system of ritual involving the whole tribe in a vast communal effort. The aim is tribal well-being, the methods are various. Some aspects of the religion and its general control are in the hands of priestly, esoteric "medicine" societies, which also function as the government and the health service. Because of their healing functions, their members are often called "doctors" in the anthropological literature. Membership is open to anyone, but because the initiation is arduous and the rituals complicated and time-consuming, there are not many members. While the whole tribe has to contribute its labor to the ritual effort, the doctors are expected to keep the effort up almost full time. They practice retreats for prayer and fasting, cure illnesses, and manage the ceremonials. They are, in the words of one writer, the "chief penitents" of the tribe. Their sacrifices help to keep the universe in balance. There are two other societies usually known as "clowns"; they appear at the public ceremonies grotesquely dressed and fool about and make fun of the crowd—particularly the white visitors. But these clowns at which everyone laughs so heartily are in fact two respected and even feared groups of men. One group represents the spirits of the dead, who are licensed to chastise the living. They are connected with some of the medicine societies and also with the two *kivas*. These are large semiunderground chambers that serve as meeting places and centers for native ceremonial. One is named for the pumpkin, a staple of Cochiti diet, and the other for turquoise, their only precious stone. Every Cochiti must be a member of one or the other kiva.

A man takes his kiva from his father and a woman joins the kiva of her husband. Kivas represent a ritual division of labor and are where the large public ceremonials are organized. The main event is the corn or rain dance, which so struck D. H. Lawrence in the neighboring pueblo of Santo Domingo. Long rows of men and women, and even some children, dance slowly and persistently all day in the hot sun in an effort to compel the clouds to give rain, the corn to grow, and all life to prosper. The drummers—there have to be several because the work of carrying and pounding the great ceremonial drums is exhausting—form a young-male cult within the kiva, while the older men form a chorus. There are a number of minor religious groups—the "river men," for instance, whose job it is to frighten and discipline the children—but the main cult, the most secret and most sacred, is that of the *katsinas*. No white man can see this cult.

At one time all the males of the tribe would have been initiated into the cult, which is looked after by one of the medicine societies, but membership has dwindled over the years. This is the real core of the Cochiti religion. The initiates put on usually abstract but often animal-like masks that cover the whole head. Wearing this mask, the dancer becomes the temporary incarnation of the god the mask represents. But to call the *katsinas* "gods" is misleading. They are not worshiped, but respected and revered. Through their human intermediaries they visit the pueblo as an act of kindness. Their dancing ensures happiness and fertility. Like the clowns, they are connected with the spirits of the dead ancestors, the *shiwanna*, who have become the clouds, the rain givers. In a way they are ancestors, but from long-ago mythological times when all men were happy. Their return brings back happiness.

Standing over this whole complex ceremonial structure, of which I have described only a part, is the cacique, the chief of the tribe, who is its chief priest. He is the only truly full-time religious functionary. His fields are planted for him and harvested by the whole tribe. He spends all his time in prayer and penance on behalf of the tribe and, most important of all, he works out the calendar of the religious year from the movements of the sun and moon. He has not much effective power, but he can wield a good deal of influence. He is assisted by two ceremonial policemen, the war captains or war priests who are named after twin warriors in Pueblo mythology. They are responsible for a variety of religious and secular affairs: the proper conduct of ceremonials, the punishment of witchcraft, the maintenance of the irrigation ditches, and the control of horses. In the old days, they were also executioners and war magicians. Actual details of warfare were in the hands of the warrior society—purified scalp takers—while hunting was the preserve of yet another "club."

This tightly knit ceremonial hierarchy was also, before the Spaniards, the hierarchy of government. It continued to be so after the conquest, but functioned behind the front of officials nominated by the medicine societies. As these societies dwindled, some becoming extinct, the puppet officials began to take over real power. They differ from the priestly officials in that they hold office only for a year at a time. A careful attempt is made to rotate offices among the various interest groups—Pumpkin and Turquoise kivas take turns with the governorship. All major secular decisions are taken by a council consisting of present and past officials.

The religious concepts of the Cochiti Indians reflect their major concerns. The pantheon includes the sun (a father), and the earth, and especially the corn (a mother), two hero twins, and the whole body of *shiwanna*. The ritual calendar follows the course of the seasons and concentrates particularly on the bringing of summer rain. Evil is explained by the practice of witchcraft and provision made to combat it. There is no aspect of Pueblo life that does not have its ritual side, and so the strength of the religion is the strength of the society. But the religion is flexible. It could accommodate enemy Indians by taking over their dances and so robbing them of power.

Christmas coincides with the winter solstice ceremonies, Easter with the spring festival, and the harvest is always celebrated. The great Corn Dance is ostensibly in honor of the patron saint (Saint Bonaventure), to whom the performers dutifully pay homage before and after the dance. But the dance itself is uncorrupted by Christianity. The church is closely controlled by the Indians and the head of the most powerful medicine society always becomes its sacristan.

The Cochiti's religion enables him to combat the weather and evil; sickness and enemies. It guides the cycle of the agricultural year and the cycle of the individual's life. It provides goals and the rituals for their pursuit. It is the basis for a well-organized system of social control; most important, it is a rallying point for cultural loyalties. Thus in the religion the values of the tribe are preserved intact. Catholicism provides a bulwark against the white-Anglo-Protestant incursion. It is an outer shell that ultimately protects the kernel of culture lodged in the traditional Indian religious structure.

The complexity of these religio-political groupings is balanced by that of the secular kinship groupings. Most prominent of these are the clans. Membership in the clan is traced in the female line, and parallels the concentration on the mother and motherhood in the religious sphere. The clan has been one of the most severely endangered of Cochiti institutions, although it still survives for some purposes. Even today, a man would not marry a woman of his clan. The clan is also a means of curing illnesses that are not attributed to witches. While clan members are technically related, it is the lineage, a group of people descended in the female line from a known ancestress, that is the effective unit. This is based on a group of women—mothers and daughters—who used to live together in the same house. Although this arrangement is now rare, it is still the basic group for domestic purposes, rather as in East London. In the old days the husbands of these women would be only loosely attached to the group, the males of the group being the women's brothers. But Catholicism and individual housing have changed all that. The Catholic stress on the permanence of marriage has reduced the importance of the brother-sister bond and increased that of the husband-wife. There are also loose alliances of families, which are the breeding ground for factions.

This brings us to factionalism, which, more than the elements of the invaders, has threatened Cochiti survival. All the complex ritual organization, the communal effort for fertility, the overlapping and balancing of group membership is not an expression of harmony, but an elaborate attempt to preserve it. Occasions for factionalism are many and are seized on. A group of "progessives" early in the century used the Indian-versus-the-Catholic issue to campaign against the traditional leaders and traditional ways. They lost, but it has taken fifty years to heal the breach. Baseball is a well-established sport in the village. There used to be one club, but, inevitably, another club was formed and the rivalry between the two has caused near violence and much bad feeling. This is expressed mostly through witchcraft fears and accusations, for that area of belief retains a strong hold. A possible ground for factionalism—the existence of ex-servicemen in the pueblo—has turned out to have a harmonizing effect because the veterans seem to take a moderate position, even a strongly nativistic one—dancing *katsina,* for example.

The secret of both the survival and possible decline of Cochiti lies in the complexity of its groups and institutions. This complexity has meant that there has always been a second string of institutions to take over when the predominant set has waned. As the clan and the maternal household declined in importance, the kiva and the extended family took over; as the medicine societies ceased to govern the pueblo, the secular officers assumed control; gaps left by the native religion could be filled in by Catholicism. But at the same time, the complexity of groupings meant a complexity of interests that could not always harmonize—hence the factions.

National service, government education and the lure of cash wages in the towns have drained the population. In the past, religious authority and the lack of any alternative way of life helped to keep the society together. Now the dissidents can leave; and not only the dissidents, but young people seeking economic advancement. This drain of human resources is fatal to a society that has to organize and man so complex a religious system; it may prove Cochiti's downfall. But to predict is notoriously dangerous where the Indian is concerned. Many young people who work in the nearby towns still return for the dances. Cochiti has a resilience and a tough core that will withstand many blows before capitulating. There may, however, turn out to be two Trojan horses, welcomed by the Indians but fatal to them: television and the vote.

TEN

Pueblo Baseball: A New Use for Old Witchcraft

THE IDEALS of harmony and co-operation and the outlawing of competition among the Pueblo Indians have become an anthropological commonplace during the past few decades. Ruth Benedict's confusion of institutions with personality traits, which led her to believe that the Pueblos were "harmonious" people, has since been cleared up. Such books as *Sun Chief: The Autobiography of a Hopi Indian* vividly show the amount of hate, aggression, and suspicion that lies behind the conscious harmony of Pueblo social life. If interpersonal relations in the Pueblos could be summed up in one word, "cautious" would be it. The power of public opinion, of "what people will say," in these crowded little communities is the strongest force for social conformity, and manifests itself in an extreme fear of witchcraft accusations. Indeed, the fear of being accused is greater than the fear of actual witchcraft. Informants are vague about the powers and practices of witches and often complain that they have forgotten what witches are supposed to do—"only the old people remember what the *kanatya* do." But everyone agrees that the most terrible thing that can be said of one is that "everyone knows he [or she] is a witch." Thus, while the cultural trappings and elaborations surrounding witch behavior have largely been forgotten, the motivational basis for this projective system remains strong. It exists, as it were, in the raw.

Everyone is suspect. The Sun Chief of Oraibi suspected his own mother on her deathbed of being a "two-heart" (witch). All interpersonal relations are fraught with danger, and there are few people who can be wholly trusted. Women in particular do not trust one another. With the Don Juanism of the males and the relative promiscuity of the women, no woman can be sure that any other woman is not her husband's lover, or has not been at one time. A woman can trust her sisters, more or less, and of course her mother, primarily because it would be difficult for members of the same household group to carry on affairs. Affines are much mistrusted, often with good reason.

What is involved is not so much sexual jealousy as, again, the fear of "talk." This is not just fear of gossip. Words have power and are not to be used lightly. Bad thoughts are believed to have tremendous repercussions in the real world. Bad words, as the manifestations of bad thoughts, "poison the air of the pueblo." There are real repercussions to accusation and insults and they do disturb pueblo peace. In societies based on extended kin groupings it is impossible to insult only one person. Any accusation may lead to a widespread split-up of the village, and this fear of internal dissension is a strong motive for not making open accusations, or at least for toning them down. In the case of a philandering husband caught *flagrante delicto,* relatives on both sides will try to patch the matter up or persuade the pair to part quietly. In the old days a woman could be rid of her husband fairly easily by ordering him out of her house. This is becoming impossible today because men are now more likely than women to be the house owners. The Catholic Church complicates matters for the Rio Grande Pueblos by forbidding divorce and remarriage. A wronged woman, taking her children, will often go to live with her sister or mother, but life is hard because she cannot remarry and she risks priestly censure if she takes another mate.

These limitations to direct action cause much frustration and bitterness among the women, so that witchcraft accusations are more likely to involve women than men. In the past, the war captains, ceremonial police of the Pueblos, would usually deal with the witches, once they had gathered sufficient proof of their activities. Death or exile would have been the punishment. Today, however, nothing would be done. One Indian said, "People just get mad and don't speak to each other, or they leave the village." Today, too, the relatively sophisticated Cochiti Indians realize that white people think these beliefs silly, and they tend to shrug them off or deny them. Some members of the ultra-Catholic progressive faction share the white man's contempt for these beliefs. But beneath the careless disbelief and outright denial lies the unchanged motivational and social basis for interpersonal fear.

Formal Pueblo institutions are a counter to, rather than an acting out of, the personality forces. People must dance together, work together, play together. They are enjoined to think good, harmonious thoughts so as not to spoil the air of the pueblo; bad thoughts are as dangerous as bad deeds. Drunkenness is feared for the aggressive impulses it lets loose. All forms of overt hostility are taboo.

In Cochiti, the intricate crisscrossing of clans, societies, the two kivas, extended families, church, and other groups helps to ensure that no permanent oppositions and cleavages can occur to channel hostilities into armed camps. The factional split between conservatives and progressives early in this century came nearest to open war, but the crosscutting of these divisions by others (particularly extended families) saved the village from complete disintegration. As long as any two groups continue to exchange women in Cochiti, it is difficult for them to remain in hostile opposition. All formal divisions within the village are divisions of labor, not of enmity. As the co-operation between the kivas is essential to the proper performance of public ceremonies, they in no way compete with each other. All medicine societies complement each other's work—there are never two societies for one cure. A careful political balance is struck so that every group is evenly represented on the council. The village is small and roles overlap, so that, despite continually recurring conflicts, there is no permanent discord.

Following this principle, the old competitive games of the pueblo were never played between any two formal groups. For races and shinny games, teams consisted of married versus unmarried, or of young men picked according to a count-out method. The social groupings were never competitively aligned and teams were not permanent. Since the advent of baseball in Cochiti, however, a new situation has arisen. The pueblo now has two baseball teams playing in the same league (Inter-Pueblo Baseball League) and in open competition with each other. The original team, now called the "Redskins," was formed many years ago; old photographs testify to the Pueblos' long-standing interest in baseball. Most men now playing grew up in a society that was already enthusiastic about the sport. Support comes from all sections of the population, including the old medicine men and the ceremonial heads of the kivas. The current cacique, the religious leader of the tribe, was for a long time a pitcher for the second team. When he assumed office, the medicine men forbade him to continue playing ball because they did not think this consonant with the dignity of his office—but he is the only exception. The Redskins, first known as the "Eagles," were the focus of interest for many years; but with the return of servicemen to Cochiti after World War II, a second team, called the "Silversmiths," was formed. This team, now the Braves, claimed independent status, built its own ball park and entered the league in competition with the Redskins. The Silversmiths were immediately successful and won the championship three years in succession. Thus a new and potentially dangerous situation occurred—the two teams had to meet each other in the village and fight it out twice a year. This was wildly at variance with the whole Pueblo ethos.

During the first game, all went reasonably well on the field, but there were fights on the sidelines—between the mothers of the players. As the momentum of the game increased, these women began to abuse one another, to brawl, and finally to do open battle. The horrified Pueblo council immediately banned all future games between the teams in the pueblo.

An examination of the original membership of the two teams shows that, because of the voluntary nature of the recruitment, the teams were a perfect breeding ground for factions. One was not constrained to join either team by kinship ties, initiation, or any other automatic factor. The Braves, when they broke away from the Redskins, broke away by family groups; that is, several families of players left the one and formed the other. Thus the choice was made not by individuals, but by families. Within living memory, there had always been two ill-defined groups of extended families that formed opposing blocks on the basis of quarrels now forgotten. Previously, these two blocks had never had occasion or excuse to come out in opposition to each other, since there had been no basis for such an oppositional grouping, and the two groups even cut across the conservative-progressive factional boundaries—but in the baseball split there was a unique opportunity for the old latent hostilities to erupt. Allegiance to the team is predominantly patrilineal, as it is in the kivas, but the two teams are by no means co-terminous with the kivas. They represent a dual alignment of families for purely competitive purposes. Families that mistrusted or disliked each other would readily line up on opposite sides. And the infection spread even to families not committed to either side. The crosscutting tendency in Pueblo institutions mitigates this, as it did with the factions, but the essential factor of the exchange of women has not had time to work itself out. What is more, the away games of the teams have increased the chances of young men to meet girls from outside the village and hence have increased the number of outmarriages. The wives of these marriages, having no female relatives in Cochiti, tend to become assimilated into the husband's mother's extended family and this widens the gap between the two teams. One year, out of eight marriages, three were to girls from San Juan Pueblo—results of the popular away game. It is not the young wives, however, but the older women who are the troublemakers. These women would formerly have had little chance to attack other women they disliked without invoking the frightening subject of witchcraft. Now they had an excuse and an opportunity to do battle royal over their sons and grandsons. The epithet "cheater" quickly became a virtual synonym for witch.

The council ban against baseball was effective in preventing open war in the village for a time, but it served only to drive the feelings underground. By 1959 antagonism had spread to the players. That year the Braves indulged in a series of rule-breaking episodes that flared into open quarrels. These were accentuated by the fact that after a trial game the year before, which rumbled but went off without incident, the council had reluctantly decided that the annual games could continue to be played. Significantly, the games were scheduled for the beginning of the week of the annual Corn Dance, on the feast day of the village saint, Bonaventure. Thus they came at a time when "all hearts are in harmony," when everyone was bending his efforts toward the success of the great communal dance for rain, good harvest, and long life.

The Braves, according to their opponents, had not behaved properly. A Redskin commented, "Rules don't mean nothing to them; they don't care." It seems that the Braves had gone to town with the rule book. They had (1) used people in the finals who had not played five consecutive games; (2) failed to turn up for games but refused to forfeit the points for not doing so; (3) used men who had previously played for other sides and refused to relinquish them even after threats of suspension; (4) cheated in the games; (5) threatened umpires (unspecified); (6) attempted to maim opponents. The rule that the Braves and their female supporters are said to have broken most often was not in the official book: influencing the course of the game by occult means—witchcraft. Particularly, it seems, they attempted to cause "accidents," to make the ball hit a runner, et cetera. When I asked why they hadn't been suspended or denied the replays, I was told, "They get their own way because the other teams are scared of them." San Juan had a good claim to two forfeited games but gave in because "they were scared." The manager of the Braves is feared as the Kwirena *nawa*, head of the powerful Kwirena, one of the "managing" societies in Pueblo ceremonials. He is also head of the Pumpkin Kiva. Some of the Redskins spoke out against the

Braves' conduct at meetings of the league, and in a confused bit of political maneuvering the Braves were suspended, reinstated, quit the league, then rejoined it. By the time of the Cochiti games they were in again but had to forfeit points for two games.

The 1959 Cochiti games, set on Sunday, were to have been a double-header—the first game in the morning after Mass, the second in the afternoon before the kiva practice for the Corn Dance. Mysteriously, the Braves did not show up for the morning game. In an attempt to be friendly and accommodating, the Redskins agreed to play the game on the following Saturday. Several of their female relatives muttered that the game should have been claimed ("The men are too soft"). But the men were making a conscious, if nervous, effort to keep things going smoothly. Several said they would not watch the game: "They'll only fight, those ladies; they'll just yell and shout and upset everybody; people don't forget easily. They don't care about the game; they just want to fight and upset other people." Some predicted that "they won't speak to each other for a year or more," others that "they are just mad in the season, they forget it in the winter." The Redskins' supporters could name only one Braves family that was consistently friendly with any Redskin family. Asked why this antagonism didn't exist between kivas, they said, "Why should it? They don't have nothing to fight about." But no one could explain why the antagonism was there in the first place—or no one was willing to risk the analysis for fear of reaching conclusions too unpleasant to bear about his beloved village. All the men agreed that it was the fault of "them old ladies. I guess they just like fighting."

The afternoon game was payed in a fit of nerves. To lend weight to the authority of the council, both the governor and the lieutenant governor sat toegther, and the war captain and his assistant placed themselves strategically between the supporters of the two sides. The men of the village deliberately chose a neutral spot behind the wire and huddled there, while the women of the teams stood around their respective dugouts.

The game progressed in a lively fashion, the women gathering force as it went on. Their comments, at first mild— "Get him glasses, he can't see"; "He can't hit what he can't see; he's blind"—became bitter, personal, and finally obscene. The men, meanwhile, made polite comments and factual observations. At one point the women became so noisy that the Redskins' manager, at his team's request, had to hurry over to quiet them. This had no noticeable effect. However, the game passed without any unruly incident, although the players were so nervous they made a phenomenal number of errors. There was some relaxation of tension because there was a neutral umpire and because the game was never in doubt. The Redskins went into an early lead and won, 18 to 8. Everyone left the ball ground quickly. Irate old ladies were hustled away by sons and grandsons.

All the following week tension mounted toward the second game. Many declared they would stay away; others were just as sure they wouldn't miss it for anything. The latter were usually women. "There's going to be a lot of accidents," a Redskin mother said, " 'cause them Braves is sure mad they lost last Sunday." In the Corn Dance of midweek, opposing families had to dance together in the communal prayer for harmony and happiness. But Saturday morning the tension was high again. Many actually did stay away. Those that came watched mostly from inside their pickups and cars. Some Redskins had just returned from drinking in the local Spanish-American town of Peña Blanca. The lieutenant governor, not a regular fan, sat between the two blocks of women and invited me to join him.

I did not have long to wait. After the game had been tied

up at 1 to 1 for four innings, the skies suddenly darkened, lightning flashed and thunder rolled, but no rain fell. A huge wind swept across the valley, lifting clouds of sand so that the whole field was obliterated. Players crouched down to avoid being blinded by the stinging grains. I took refuge in a Redskin car, where it was quickly pointed out to me that if the other ground had been used (the Redskins') this would not have happened, because there was less loose soil there. But the Braves had insisted on using their own inferior ground, "so that they could work more of their magic." (Twice in the previous week I had been cautioned to watch out for their, the Braves', "magic.") I failed to see how this complete halt was to the Braves' advantage.

The game should have been stopped until the sand cleared, but the Braves insisted on continuing to play. They played between sharp bursts of wind, swirling sandstorms, and the crashing of thunder. And still no rain fell. Sun Chief says that if, instead of rain at the end of a *katsina* dance, only a strong wind blows, spreading sand, this shows that those who sent for the *katsinas* had done evil. This was the feeling at the Cochiti game, amid the storm clouds and dead dust and absence of rain. One Redskin going out to bat fell on his knees, crossed himself, and muttered a prayer.

There was a nonneutral umpire of the Redskin faction, but he was courting the daughter of a prominent Braves family. The only reason he was made umpire was that he was on leave from the Navy and so would be taking any bad feelings away with him when he left. He gave a faulty-seeming decision that cost the Redskins a base. Immediately the Redskin women called out to him: "Some of her dirt has rubbed off on you! She's got you under her skin, that girl." Among themselves they used epithets other than "girl," and muttered about "influences." But it stopped there; the umpire was the son of the lieutenant governor, whom no one wished to offend.

In between sandstorms the game continued; the score leveled to 2 to 2 at the bottom of the eighth inning. In the final innings the Redskins seemed to go to pieces as the sand lashed their faces, while the Braves hit two runs to win the game, 4 to 2. The players ran to shake hands, although some refused—an unheard-of thing in previous games. The male participants tried to keep things calm. The Braves women were screaming with delight at the victory of their side. The Redskin women went away tight-lipped and furious, convinced that dirty work had been done. The storm, the "influenced" umpire, the unaccountable reversal of the Redskins (an admittedly superior team under normal conditions), all added up to—witchcraft.

In the weeks following the games, rival families went about not speaking. About three weeks later, an incident occurred that reactivated the whole business. The Redskins had just lost a game and were returning home disconsolate when a Braves mother accosted one of them entering his house. The burden of her remarks seemed to be that he had lost the game because his love life was sapping his strength. All this was said in the presence of the Redskin's wife, who was furious but remained mute. The Redskin spat out a few replies and went indoors. The Braves mother had not finished, however; she stood on her own rooftop and hurled insults across at the neighbor. The Redskin took his whole family to the governor's house and asked for the council's protection against these onslaughts. That evening a council meeting was called, and, in typical Pueblo fashion, the combatants were told to shake hands and apologize to each other. An announcement was made to the pueblo to the effect that this antagonism over baseball would have to cease or the sport would be discontinued. This was a desperate measure and a test of the council's authority. The young people were not at all likely to give up baseball, whatever the council said. However, as harvest and winter approached and the baseball season drew to a close, hard feelings began to soften. There would be time during the winter to forget the summer's quarrels.

Competitive Western games that have been introduced into primitive societies have usually taken the place of more violent forms of competition. For example, football in New Guinea replaced intervillage spear-fighting. But baseball in the pueblos was a competitive intrusion into an essentially noncompetitive social system. As long as competition remains between villages, no untoward events occur, as this in is line with tradition, but competition within villages is potentially destructive. Pueblo institutions are constructed to eliminate and nullify aggressive conflict by placing individuals in automatically determined, overlapping-role situations. The baseball teams, based on voluntary recruitment and stressing competition, allow the acting out of competitive and aggressive tendencies. The Pueblos have taken various steps to neutralize this effect but the participants seem just as bewildered by these steps as by the turn of events that necessitates them. Resort to naked authority in the settlement of interfamilial disputes is a new thing to Cochiti and, in a way, a confession of weakness in the social system, previously so ingeniously adequate to deal with conflict. It looks as if the male forces of authority and order may be able to keep the peace. But the women have married the old witch fears to the new sport and thus directed a whole body of deep-rooted motivations into new channels. When the tension is high, the old cry of "Witch!" flies from the women and long-suppressed rages are given full vent. Of course, it may prove therapeutic.

ELEVEN

Veterans and Factions

ONE OF THE most important questions for the student of Pueblo society is the survival of the Pueblos—not only in the face of outside interference, but in spite of internal dissension (although to a large extent the latter has been the result of the former). It is interesting that many of the pueblos have not presented a united front to the outside. Some factions have often been only too willing to accept the ways of the various conquerors, and even in those villages that have consciously tried to keep their culture intact, pervasive factional disputes have threatened the social fabric. These factions are usually labeled "progressive" (those who are willing to accept Anglo ways, reject the authority of the traditional leaders, and generally concur with the breaking up of some of the traditional Pueblo way of life) and "con-servative" (the supporters of the old ways and the old leaders). Each pueblo adds its own flavor to this basic recipe —Protestantism versus Catholicism and democracy versus theocratic authoritarianism are two of the issues.

An additional factor that seems to threaten the integrity of the Pueblos' culture is the influence of returned veterans, with their taste of wider experience and their broader knowl-edge. It has been pointed out that these veterans have been "oriented to more reference points more intensively than have the prevailing theocrats." In Taos Pueblo they represent one of the major sources of factionalism because they have been "at a disadvantage in gaining experience requisite for traditional power positions." What is more, it has been main-tained that none of the pueblos are "organized to cope with factional disputes in any constructive way." I want here to examine the impact of veterans in the pueblo of Cochiti and the consequences for the factional situation there.

At about the turn of the century several Indians who had been educated in schools away from the pueblo returned with adopted Anglo names and with proposals for several changes in pueblo life. These were: refusal to accept the authority of the traditional officers of the pueblo (cacique, war captains, medicine-society leaders and their nominees, the civil officers); repudiation of all aspects of the native religion, in particular the *katsinas* (the masked dancers rep-resenting the tribal deities) and the supernatural powers of the medicine-society heads; strict adherence to the doctrines of the Catholic Church. They found a number of supporters, largely from one moiety (usually referred to as a "kiva" after the semi-underground chamber the moiety uses for ceremonies), the Pumpkin Kiva. Many Pumpkin members and most of the members of the other moiety, the Turquoise Kiva, remained conservative and opposed the stand of the self-styled "progressives." The Church and Indian Service backed the progressives, but the latter seemed to get the worst of the battle because the pueblo officers still had some means at their disposal to bring the offenders into line—mainly the confiscation of land. As the original leaders of the progressive movement died, the faction lost its impetus and members gradually slipped back to the old ways. At the same time, the medicine-society heads and older conservatives had also died, and a more moderate state of affairs prevailed.

Progressives now help to manage ceremonies even if they do not actually take part, and some, as old age overtakes them, return to the religious practices of their youth. But the two poles of opinion remain, and, occasionally, bitter disputes bring out latent resentments and align families against one another. That great leaven of disputes—intermarriage—has succeeded in bringing together several families otherwise opposed. Most of these marriages are, however, contracted by veterans, which raises the question of the place of ex-servicemen in the system.

World War II caused considerable disruption of pueblo life. Many adult males from Cochiti were drafted and some never returned. The figures below are for World War II, 1940-45, and for the Korean War, 1951-53.

	In service	Died	Re-enlisted	Returned to Pueblo	Returned to near Pueblo
1940–45	33	3	5	14	?
1951–53	24 (incl. 5 from 1940–45)	1	2	12 (incl. 3 from 1940–45)	4

In 1958-59 there were still some twenty veterans living in Cochiti, out of an adult male population of approximately one hundred and seven. Few had returned to their previous occupation of farming; most were either working for wages outside the pueblo or doing paid work of some kind in and around it. Several were silversmiths, timber workers (at a nearby sawmill), draughtsmen, janitors, school-bus drivers, workers on Anglo farms, and as such had permanent contact with the outside world. Many could not participate in pueblo government, owing to the rule that officials must reside in the pueblo and have no work outside it.

What has happened to the veterans in the pueblo is interesting in terms of the factional situation. Many were the sons of conservatives and their parents' early teaching does not seem to have left them. Of the veterans of 1940-45, most have resumed active participation in the ceremonial life, dancing *katsina* and becoming members of the kiva drum cults and managing societies. Even so, they have tried to introduce many innovations into the pueblo, often in the face of opposition from their older conservative relations. But the fact that they are themselves the sons of conservatives has helped to lessen the old people's opposition. In a sense they are a disappointment to extremists in both factions. They are avowedly nativistic, but also demand material improvements and changes in organization that are at variance with the ideas of the older, more conservative men. Their nativism antagonizes the hard-boiled progressives, who would like to see them go the whole hog with their "Anglo-cization" of the pueblo. It is fascinating to see how some veterans treat the progressive attitude as old-fashioned. Their effect has been to produce a third force in Pueblo life, a nativistic but progressive force that seems to be providing a vigorous alternative to the other two spent factions and to the moderates who either sat on the fence or took a plague-on-both-your-houses view. What is more, they have provided a reference group for younger people, who can now avoid being torn between the more extreme demands of the factions. The prestige of veterans as returned warriors is high and they are listened to with respect.

What all this suggests is that a unidimensional view of factionalism in Cochiti is no longer valid. The two factors of nativism and progressivism have to be separated in order to explain all the positions taken (see figure).

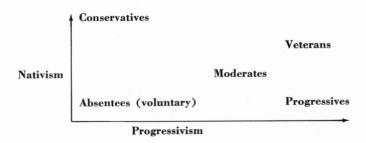

Nativism means the acceptance of the positive value of the native religion and ceremonialism, a pride in Indianness, and a desire to preserve the old ways as much as possible. Progressivism means the acceptance of changes made necessary by the assimilation of all the material benefits of Anglo culture, including electricity, water, sanitation, hospitals and doctors, motor transport, et cetera. Progressives and moderates tend to be more tolerant of anthropologists and to have a more positive attitude to many aspects of Anglo life. The veterans have managed to combine both these attitudes and therein lies their strength. But the question of why they were able to do this in Cochiti and not elsewhere still remains to be answered.

One clue lies in the decline of the medicine societies. No veterans have joined any of the medicine societies, which are the most conservative of the religious and political institutions in the pueblo. They have failed to recruit new members, and it is contrary to Pueblo ethics to force membership. Had they still been flourishing, the veterans might well have had more trouble settling in after their return. The medicine societies, unlike the *katsina* cult, are also political organs, and nominate the secular officers of the pueblo. As their ritual functions are concerned largely with healing, they came into specific conflict with the Indian Service medical program and also helped to keep alive belief in witches as sources of illness. In their political role, they conflicted with the Indian Service Administration and with outside influence generally. If the medicine societies had flourished, to accept hospitals and health services and Indian Service Administration aid wholeheartedly would have made it impossible to be fully nativistic. The *katsina* and kiva dance rituals, on the other hand, are less specifically in conflict with Anglo institutions. Their conflict is with the Catholic Church. This has been resolved by keeping the *katsina* dances secret and by incorporating the animal and rain dances into the calendar of the church. Thus, in the absence of pressure from the once all-powerful medicine societies, the returning veterans could fit into the nativistic side of Cochiti life without too much conflict. In Rio Grande pueblos where the medicine societies are still powerful and yet have failed to gain veteran support there is a great deal of conflict; at Santo Domingo, for example, the veterans have been forced into the ultraprogressive camp and have formed a branch of the American Legion. There is no American Legion branch at Cochiti.

The decline of some of the functions of the clan system and of agriculture also played a part in rendering veteran participation easy. Through the lack of extensive agricultural activity, traditional demands and sanctions have lost their force. Thus the veteran has little occasion to resent the old ways. It is important to note that the changes resulting from that decline took place before World War II and are not a consequence of veteran activity. Had agriculture and the clan system still been effective social forces when the veterans returned, the rule that pueblo officials have to live and work in the pueblo would have been, to say the least, irksome to them. Most of them want to earn more than would be possible under a system of subsistence agriculture and co-operative farming, with obligations to clan and other relatives and to the community with respect to irrigation works. The absence of these pressures has enabled veterans to take up money-earning occupations within the pueblo and so qualify for official posts there.

The Catholic Church occupies an important place along with nativism and progressivism. Becoming less nativistic does not necessarily mean becoming more Catholic. However, the older factional dispute led to a cleavage between the progressive supporters of Catholicism and the conservative supporters of the native religion. When the struggle was flaring, there was almost a complete split, and the conservatives were at the point of leaving the church. But in a curious sense the church has been a point of unity rather than dissension. As long as the Franciscan fathers kept within what the majority of Cochiti thought were their proper bounds (serving Mass and performing the other church rituals, and "leaving us to run our own lives"), the Indians were ready to pronounce themselves devout Catholics and support the church. So, most of the time, there was a common meeting place and a common ritual for all sections of the village. The veterans, too, are devout Catholics (with some exceptions), but their wider experience of the world has helped them to be more vigorous and positive toward the church than the non-veteran villagers. They feel less intimidated and overawed than the natives, and, in many cases, the priests themselves. They are able to take the church in their stride; it looms less important to them than to the others.

Thus it is that the experience gained by the veterans, far

from disrupting them, and hence the pueblo at large, has given them the knowledge, ability, and confidence to make the best of several worlds, or rather to make a new world out of the remnants of the old. As one veteran said to me, "I'm a good Catholic and a good Indian, and I'm going to be both." In one or two interesting cases, however, there has been an even more extreme reaction against the church than the most ultraconservative would have contemplated. The attitude of one young ex-Navy veteran has shocked the nativistic in its extremism. The young man, son of a much respected moderate who swung between the two factional extremes, had had some college-level education on the GI Bill. He studied philosophy and the history of New Mexico, and the combination had turned him not only against the church, but also, peculiarly, against those conservatives who desired no changes at all. He had considered the relative merits of Catholic and Indian philosophy and found the former deficient. He has worked out a theology of nativism that, despite its anti-Catholic flavor, includes God as an explanatory principle. (He is equated with the Sun Father, and the *katsinas* are "like saints.") To him all aspects of nativistic religion were symbolic of various aspects of Pueblo life and "celebrated" these. His objection to Catholicism was that it failed to symbolize properly the Indian way of life. He read books on Pueblo religion and made copious notes on prayer sticks and *katsinas*. When he knew enough, he claimed, he would begin practicing the religion. He told the priest to his face that he didn't need the Catholic religion. He never went to church and urged his peers not to—with conspicuous lack of success. They resented him and, while showing the typical Pueblo tolerance of opinion in these matters, they laughed at him behind his back. In some ways they seemed to fear him, and most avoided him with a muttered "He talks too much." They were always reluctant to enter into discussion with him, one of them maintaining, "It doesn't do any good to talk about these things we don't understand, anyway." The unity that they were busily forging for themselves was a unity of practices, not of concepts. They had no need for, and were rather annoyed by, the ex-Navy anti-Catholic veteran's attempt to make a rational system out of what was a pragmatic behavioral compromise.

This was one kind of deviation from the veteran norm. Others who could not adapt either left the pueblo or took to drink—usually at times of stress; for example, just before ceremonies in which they were to participate. The firm veteran stand is typified by the silversmith who set up a workshop in the pueblo and sells his work outside the community as well as to visitors. He goes to museums to study old Pueblo designs to incorporate into his work, but he also makes rosaries, crosses, et cetera. He has modernized his house and become a member of the civil government, at the same time joining his kiva drum cult and participating in *katsina* rituals. Along with other veterans he has held various posts in the village government. At one change-over of officials, veterans occupied all the major posts in civil offices; they had also participated in all regimes since World War II.

There is no class consciousness among the veterans. They have never recognized themselves as a group with interests. They tend to think of their relations to one another in terms of the ready-made categories of group membership and even as deadly rivals (on the baseball teams). But there is a covert unity of attitude and action among them that is having a marked stabilizing effect on Pueblo life and helping to make the transition from the old to the new less painful. They provide the bridge across which acculturation can travel, rather than the spearhead of change as in other pueblos.

The integrating influence of veterans in Cochiti has shown

the importance of timing. The veterans became a potent force in Cochiti society at a time when the various institutions that might have pushed them into an extreme position were dead or on the wane. They were also aided by the fact that they were mostly the sons of conservatives. This combination of circumstances, coupled with the immense prestige accruing to them, has made them the best hope for painless acculturation in Cochiti. A comparison with Santo Domingo and Taos would show how the reverse could easily have happened. Probably the small size of Cochiti (less than three hundred permanent inhabitants) has a lot to do with it, because this helped to undermine the older institutions by restricting the number of recruits for the medicine societies and by making unworkable a complex system that was suited to a larger population.

The full story will be known only after a thorough comparative study has unearthed all the important variables. What the Cochiti case has shown is that it is possible to be progressive, that is, to embrace positively many aspects of Anglo material culture and organization, and yet to be nativistic, that is, to enter enthusiastically into many aspects of the native religion and to preserve much of the traditional way of life. In all pueblos there are moderates who are unenthusiastic about any extreme position. The Cochiti veterans and their followers differ from these in seizing both extremes, and in their active enthusiasm they have managed to steer the pueblo away from a state of apathetic moderation, which could have led to withdrawal and decline. However, it may well be that even the veterans will not be able to stop the drift of the most able members away from the pueblo.

TWELVE

Witches, Clans, and Curing

ILLNESS, both mental and physical—although based on universal psychobiological factors—is in its expression culturally patterned. One becomes "sick" or "crazy" in a well-defined, culturally delimited way. Illness is defined differently from culture to culture. Behavior labeled as "sickness" in one culture may count as religous ecstasy in another. The sociocultural system of which the individual is a member provides the stresses that cause the illness; the medium of expression of the illness; a theory of disease (spirit possession, soul loss, witchcraft, or attack of gods, ghosts, or germs); the basis for mobilization of help for the patient; a cure, and, in varying degrees, insurance that the cure will be permanent, that is, without relapse. In many primitive societies, fine balances have been achieved among these factors. Personality traits, cultural traditions, and social groupings combine both to cause and to cure disease. In many other societies, however, these factors fail to coalesce. The society provides the stress, but fails to find a cure; or, if it finds a cure, it fails to provide continuous reinforcement. Our own culture sharply dichotomizes the hospital and the society, and, in the case of mental illness, the society is often directly or indirectly hostile to the patient and the hospital. Primitive societies and religious healing groups frequently have the edge on hospitals in that they incorporate the sick person into the society and, indeed, utilize the sickness in some cultural sphere.

Kilton Stewart gives a detailed account of one type of hypnotherapy, practiced by the Negritos in northern Luzon (Philippines). The shaman induces a trance in the patient and instructs him to fight and overcome the demon that is attacking him. Having mastered the demon, the patient demands from him a dance and a song. The shaman then ends the trance, and the patient is told to perform the dance and sing the song just learned in front of an assembly of Negritos. The important thing about this type of cure is that all the aesthetic life of the Negritos is derived from it. That is, all the songs and dances of the Negritos are originally learned in such therapeutic trance conditions. These songs and dances are then regularly performed; each person does a dance drama in which he illustrates how he overcame his illness (the demon), receives the support and applause of his fellows, and in turn appreciates and applauds their dance dramas. The likeness to certain types of group therapy is striking, but with the difference that, among the Negritos, a large area of the total culture—aesthetic and recreational —is involved in, indeed derived from, the therapy. Reinforcement is built into a continuing cultural process in which everyone participates. The therapy involves the whole social group acting in a whole cultural area; it is not divided between clinic and outside.

In the American Southwest, the home of the Cochiti, the Navaho Indians have an ethnographic reputation as expert curers. Their "nine night sings," involving complex rituals and the assembly of thousands of Navaho, have a Durkheimian grandeur. Such a huge effort to achieve a curing success is bound to have a supportive influence on the patient and therefore help to effect a cure. But the cure does not necessarily last. When the guests have packed up and gone home, the cure is over. Cochiti cures are less spectacular but are, I think, more subtly successful, especially in reinforcement.

The distinctions in Cochiti thought between various types of disease and their appropriate cures are not always easy to see. There seem to be three main types. First and simplest are natural diseases (burns, fractures, and so forth), which are largely curable by natural means—herbal treatments, elementary first aid, and sometimes treatment by U.S. Indian Service doctors. Then come illnesses caused by witches, which are treated either by a member of a medicine society or, in severe cases, by the entire society. Each medicine society specializes in certain types of cure. The various diseases are characterized as "sharp" (*tsiati*) and "dull" (*tsatsi tsiati*—literally, "not sharp"). Sharp illnesses generally seize patients suddenly, and are always considered the result of witchcraft. Dull illnesses are those that, in the words of an informant, "just go on and on and don't seem to get better." For these illnesses, the medicine society cures are considered too drastic and clan cures are employed. While not able to verbalize clearly the distinction between these two types of disease, the Cochiti Indians know one kind from the other. In practice, the drawn-out dull diseases are not treated as though they had been caused by witchcraft, although it is impossible to pin the Cochiti down to a coherent theory of the causation of disease.

There are, in the literature, many details of Pueblo curing ceremonies, although no anthropologist seems to have actually attended a cure. Some of the medicine societies and their methods are common to all the Keresan pueblos. I shall concentrate on Cochiti, but much of this material is true for all the Keresans.

There are societies proper and degrees within them. In the important Flint society, its two degrees of Snake and Fire are now inextricably merged. The Flint is powerful because it maintains associations with the Koshare managing society and because the cacique is chosen from it. It also nominates the war captain and his assistant. The Giant society is next in importance, and its head is first assistant to the cacique. The Giant, which nominates the governor and his assistant, is also closely associated with the Shrutzi society and the management of the *katsina* cult. The Shikame society is loosely associated with the Kwirena and nominates the *fiscale* and his assistant. The medicine societies are thus intimately bound up with the ritual and political life of the tribe, and form a theocratic hierarchy of government as well as an agency of medical and spiritual well-being.

Recruitment to the medicine societies is voluntary, by "trapping," or by cure: an individual can join as a result of vocation, because he was trapped through entering a forbidden area during a ceremonial, or from a desire to perpetuate a cure. There is an elaborate initiation that often lasts many years and involves abstentions, fastings, and retreats.

There are three primary functions of the societies: curing, rain making, and government. The last is largely delegated to the secular officials, and the medicine men concentrate on the first two. In general, they are the guardians of tribal well-being, ensuring its continuing fertility and health, although they function only in a context of immense communal effort. While sacrifice and prayer, mainly through dance and ritual, are required of all Cochiti, the medicine men are, as Adolph Bandelier says in *The Delight Makers*, the "chief penitents of the tribe." They continually fast and pray on behalf of the Cochiti and indeed of all Pueblo Indians. Most of their time, however, is spent in curing. There is evidence of some division of labor among the societies. The Flint society is primarily for curing illnesses, setting fractures, and helping the people combat witchcraft. They are called on to preside at births and deaths and are particularly proficient at curing wounds. The Snake society cures snake and other bites, while the Fire society specializes in burns and fevers. The Giant society also treats fevers and is perhaps preferred for births. The societies collectively lead communal fasts and purifications.

In their general role as penitents, members of societies fast, pray, and make prayer sticks in seclusion, thus gaining the good will of the tribal deities, and ensuring rain, fertility, and good health. To understand their specific curing methods, one must understand the nature of witchcraft and its place in the theory of disease. Some diseases are to the Cochiti natural. The medicine men have considerable knowledge of first-aid measures and herbal cures for these illnesses. Others are not so obviously due to natural causes and are attributed to the supernatural malevolence of witches. In Cochiti thinking, witches are almost exclusively concerned with causing disease. In Pueblo cosmology, there is an uneasy balance of forces in the universe. The forces of good—the *shiwanna* and the various other deities and spirits—are only precariously in control. Even they have to be compelled by elaborate rituals into producing rain and health. The witches represent a vast conspiracy of ill-defined but definitely malignant beings that seek to destroy Pueblo civilization by attacking the health of its members. They are of various types, appearing as humans, animals, and birds (especially owls), or as fireballs. Living humans can be witches by being born with two hearts, one good and one bad. Practically everyone is suspected by someone at some time of being a witch or of practicing sorcery. The distinction between witchcraft and sorcery is not clearly made in ethnographic writings or in Pueblo thinking; a person actually practicing sorcery (as opposed simply to being a witch) is himself a witch, or "two-heart." In the old days, persons found indulging in sorcery would have been clubbed to death by the war captains after a trial before the pueblo leaders. Such evidence as proof of possession of owl feathers or other sorcerer's devices would be required. Witchcraft mythology is riddled with inconsistencies, and it is often difficult to know whether an accused person is a passive witch, an active witch, or an ordinary human in league with witches. Witchcraft accusations are rarely specific as to the nature of the witchcraft or the identities of the victims. The accusation is simply that he or she is a witch. Such an accusation can gain sympathetic hearing only if feeling generally is roused against the accused on some issue. Charges have to be made with care because the strong notions of matrilineal heredity make them, by implication, indictments of the accused's matrilineal kin.

It is against this terrible conspiracy of evil that the people, helpless in their lack of ritual knowledge, seek aid from the medicine societies. The societies possess the knowledge, paraphernalia, and courage to combat the witches, and these are the sources of their great power among the Pueblos.

The witches cause illness by two basic methods. They either steal the heart of the victim, or they shoot objects into his body. To cure him, the medicine societies must suck the objects from the body or recover the heart by fighting the witches. To understand the nature and effectiveness of this curing process, one must enter sympathetically into the Cochiti imagination. Most of the time they feel that there is an uneasy balance in the universe and that it is only the enormous ritual efforts of the tribe and the vigilance of the medicine men that keep the universe on an even keel and the witches at bay. But threat is always there. When someone falls ill or behaves violently or erratically, it means that the witches have broken through, in the same way that a drought means that the *shiwanna* have withdrawn—usually because of faulty ritual, which can itself be the result of witchcraft. When one is ill, the terror produced by the feeling that one is in the grip of the witches is real and profound, and is accentuated by the fear that everyone else feels. It is equivalent perhaps to the medieval terror of feeling irredeemably damned. That this conspiracy of evil has allies in the pueblo and even among one's own relatives is doubly terrifying. Even the doctors can be suspected, and the *katsinas* themselves are not above suspicion. Sometimes people fear that they may be unconsciously guilty of witchcraft—for example, when their bad thoughts about someone seem to have resulted in his death or illness. The over-all atmosphere in the face of sickness or violence or anything completely untoward is one of helpless fright. Into this situation step the medicine men. Their curing method consists of pitching the terror almost to breaking point, triumphing over the witches in a fight, recapturing and returning the heart to the victim, or removing the objects from his body. Here is Leslie White's matter-of-fact summary of the process.

When a person is ill he may ask to be treated by a medicine man or by a society. If the illness is not severe, one medicine man only will come. But if the patient is very ill, or wishes to become a member of the curing society, the whole society will come. The father of the patient summons the doctor (or society) by taking a handful of meal to the doctor selected or to the head-man of the society.

When one doctor only comes to treat the patient, the procedure is simple. He smokes, sings, mixes medicine in a bowl of water, puts ashes on his hands and massages the patient's body, and sucks out any objects that he locates. But when a whole society comes, there is an elaborate ceremony in which considerable paraphernalia is used. Usually a society spends four days in its house in preparations before visiting the patient. Then when they go to his house, the medicine men smoke, sing, and pray over the sick one for three nights, and on the fourth have their final curing ritual. But if the condition of the patient is critical, they will perform the curing ritual at once. . . . A meal painting is made and paraphernalia laid out. The chief item of paraphernalia is the *iarriko*, the corn-ear fetish. Each doctor receives one at initiation. It is returned to the head-man at death. It is the badge *par excellence* of the medicine man. Stone figures of *Masewi, Oyoyewi, Pai yatyamo, K'oBictaiya*, and of lions, bears, and badgers, etc. are laid out on the meal painting. The medicine men do not possess power to cure disease in and of themselves; they receive it from animal spirit doctors (the bear is the chief one, others are mountain lion, badger, eagle, etc.). Meal lines are drawn on the floor from the door to these stone figures; when the songs and prayers are begun, the spirits of the animal medicine men come in, pass over the "roads" of meal, and invest the stone images. Medicine bowls, skins of the forelegs of bears, flints, eagle plumes, rattles, etc. are used. A rock crystal (*ma cai'yoyo* or *ma coitca'ni*) is used to obtain second sight.

The medicine men wear only a breechcloth. Their faces are painted red and black, and they wear a line of white birddown over the head from ear to ear; songs are sung, the head-man tells the people present to believe in the medicine men that they are doing their best, etc.; water is poured into the medicine bowl from the six directions, each doctor puts some herb medicines into the bowl. The doctors rub their hands with ashes, and massage the patient. When they find some foreign object they suck it out and spit it into a bowl. The rock crystal is used to locate objects in the body and to "see witches." Witches gather about a house during a curing ceremony; they wish to harm the patient further or to injure the doctors. They have been heard to rap on the door (at Cochiti) and call to the doctors, defying them. The War Captains and their assistants always stand guard outside the door during a curing ritual. They are armed with bows and arrows since rifles would not hurt a witch.

Frequently the doctors decide that the heart has been stolen by the witches. Then it is necessary to find it and bring it back. This almost always means fighting with the witches. They go out armed with flint knives; they wear a bear paw on the left forearm, a bear claw necklace, and a whistle of bear bone. The War Chief's guards try to accompany the medicine men when they leave the curing chamber, but the doctors travel so fast it is impossible; sometimes the medicine men leave the ground entirely and fly through the air.

These combats with the witches are occasions of great moment. Cries and thuds can be heard in the darkness. The witches sometimes tie the queues of two or three doctors together and leave them in a tangled mass on the ground. Or, a medicine man might be found lying on the ground bound with baling wire, his knees under his chin. The witches try to overpower the doctors by blowing their breath, the odor of which is unbearable, into their faces. Sometimes the doctors have to seek refuge in the church, when the witches "get too bad."

But sometimes the medicine men capture a witch. He is usually man-like in shape and about a foot and a half long (although he may be as large as a man, or he may be in the form of some animal). Often he looks like a Koshare. He squeals when they bring him in. They place him before the fireplace and then call the War Chief in to shoot him with a bow and arrow. The medicine men frequently return smeared with blood or "black" after a fight with witches. Often, too, they fall into a spasm or lose consciousness upon their return.

The medicine men come home with the heart (*wi nock*). This is a ball of rags with a grain (or four) of corn in the center. The patient is given this to swallow.

When the ceremony is over and everyone has been given medicine to drink, food is brought out (stew, bread, and coffee). The medicine men eat first, then the people. Baskets of cornmeal and flour are given to the medicine men in payment for their services. They gather up their paraphernalia and go home.

This account seems to fit pretty well the experience of both doctors and patients in Cochiti. The sequence of a full-scale cure is interesting. The doctors spend four exhausting nights preparing. They do not eat or sleep during this time, and they smoke a great deal. They can be heard chanting in the society house. Witch phenomena (fireballs, owls, and so forth) increase during this time, and everyone becomes agitated. Then the doctors go to the house where the patient has been waiting—an agonizing wait—and repeat the performance. They manipulate the paraphernalia, invoke the spirits, smoke, chant, and build up more tension. By the fourth night of this ceremony, the tension is almost unbearable. The witches are gathering to thwart the efforts of the doctors. The doctors maintain that they can only do their best and that the issue is still very much in doubt. Then a final supreme effort must be made. The monotonous rise and fall of the chant, the flickering fire in the deep dark, the hideous make-up, the cries in the night and rappings at the door and windows, the elaborate precautions—all these elements crescendo until the doctors, worked into a controlled frenzy, dash from the house to do battle. Patients describe how they have been nearly mad with fear by this time, unable to move or even cry out, convinced that they are to die. Then comes the terrible battle in the darkness. The doctors claim that, although of course they do a lot of the business themselves, it is the witches who get "inside them" and make them do it. They do indeed roll in convulsions and lacerate themselves. One explained, "We are more scared than they are [those in the house]. The witches are out to get us. They get inside us and make us do these things until we don't know what we're doing. We run to the church sometimes." Finally, exhausted, they return. Those in the house are by now in a state of extreme fright. "Sometimes we think the witches have got them [the doctors] and that they will come for us." The doctors reappear and enact the ultimate horror. They come in the semidarkness, huddled together, fighting with something in their midst that screams horribly. It is the witch who stole the heart. Then, by the firelight, the war chief shoots the witch, and it disappears. The effect on the patient can be imagined. The incredible relief, the joy, the gratitude leave him "feeling like all the badness has gone out." The heart has been returned. Then, almost nonchalantly, the doctors and patients eat stew and drink coffee. Life returns to normal; the universe is on an even keel again.

There is no doubt that much Cochiti illness is psychosomatic. They do not distinguish formally between physical and mental illness. All illness is abnormal. Belief in witches provides a cultural medium through which illness can be expressed. Also, in many cases, a pathological fear of witches can itself bring on illness. Any Cochiti who suffers from certain illnesses will believe himself bewitched, but not all Cochiti are so afraid of witches that the fear drives them to sickness. In the more markedly paranoid, intense fear of others is expressed, indeed felt, as witch fear. The paranoiac trait and the cultural belief in witches obviously reinforce each other. When a person feels ill, he suspects witchcraft, which in turn accentuates the illness. But the tribe has, in the medicine man, a cultural mechanism to deal with this situation. Terror of witchcraft is utilized to provide a kind of shock therapy. The patient is put through a terrifying experience, "saved," and his "heart" restored. His relief is so great that, in many psychosomatic cases, the ceremony itself has sufficed as a cure. He does not have to join the society that cured him, but he may want to do so out of gratitude or to help perpetuate the cure.

Cures of this type have usually been for men. The complaints are various but most of them seem to be abdominal pains, rheumatism, and respiratory troubles, as well as anxiety and erratic behavior, insomnia, and vomiting. At least two men described as having recurrent fevers appeared to be mentally abnormal; the fevers (rises in temperature) were accompanied by violence and hallucinations of such ferocity that the men had to be restrained. The hallucinations were, of course, mostly about witch phenomena. The witch theory accounts neatly for all symptoms.

The other type of cure involves the clan, rather than the medicine society, as curing agent. The question of how is it decided whether a clan or society cure should be employed has never been pursued, perhaps because data are scarce; but several striking facts emerge. The most obvious is that in cases where a clan cure is selected there is never any mention of witchcraft as the cause of the sickness, and so witchcraft is not called upon in the curing process.

The clan cure is a variation of the clan adoption ceremony. Clan adoptions are performed, for example, for anyone coming to live in the village who does not have a clan. His head is washed by a woman who becomes his clan "mother," and from then on he is a member of her clan. He is given a new name, and feasting takes place among his new-found clansfolk. Tewa wives are usually treated in this way in order that their children may have clans. A man can be adopted, too, but it is not so important for him as for a woman. Since the clan organization is matrilineal, she must have a clan to pass on to her children. For a man, it is membership in one of the moieties (kivas) that is important.

The whole notion of adoption in Cochiti is interesting because it is bound up with a preoccupation with health. A child is often adopted into a clan or clans other than his own as a kind of insurance policy. The child may be perfectly healthy, but he should still acquire some extra clans. He or she does not become a full member of these clans (for example, a girl does not pass on membership in her adopted clan to her children), but does stand in a very special relation to their members. They care for the child in a spiritual sense. Clanless immigrants are believed to enjoy better health as a result of being adopted. One does not have to be ill in order to benefit from adoption. I was able to trace the case histories of some of the patients cured by this method, of one in particular.

The patient, whom I met in 1958, was a woman of forty. Her immediate family at that time consisted of her seventy-five-year-old father, who had begun to go blind in about 1945; her sister, three years younger; and her illegitimate son of sixteen. Her life history revealed that her mother had died in about 1930. Her father then remarried. (His second wife was a Cochiti woman who had been married to a man from the Zia pueblo. After his death, she had returned to Cochiti, bringing her son, who married a Cochiti girl.) Neither the patient nor her sister was considered attractive by the men of the village, and neither ever married. The patient, however, had borne a son in 1942. Her sister got into trouble in 1945 with the pueblo council for giving information to outsiders on some ceremonial matters. Her father was totally blind by 1948. Her cure took place in 1951. Shortly after that, her stepmother died, following a long period of declining health.

The patient's early family life had been overtly secure and happy. The mother had been a beautiful, energetic woman, and the father an important ceremonial official. The patient, while of below-normal intelligence, was a serious and conscientious girl who, with her mother's help, looked after her younger sister. The patient was about eleven or twelve when her mother died. The running of the household and the care of her sister were thrust upon her. She evidently took the death of her mother very hard. Her relatives say it was useless to console her. Her father's remarriage did not help. While it is difficult to ascertain the relations between the patient and her stepmother, they were evidently strained and distant. This was attributed to the patient's "queer" behavior, which began shortly after her mother's death.

The first symptom was apparently insomnia. She would

wander about at night and complain constantly that she could not sleep. During the day, she was too tired to do anything, and simply sat around. At first she was censured for this behavior. According to her sister, "She used to put on her best clothes in the morning and just sit on the step combing her hair. Then she put on her jewelry, all of it, and sat there all the rest of the day. She'd cry and moan and she was always sick around the place. She had pains in her stomach and couldn't eat anything. She sat and talked to herself all the time, crying and talking." She had vague fears, but "not about anything in particular"; she simply "acted scared" all the time. She was afraid of relative strangers and unable to recognize people. The pains and vomiting became acute, and she was taken to the Indian hospital, from which she was eventually discharged without being fully cured. "Them doctors couldn't do anything for her, she was sick in her mind."

The content of her talk consisted almost entirely of complaints about her lack of a home. Her father's rapidly failing sight made him utterly dependent on his daughters and other relatives. Under the old matrilocal system of residence, a man was always dependent on his wife's mother for a house. This man had never had a house of his own, but had always lived in one supplied by his affinal relatives. At the time of the onset of his daughter's serious symptoms, he was living in a house owned by his stepson, the son of his second wife. It had been built by the stepson for his mother on her return to the village, and it was legally his. As the stepson was himself living in a borrowed house at the time, the two sisters and their father were under threat of a possible eviction. This threat was not serious so long as the stepmother was alive, but she was a fragile woman whose health was progressively failing throughout the period. Under the matrilineal system of inheritance and the institution of female house ownership, the two sisters would inherit their mother's house. But in this case, as in many others, rules and practice did not coincide. Houses are not infinitely divisible, and the house that could have come to the patient in the female line went instead to the children of her mother's mother's sister. Since newly married couples now prefer to set up a separate home, it has become less common for sisters to share houses. The onus of providing a house in most instances falls on the husband, unless his wife is senior of a group of sisters and inherits her mother's house. The father of our patient was unfortunately caught between the two systems, and his sight began to fail before he could adapt himself to the newer system of male house ownership.

The result of this potential housing problem was to create actual insecurity for the patient, who was already subject to emotional insecurity. It is doubtful that the stepson would ever have turned them out (in fact, there is evidence to the contrary), but the patient seized upon the uncertainty of the situation and used it to express the deep feelings of abandonment and insecurity consequent upon her mother's death. The house that she fretted over should have come to her from her mother; that it had not was a reinforcement of her anxieties over the discontinuance of the mother's love.

There is some evidence that, for all its outward calm, the early life of the patient may have contributed to these feelings. Her younger sister took her place as the spoiled baby of the family, and there was some resentment on the patient's part at having to play nurse to her. During the mother's final illness, the patient had both to look after the unruly child and attend the sick woman. It was during this period that she first became sullen and withdrawn. The nature of the mother's continuing relationship with her daughters must be appreciated in order to understand the patient's fright at the thought of her mother's death. This relationship lasts as long as the mother lives. All advice and help in personal and family matters that a woman may need are obtained from her mother. Particularly in regard to marriage and childbirth and the rearing of children, the mother plays a crucial part and is constantly at her daughter's side. Even today, when there are very few matrilocal households left in Cochiti, this bond remains as firm as ever. Mothers will trudge miles and ford the river in order to help daughters, and vice versa. It is not simply a matter of practical help, but of emotional dependence of an intense nature. With initiation, the boy is to some degree weaned of this dependence, but the girl remains at home with her mother all her life—in feeling, if not in fact. Bearing this relationship in mind, we can appreciate the acute anxiety that the sickness and death of her mother must have aroused in the patient. All informants agreed that the spells became worse during her pregnancy and after the birth of her child. She was assisted in childbirth by her mother's mother's sister's daughters—one of whom owned the disputed house. The Cochiti's fear of going through a first birth without the help and emotional support of a mother has been noted in a number of other instances. It is one of the reasons girls refuse to go to a hospital for the delivery. (This prejudice is breaking down in the present generation.) Shortly after the birth of her son, the patient's father began to go seriously blind, although his sight had been bad for some time. At this point, the patient was taken to the hospital, as previously described. Since she was essentially a dependent person, the responsibilities of a blind father, a sickly stepmother, an irresponsible younger sister, and a fatherless baby —combined with the lack of a home of her own—were too much, and she broke down completely. She failed to give milk properly just before leaving for the hospital, and this function was handed over to a female relative, as is the Cochiti custom.

After her dismissal from the hospital the girl's relatives decided to take positive action. To understand what was done, the network of extended family and clan relationships surrounding the patient must be examined. In the figure, the relatives are indicated with the patient (P) as reference point. In generation 1, there are two sisters who own a house. In generation 2, two brothers married the daughters of these two sisters, one brother being the father of the patient. The house went to the wife of the other brother, as she was the older of the two cousins and had married first. Finally, it went to the patient's second cousin (her mother's mother's sister's daughter's son), who was also her father's brother's son. The patient's mother died, and her father married a woman from the patient's own clan—Oak. The patient's father's sister's daughter married the patient's stepbrother. It was this stepbrother who had built the house for his mother in which the patient, her father, stepmother, sister, and son were living.

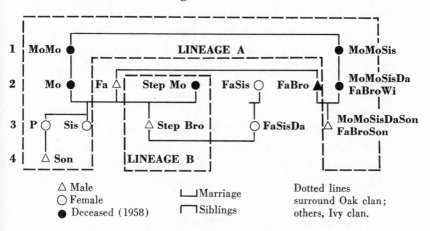

The Patient's Extended Family and Clan Relationships

The surviving relatives who could be considered to have some responsibility for the fate of the patient and her family were her maternal second cousin (who was also her father's brother's son); her father's sister's daughter; and the latter's husband, who was also the patient's stepbrother. The first move was made by the cousin who had the house that was ostensibly the cause of the trouble. He made a deal with his father's brother, the father of the patient. The latter owned some land that was suitable for building, and the cousin agreed to trade the house for the land. The patient and the other members of her household were thus able to move into a house that was indisputably theirs; now they had a home. This solution, however, was not in itself a cure. A fuller cure was arranged by the patient's stepbrother. It had to be a clan cure; that was the only type that would fit the circumstances. Meanwhile, the cousin's own stepmother had provided him with a house until such time as he could build his own.

To arrange for the clan cure, the stepbrother had had first to find someone who would be willing to bear some of the expense—and who knew the cure. Ironically enough, the person best qualified to do the cure—the one who knew the ritual best—was the patient's own father. But it was impossible for him to carry out the cure on his own daughter: central to the idea of the clan cure is the acquisition of new relatives, so that it is obviously a disadvantage to use as curer someone as closely related as a father. The Cochiti did not rationalize it in this way, however; they simply said that it would be "unthinkable" for a patient to be cured by her own father or mother. But a complete outsider to the network of relatives would probably be unwilling. In these circumstances, the stepbrother turned to his mother's brother for help. This man was under no obligation to undertake the cure, but he and his wife nevertheless agreed to do so. The relation of curers to the patient is outlined in the following figure.

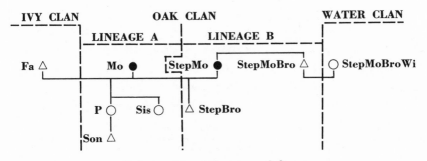

Relationship of Patient and Curers

The stepbrother was right to consult his mother's brother as the proper adviser on clan matters, and the mother's brother was right to help his nephew out. If, however, the central part of the cure is the adoption of the patient into two clans other than her own (the clans of the curer and his wife), then half this advantage of the cure is foregone in this instance. This compromise has occurred in other Cochiti cures: there are fewer people these days willing to undertake the cure and the Oak clan has many more members than the others. There is no indication that the patient's father deliberately chose his second wife from the Oak clan; because this clan is so large, the chances of his drawing a wife from it were quite high. But how will the cure proceed if one of the curers is of the same clan as the patient? How can the patient be adopted into her own clan? Some say that "you just go ahead with the ceremony, anyway, like she wasn't an Oak." I think the clue to this apparent anomaly lies in the gap between theory and practice. Although in Cochiti there are many people with the title of *ha'panyi* (Oak), and they are members of the same clan and so theoretically related, the relationship is in many cases either tenuous or nonexistent. More cases of endogamy occur within the Oak clan than within any other, and there is apparently little censure of such marriages. (Another clan cure involved both an Oak patient and an Oak curer.) It seems that among the Oak there may be overlap in membership, and as long as the curer is of a *lineage* that is not related to the lineage of the patient, the common clan is overlooked. In this case there was no known relationship between the stepmother's lineage (B) and the patient's. This kind of compromise has to be effected on many occasions in a small community carrying the burden of an archaic social structure intended for a much larger community. The other clan involved in the cure, that of the stepmother's brother's wife, was the Water clan. Initiation into this clan was especially beneficial for the patient, since it contained important medicine men.

The stage was thus set for the cure. It took place at the home of the sponsor (the patient's stepmother's brother). An announcement was properly relayed four days before with a pinch of corn meal to the clan members concerned (Oak and Water). The Water clan and the members of the Oak lineage B were present. The patient's lineage gathered at her home, along with members of her father's clan, Ivy; after a great feast, the patient was conducted to the curer's house, where everyone joined in washing her head with amole suds, the traditional method of sanctifying adoptions. (It is also the method used to indicate and sanctify any significant change in status, such as that undergone at initiation.) There were presents for the patient, including melons, rabbits, and corn. Then the patient was given new names, and returned to her own house. The curer's wife and her sisters and all the women of her clan would henceforth be mothers of the patient. Similarly, the women of the stepmother's lineage would be mothers and would be addressed as such by the patient. One informant describes the status of a patient after such a cure: "If an Ivy is cured by Sage and Oak, he is still Ivy but also he is a little Sage and a little Oak. Later if a Pumpkin asks the Sage or Oak to be cured, then the Ivy who is a little Sage or Oak goes along to help out." The cure is unlike an adoption, however, in that the patient's children will not inherit her "little" clans.

This cure took place in 1951, and shortly afterward the patient and family moved into the house that had been given up to them. Since then, the patient has never had a spell; she shows no organic symptoms and behaves normally. Before the cure, she was "wasted away to nothing" and "pretty near dead sometimes."

It can be seen how the institution of clanship is utilized to affect a cure and to help maintain it. The patient is now a member of the Water clan and a different lineage of the Oak clan—she is a "little" Water and is dependent on continuing membership in the Water clan for her continued good health. By becoming a member of this clan she was cured, and by continued membership she stays cured. She has acquired a relationship of dependence with a previously unrelated set of people. What is more, her faith in the efficacy of the cure is reinforced when she goes along to participate herself in cures conducted by the Water people. Clan, or rather lineage, membership is also of practical importance in mobilizing help for the patient.

I have no other case recorded in such detail, but in three other cases (all involving women), the data do suggest a striking similarity in the total syndrome: a hiatus in the mother-daughter relationship leading to considerable anxiety and consequent illness. In all cases, insomnia, erratic behavior, withdrawal, and amnesia predominated. In other cases, the data were sparse or showed no conclusive evidence of mother-child problems. But it should be remembered that the adoption cure is thought to be generally effective in ensuring health and is not specifically confined to the type of illness based on problems of maternal deprivation.

An interesting problem revolves around the fact that there

are two kinds of cure for two types of illness: an illness thought to have been caused by witches is cured by an elaborate shock therapy; an illness not associated with witchcraft is cured by adoption into a social group.

Interpretation is bound to be speculative, for there is no proper clinical data for these people, but some conclusions, however tenative, may aid in sorting out the problem.

I have suggested that paranoia may be at the root of the witch-illness complex. This analysis excludes, of course, the purely physical illnesses, to the degree that there are such things. In any case, even if the primary cause of the illness is physical, the fear of witches engendered by it produces secondary mental symptoms that serve to intensify it. Either an individual is to some degree paranoid, with stress inducing physical illness, or he is physically ill, which induces a state of acute paranoia. In either case, the paranoia must be dealt with, and the witch theory offers a medium for the expression of the illness, an explanation of its cause, and, through the societies, a means for its cure. Elaborate shock treatment attacks the cause of the disease and, by conclusively eliminating it, restores the patient, even if only temporarily. There is no provision in Pueblo cosmology for the final overthrow of the witches.

The sources of paranoia in the culture are hard to trace without clinical data. In a sense, the elaborate witch fears are a kind of customary paranoia. But it cannot be imagined that they would persist unless a good many individuals were motivated by an exaggerated fear of others and of the world generally, independent of the cultural beliefs about spirits, witches, and so forth. As I have suggested, the two are mutually reinforcing. Excessive paranoia may originate in the projection of hostility as a result of anxiety over aggression induced in childhood. This is present in Cochiti to some degree. The child is indulged initially by a body of females and later is partially rejected in favor of a younger sibling.

Even without this rejection, it would be impossible for the degree of indulgence the child receives initially to be sustained, and a perception of rejection is inevitable. Overindulgence has given him no training in self-control, and he is ill prepared to restrain his aggressions later. But he must restrain them. Aggression is the cardinal sin in Pueblo eyes. At times, the society seems to be geared entirely to reducing, controlling, and repressing it. Pueblo institutions stress cooperation and friendliness, but this stress is a counter to aggressive tendencies, rather than a channel for acting out of harmonious ones. Individuals driven too hard by this child-rearing system will probably develop real paranoia, but most individuals will have at least a streak of it. This deep motivational aspect of paranoia is reinforced by the stories and experiences of witchcraft with which the child is fed and frightened as a disciplinary technique.

It is possible to speculate, then, that this is the framework in which the society develops its typical illness. The witch-illness complex illustrates the whole cycle of the society, providing the strain that causes or aggravates the illness, giving it a culturally approved and patterned mode of expression, and using this mode of expression as the basis for a cure by a social group—the medicine society, which the patient can then join.

The clan cure, along with its associated types of illness, should be seen against the background of the adoption system and its ideology and the ideology and sentiments of the clan. Why do the Cochiti adopt a child into a clan to ensure his future health, or adopt an adult to restore his lost health? For the former, the Cochiti have the readier explanation. The most terrible thing that can happen to a child, they say, is to lose its mothers—its own mother and her female matrilineal relatives. The adoption gives it a set of reserve mothers if its own are lost, and one cannot have too many mothers, anyway. The clan is matrilineal, which means that an individual's pivot is his mother, through whom he acquires his clan relatives. The clan is strongly identified in the Cochiti mind with the mother herself and therefore with nurture and security. When the loss of a mother is feared, or actually occurs (through death, estrangement, or remarriage), the breach is healed by the patient's adoption by another clan——which gives him new mothers, who perform such symbolic acts of nurture as washing the head, giving food, and renaming. All these acts are associated with a ritual of change in status (initiation), and symbolize the shedding of an undesirable personality and the acquisition of a new and healthier one. At initiation, it is the status of child that is shed; at the clan cure, it is the status of motherless person.

The Cochiti do not verbalize it in this way, but they do express sentiments that are revealing: "We get our clans, like ourselves, from our mothers"; "Our clans come from our mothers like all good things"; "Why do we have clans? Because we have mothers"; "My clan is my mother's name." The idea of uterine kinship is the most popular in explaining the notion of clanship. Clansmen ultimately come from the body of the same woman. If this sentiment is coupled with the extreme dependence, especially in women, on the mother herself, it becomes easier to see both the sources of the nonwitch disease and the basis of its cure. As in the case of the witch disease, the society provides the strain—the mother-child (particularly daughter) relationship and its imminent breakdown; the ideology—of matrilineal descent and the sentiments associated with it; the mobilization of help—the clan and lineage; and the means of cure—adoption into a clan and the acquisition of mothers and maternal nurture. Even in cases where the source of the disease is not the same as the source of the cure (mother-child relations), maternal nurture is still thought to be effective. It should be noted that the acquired clans do not do anything material for the patient. The whole process is symbolic. What they do is spiritual. They restore lost security by accepting the patient as one of themselves.

The whole complex of mother symbolism is interesting. What Fred Eggan says of Acoma is in general true of Cochiti.

One important pattern at Acoma, which is characteristic of Keresan villages generally, and which contrasts with the Hopi and Zuni to a considerable extent, is the emphasis on the concept of "mother." In the Origin Myth we have seen that the central figure is Iatiku, who is the "mother" of the people whom she created and whom she receives at death. The corn-ear fetishes represent her and have her power; the cacique is her representative and is referred to as her "husband" in the mythology. In the kinship system the term "mother" is widely extended, and recent changes have extended it still further. In ritual relations the wife of the "ceremonial father" performs many of the ritual functions performed by the ceremonial father's sister among the Hopi and Zuni. In the Scalp Dance it is the mother of the twins who dances rather than their sister or aunts.

In Cochiti, the cacique is in fact referred to as "mother," as are the medicine-society heads. The fetishes of the medicine men are also their mothers, and in the ritual addresses both to them and by them the concept is elaborated at length. The sentiment and the symbolism are more elaborate among the Keresans than in Hopi or Zuni.

It may well be that the strength of the sentiment is a reason for the persistence of the clan ideology and some associated practices (exogamy, curing) even after the economic and social bases of clan organization have disappeared.

What is striking in this role of the clan is the unconscious cultural insight, namely, that the motivations involved in the clans' persistence and those involved in much nonwitch illness are the same. The neurosis of the patient I have discussed was based on a breakdown of those sentiments and social relationships on which the clan system depends in large measure for its effective persistence. The breakdown was repaired by restoring the disrupted relationships (by adoption) and so reinforcing the shaken sentiments. Durkheim and Radcliffe-Brown have argued that ritual serves to emphasize and reinforce those sentiments on which the social structure depends for its continuation, and here we have an example of the truth of this assertion. The cure is built into the social structure.

Cochiti culture not only provides the sources of its people's illnesses; it provides the media of expression for them, it mobilizes help for them, it effects the cure and ensures its reinforcement. It distinguishes the illnesses that require dramatic shock treatment from those that require more peaceful nurture treatment, and in each case it utilizes the motivational source of the illness as a means of cure. This system is not the result of individual insight, but rather of the slow working out of cultural patterns over the centuries.

Already, however, these patterns are changing. The medicine societies are becoming extinct, and American education does not encourage confidence in "witch doctors." The clans are ceasing to function effectively even in their limited spheres, and changes in household composition are complete. All these forces bear on the efficacy of curing techniques. They affect the causes of illness more slowly. The Cochiti therefore face the prospect of a persistence of traditional illnesses without the benefits of traditional cures—a situation that necessarily faces many primitive societies in transition. Those concerned with health and sickness in these societies would do well to take a hard look at the relations among sentiments, culture, and social relations before doing anything to upset their delicate balance. In many cases, the hospital and the physician are but indifferent substitutes for the society and the shaman on which the patient has learned, and is moved, to depend.

Language and Religion

THE ESSAY "Language in Two Communities" serves two purposes: to introduce the subject of sociolinguistics and to compare the societies of Tory Island and Cochiti. It is difficult to introduce linguistics to the nonspecialist, but this discussion of language use will illustrate some of the problems facing the anthropologist who is concerned with the role of language in society, rather than merely with the technicalities of language structure.

Speculations on the relationship between language and society are old and often quite peculiar. Herbert Spencer thought that language reflected national character. The Spanish language, with its excessive use of the subjunctive,

255

showed that the Spaniards, in never wanting to make simple declarative statements, were excessively suspicious of one another. This was a natural reflection, Spencer thought, of the autocratic and tyrannical Spanish society. English, on the other hand, with its attenuated subjunctive and its preference for the indicative, reflected a free and democratic society where people were not afraid to speak their minds. One suspects a little bias here, but the point —that language is the major carrier of culture—is well established in anthropology through the work of Benjamin Lee Whorf and Edward Sapir. There is, however, some controversy about the details—about how specific are the connections between language, thought, and reality. But philosophers join with anthropologists in stressing these links, and it is probably at the level of idea systems that the influence—or, if one is a Wittgensteinian, the disease —of language is most easily perceived. People's worlds are rendered through their language rather than directly through their senses; they react to a world constructed for them by language. For the speaker of what Whorf dubbed "Standard Average European," the world is composed of actors who do things—not necessarily because this is how the world really is, but because this is how their languages make them talk about the world. So we say, "The lightning strikes"—and some clever Greek philosopher is bound to ask what the lightning is doing when it isn't striking. Thus there arises the idea of an essence of lightning, and a concept of essences and causes generally. Ultimately, there has to be a first cause that caused everything else for the same reason. Many American Indian languages construct the world differently. They are what Bertrand Russell would have called "event languages"—such as those he tried to construct mathematically to get around the "substance" languages that did not mirror the world as a world of events, the way physicists saw it. Had Russell been a Hopi Indian, he may not have had this problem. Lightning would have been an event with its modes, not a noun with its attributes. The Hopi verb simply states that lightning occurs and how. But then there are no Hopi physicists, and it may be that the very structure of our language encourages us to search for the causes of things.

It was the implications of this thesis that aroused my interest in bilingual and trilingual communities. If people spoke two or more languages with very different metaphysical implications, how would this affect their behavior and their culture? One answer was that they compartmentalized the languages—assigning some to one cultural or social sphere and some to another. *"Language in Two Communities"* explores some of the ways in which this happens.

As for "Religion and the North American Indian," which begins with some general comments, an interest in religion was, as I described in the introduction, my way into anthropology. This experience of mine parallels Malinowski's, since it was his reading of *The Golden Bough* that turned him from natural science to the study of man. Edmund Leach has, with his usual charm, dismissed Frazer as nothing more than "an assiduous literary mole." But a giant like Frazer can stand the petulant buzzing of these gnats. As a rational explorer of the bizarre world of ritual and belief, and as an analyst of, for example, totemism and exogamy, he ranks, despite the sniping of lesser men, as one of the great originals. If a student were to ask me where to start in the study of religion, I would unhesitatingly recommend that he begin where so many of us began, with *The Golden Bough*. Then he might look to the much neglected Henri Bergson—a name that no doubt rings as oddly in our ears today as Frazer's ornate but impeccable prose. But the seeds of a theory of religion, rooted in a study of life processes, are to be found in Bergson's work.

THIRTEEN

Language in Two Communities

THERE IS OBVIOUSLY a considerable overlap between the interests of a linguist and those of a sociologist engaged in the study of multilingual communities. But the focus and the end product are quite different. The linguist's focus is ultimately semantic and is concerned with theories about language per se. Hence situations and contexts are important for him in his study of the processes of communication. The sociologist, on the other hand, is interested in social structure; for him communication is important insofar as it throws light on the structure of social relationships. But the material used by both is similar and to some extent the methods, too, must be the same. It is interesting then to see what each can give to the other.

In the study of codes and customs or of speech and society, multilingual communities have a special importance. In any individual language there are different registers, styles, or codes; these are used in differing circumstances by the same people, or they serve to mark off one set of people from another, and so on. But in a multilingual community the different languages themselves can serve these functions, and it is easier to pin down the code-switching under such conditions.

The juxtaposition of two or more languages within a community usually goes along with the interaction of two or more cultures, or at least with the interaction of different culture elements. Thus the distribution of language use may tell us a good deal about the relations between the cultures. More important, the interpenetration of the languages and their different usage may have feedback effects that help to change the culture and produce a new, modified, or composite culture. Not that language should be turned to simply for clues to cultural and social relationships, for language is a part of culture and is essential to social relationships; it must be studied as part of the sociocultural scheme.

Nevertheless, it is probably best to start by looking at simple correlational aspects of language and other forms of culture. For example: Does the degree of assimilation of loan words—or even the sheer proportion of loan words—indicate a degree of assimilation of other aspects of an alien culture (norms, values, techniques, et cetera)? Does the variation in the special-vocabulary penetration of loan words carry similar implications—for example, deep penetration in technological vocabularies but shallow penetration in ritual vocabularies? Similar questions could be asked concerning language use, as opposed to simple questions about vocabulary.

But the feedback effect must not be forgotten. The acceptance by a community of *lexical* penetration in one sphere may well help to accelerate total *cutural* penetration. Hence language may be a causative element in acculturation, and not simply a barometric indicator of the degree of acculturation. It could in some cases be the essential softening-up factor that predisposes a community to accept alien norms and values.

I want here to map out, at a fairly high level, the ethnography of language use in two communities, one trilingual and the other bilingual. The aim is to see if there are any meaningful patterns in the differential use of the various languages within the communities.

Cochiti is a small village of Pueblo Indians some thirty-five miles southwest of Sante Fe, New Mexico. Its three hundred Indians live mainly by agriculture, but they also commute to nearby towns for various forms of wage work. Despite an obvious adoption of white (Anglo) civilization (cars and trucks, combine harvesters, television, artesian wells, et cetera) there is still a flourishing native culture. Matrilineal clans continue to be exogamous units arranging marriages; there is a complex cycle of ceremonies for rain and curing organized by two moieties and a number of medicine societies; a theocratic-secular hierarchy of officials exercises control. Three languages are spoken regularly in the village: the indigenous Keres, Spanish, and English.

Keres is sometimes regarded as an independent language, but was placed by Sapir in his Hokan-Siouan phylum. It is divided into two distinct dialects: Western (spoken in Acoma and Laguna pueblos) and Eastern (spoken at Cochiti, Santo Domingo, Santa Ana, San Felipe, and Zia pueblos). It is estimated that the Western and Eastern dialects separated about seven hundred years ago. As a language, Keresan is characterized by the following features: a distinction between inflected and noninflected roots, the inflected roots covering most of the nominal and verbal elements; inflection for tense (although only one tense—future—is marked by the morphology), aspect, mood (affirmative, dubitative, and hortative), number (singular, dual, plural, collective), and person (a complex set of affixes and verbal auxiliaries is used for expressing all combinations of subject and object persons). Phonetically, it is extremely unlike any European language. Stops, for example, can be simple, aspirated, glottalized, palatalized, retroflex, palatalized-glottalized, and so on. Vowels are both voiced and unvoiced.

Spanish first came to Cochiti with the earliest conquistadors in the 1540's, but was not entrenched until later—probably about 1650. In 1680 the Pueblo Indians rose in revolt against the Spaniards and threw them out, but they returned and established their rule firmly from the beginning of the eighteenth century. It can be assumed that Spanish was stabilized in Cochiti after that. It was, of course, the language of the Catholic Church, and no attempt was made to translate the catechism into Keres. It was also the language of the secular hierarchy of government, set up by the Spanish but kept under the covert control of the theocratic officials. Spanish was reinforced in Cochiti when a small colony of Spaniards took root there, probably at the end of the eighteenth century, perhaps earlier. They were predominantly traders, and Spanish must early have become the language of trade. It also took the place of sign language as the lingua franca of the Pueblo Indians. There are a very large number of Spanish loan words in Keres, but the Cochiti, at any rate, have no difficulty in knowing which of their words are indigenous and which are of Spanish origin. A joke they play on outsiders is to maintain that they "don't speak Indian at all," and to cite a long list of words that are derivatives from Spanish. Favorites are *wakash* ("cow"), *kawahyo* ("horse"), *shiri* ("chile"), *pa* ("bread"), *kanasti* ("basket").

English first came to the village almost three hundred years after the appearance of Spanish, but was probably not well established until the end of the nineteenth century. In the same way that Spanish infiltrated largely as the language of the church, English has made headway largely as the language of the school. It has also replaced Spanish as the lingua franca of the Pueblo Indians, except among the very old. As the village has become more and more drawn into the various bureaucratic nets (Indian Service, state-government departments, U.S. Health Department), the use of English has increased. Cochiti is not on the normal tourist routes, but there are enough visitors to make it worthwhile to trade—that is, to use English.

Some speak either fluent or pidgin versions of Navaho, Tewa, and (less likely) Hopi and Zuni. One old man spoke fluent Keres, Spanish, English, and Tewa, fairly good Navaho and some Zuni. A smattering of Kiowa and Comanche and some of the Athapaskan languages other than Navaho is known largely through song-borrowing.

Within Keres itself there are two distinct registers, secular and sacred. Colors, directions, animals, places, et cetera all have special, sacred names that are used in ritual. This ritual language is known only to the "cooked" people, that is, the ritual specialists. The "raw" people (Spanish: *crudos*) are those who "know nothing," the nonspecialists, who have no esoteric knowledge and, in particular, no knowledge of the ritual language. As far as I could judge—and it was difficult for obvious reasons—there has been no penetration at all of Spanish or English into this sacred language. This certainly reflects the real situation insofar as there has been a consistent compartmentalization of cultures in the area of ritual. Instead of producing a mishmash version of Catholic and native religion, like, say, the Yaqui, the Pueblo Indians generally have simply continued to run two religious systems—native and Catholic—side by side. Linguistic purity here is perhaps an important element in the notorious conservatism of Pueblo Indian religion, which is at the heart of Pueblo Indian conservatism generally. Thus, to speak anthropomorphically, the village has cheerfully assimilated words, and with them ideas and techniques, in the secular sphere, while it has rigorously excluded both words and concepts from the sacred. Thus secular life can vary and be flexible, while the sacred core of the native culture remains inviolable.

As far as the mixing of languages is concerned, I often heard Keres conversation interspersed with English and Spanish phrases and, less often, the other way around. Perhaps I can roughly summarize the uses of the three languages as follows:

Keres is the language of the home and early socialization; of native ritual and government; and of intra-Cochiti affairs generally. It is the language most readily spoken by one Cochiti to another under normal circumstances.

Spanish is the language of stores and trade; of dealings with Spaniards (Spanish Americans, to be technically correct); of Spanish activities such as *gallos* ("rooster pulls"), Spanish dances, gambling in the stores (cards), et cetera. It can be the language of the church but this depends wholly on whether or not the priest is Spanish-speaking. When I was there, the priests, who visit the village but do not live there, spoke English.

English is the language of school; of dealings with Anglos; of dealings with government in its various guises; of dealings with employers and tourists; of dealings with other villages (non-Keresan). It is also the language of baseball, which is now very important in terms of both internal strife and external relations. The Indians have picked up the whole stereotyped language of baseball—including the abuse—and they use this rigorously during the games. When the Cochiti play non-Keresan teams (Tewa, for example), they censure the other sides for using the native language instead of English for giving instructions. This is thought of as cheating. Spanish is being squeezed out. Keresan is the language of Indian identity, and great pride is taken in it. Spanish was the language of Catholic identity, and, paradoxically, there is also great pride taken in being Catholic. Catholicism (and thus the Spanish language), in fact, became a kind of protective crust around the basic nativism. When the Spanish dominated and forced the Indians to be Catholics, Spanish was the enemy language. But when the Americans took over and sent in Protestant missionaries, nativism went even further underground and Catholicism became the projected self-image, which shut the door to Anglo-Protestant missionizing. Spanish was the protective language at this stage. This protective function has been eroded both by factionalism (Catholic versus native) and by the progressive bilingualization of the Spanish Americans themselves. Then, too, the church has ceased to be a predominantly Spanish-speaking institution.

The language situation at the moment can perhaps be viewed most graphically in terms of the distribution of fluency by age, as shown in the table.

	Keres	*Spanish*	*English*
Age group			
80+	Fluent	Fluent	None
60–79	Fluent	Fluent	Little
40–59	Fluent	Moderate to Little	Good to Moderate
20–39	Good to Fluent	Little	Fluent
10–19	Fluent	Little to None	Good to Fluent
6–9	Fluent	None	Little to Fluent
0–5	Fluent	None	None

Language Fluency by Age in Cochiti

The order of fluency here is none, little, moderate, good, fluent (impressionistic but, I feel, not far from the truth). As regards Keres, some men in the 20–39 age group who have been away from the village for a time, either in the armed forces or at work, may have lost some of their fluency. Spanish is simply dying out with the older generations; the young are not bothering to learn it. The situation with English is a little more complex. The older people know little or none. The young and middle-aged vary among themselves from moderate to fluent. The youngest children—that is, preschool—know nothing but Keres. ("Fluent" on the table is of course relative to age. By calling the 0–5 group "fluent" in Keres, I mean they have achieved a degree of fluency that can be expected for that age.)

The distribution is much the same for both sexes, except that old women (sixty and over) may not even know much Spanish, while women in the 20–39 age group would be fluent in Keresean but, lacking the outside experience of the language, not as practiced in English as their menfolk.

In general, then, the normal language of the community when it is closed and working within itself, is Keres. (A minor exception to this is the group of Tewa-speaking wives who speak Tewa among themselves and English to the rest of the village. But they tend to pick up Keres very quickly.) Other languages come into play to handle specific situations. However, school English is gradually eroding this solidarity, as are baseball and television. Spanish is fast disappearing and English is on the increase as a language of normal use. Even so, while watching baseball on television, the Cochiti will normally discuss the game in Keres interspersed with English expressions. "Pinch hitter *háti kaku?*" "Third base *s'atyumshe.*" ("Where is the pinch hitter?" "On third base, my brother.")

Tory is nine miles off the coast of Donegal at the extreme northwestern tip of Ireland. Despite its location, it is in fact part of the Republic of Ireland (Éire). It is isolated and in the winter can be cut off altogether. The population varies because of migrant labor, but there are approximately two hundred and fifty people, all Roman Catholics. They live by crofting and fishing, government subsidies, and remittances from migrant laborers in Scotland and England. Many aspects of their social structure reflect the general archaism of the culture.

The two languages spoken on the island are Irish Gaelic and English. Gaelic (alternatively referred to as Irish) is an old Indo-European language, with a long literary tradition. In this it differs enormously from Keres, which is not written and which no one but the Indians cares much about. Gaelic in Ireland is in a different position. During the English occupation, the fortunes of the language fluctuated, but on the whole it declined rather rapidly from the beginning of the eighteenth century, until some areas of Ireland became completely English-speaking. During the nineteenth and twentieth centuries, Gaelic as a language of everyday speech and literature continued to decline. At the end of the nineteenth century, however, there came the great Gaelic revival and the attempt to create a living language out of what remained of the peasant speech in a few remote parts of Ireland, and out of the considerable wealth of the literary tradition. The revival of the language where it had died, and the preservation of it where it existed, became part of the national resurgence that culminated in the independence of Ireland (Éire) in 1922. "An Ireland Free and Gaelic" was the slogan. In this scheme of things, the *gaelgeorí*, or "native speakers" (fondly known as "aboriginals" to the cynics in Dublin), had a very special place. Areas where Gaelic was still naturally spoken (*gaeltachta*), as on Tory Island, were recently placed under a special ministry (Roinn na Gaeltachta), and are subsidized and specially treated in various ways. It is against this background of national revival and government encouragement that the seeming contradiction of the continuing decline of Gaelic on Tory and in other *gaeltachta* must be viewed.

There is a typically Irish paradox in the use of Gaelic: those who speak it do not write it; those who write it do not speak it. (This is not strictly true but will do as an approximation.) The native speakers, although they learn to write Gaelic in the schools, by and large do not use this skill; many forget it completely once they leave. The people who learn Gaelic in a literary context at school—virtually as a foreign language—retain some degree of literary skill but do not use Gaelic as a normal language of communication and often lose any skill in speaking it. The exceptions are nationalist enthusiasts, who speak it among themselves and try to convert non-Gaelic Irishmen.

A corollary to this paradox that helps explain it is: in the *gaeltachta* there is a strong economic motivation to learn English; in the English-speaking areas there is a strong economic motivation to learn Irish. Since most of the native-speaking Gaels are driven to seek work in England and Scotland, it is a great advantage to them to learn English. Many will maintain that, although it is nice to have the Gaelic, it is useless; to get anywhere they have to learn English. This is because they are not ambitious for anything more than well-paid laboring jobs. On the other hand, for an Irishman who aspires to rise in government service—which is a major source of higher-income employment in Ireland—knowledge of Gaelic is compulsory. Most of these aspirants, however, come from English-speaking areas and homes. They learn to write Gaelic often as a convenience in order to get jobs and promotions, but in all normal usage they speak English.

The combination of these factors leads inevitably to an overall decline of Gaelic as an effective language, despite nationalistic fervor and government encouragement.

On Tory Island, however, English has never been firmly established. In the past it was used almost solely for dealing with the landlords, who went out of evidence in 1861. There were some priests who had never spoken Gaelic, but they did not last very long. Even in the 1960's there were still some old people on the island who spoke virtually no English except a few words of conventional greeting. The table below, comparable to the one given for Cochiti, shows the situation now.

	Gaelic	*English*	
Age group			
80+	**Fluent**	**None to Little**	
60–79	**Fluent**	**Little to Fluent**	
40–59	**Fluent**	**Little to Fluent**	wide variation
20–39	**Fluent**	**Little to Fluent**	
10–19	**Fluent**	**Little to Good**	
6–9	**Fluent**	**Little to Moderate**	
0–5	**Fluent**	**None**	

Language Fluency by Age on Tory Island

As in Cochiti, there are some differences according to sex, with some old women knowing no English and some of the younger and more island-bound women knowing little or only a moderate amount.

Gaelic, then, is the language of the home and of all normal dealings with fellow islanders. English is learned originally as a foreign language in school, where all lessons are "through the medium of Irish." The English learned in schools is steadily reinforced in some speakers and virtually lost in others, although there is high prestige attached to being able to read and write *both* languages—a rare achievement. The ability to sing songs with equal facility in both languages is also highly regarded. Even so, people tend to specialize: those who sing in English cannot usually sing in Irish, and vice versa. This may be because some of the younger men enjoy singing only "rebel" songs, which are all in English; there is no point abusing the enemy in a language he does not understand. Many of these young people express a dislike for the "old-fashioned" Gaelic songs, with their repetitive themes of love, death, shipwreck, and cows. Needless to say, these singers of English songs are mostly the successful migrant laborers. There is a group of chronic nonmigrants on the island who for various reasons have never mastered enough English to operate successfully in Great Britain. These tend to be homekeepers and Gaelic speakers and singers, who are regarded as "backward" for this reason by the more energetic. While some are indeed educationally subnormal, most of them are simply introverted fellows who lack the urge to taste the delights of Glasgow.

There are several reasons for the steady and progressive reinforcement of English on the island.

(1) Many officials and official forms use English, despite the official policy of Gaelic in government.

(2) There is an increasing number of summer visitors who speak English. Also, the very influential lighthousemen are all English-speaking. (There has been a lighthouse on Tory since 1832.)

(3) The Irish of Radio Eireann ("Civil Service Irish") is not easily understood because it is based on a dialect different from the Tory version of Irish. In recognition of these dialectical differences, the radio does try to vary its announcers but even so the Tory Islanders find this Irish hard to follow. It is "Dublin Irish" not only in dialect, but also in general vocabulary and usage. The upshot is that the islanders listen mostly to the BBC and the English-language news services. A curious ritual in Tory, where the inland weather reports are irrelevant and the shipping forecasts vital, is the solemn listening to the BBC forecast for coastal waters at

midnight, a broadcast preceded by the playing of "God Save the Queen." The whole event has a decidedly Irish air.

(4) If the islanders are literate at all, it is usually in English. This literacy is forced on them, often enough, by living for long stretches in England. Hence most of their reading—books, newspapers—is done in English. And it is a striking fact that all letters home from migrants to parents are written in English. Even the most fanatical Gaelic speaker would not dream of writing to his parents in Gaelic. As a result, the only increases in vocabulary that occur are through English, with the effect that the number of loan words is incalculable. In some areas of discourse, there is virtually an English vocabulary set in a Gaelic grammar—in talking about marine engines, for example. And this vocabulary is a vigorous one. English words are Gaelicized and assimilated and made subject to all the mutations necessary. It is often the case that even when a Gaelic word for something exists, the islanders will not know it. For example, a dead elephant from a circus ship was washed up on the shore once and covered with concrete. I was told this on the mainland and when I arrived on Tory I asked about it in my best book Gaelic: *"Cá bhfuil an trod?"* ("Where is the elephant?") This was incomprehensible to them. I explained further, the light dawned, and amid laughter I was asked, *"B'é sin an t-elephant, narbh é?"* ("That was the elephant, wasn't it?")

Most of the islanders, then, live in two worlds, each strangely cut off from the other. On the island they speak only Gaelic; off the island they speak only English (except occasionally among themselves). There are strong pulls in both directions: economic and rational pulls toward English, sentimental and patriotic pulls toward Gaelic.

On Tory, there is not much need for English as a total language in any context, unless there happen to be English-speaking people there. The nurse and lighthousemen speak English, but most islanders are not in constant interaction with them. It is now the policy of the church to appoint only Gaelic-speaking priests. Thus most of the conversation among the islanders is in Gaelic, even though it is laced with English words. Personal names are a mixture of Gaelic and English, but the English versions are always Gaelicized when, for example, they appear in the genitive, vocative, or dative cases.

This situation contrasts with the more thoroughly bilingual *gaeltachta,* where not only are both languages known, but both are in constant use. Two other areas I am familiar with (both in County Donegal) reflect in their language use differences in cultural situation. Gweedore is assertively Gaelic and pursues a self-conscious policy of Gaelicization in most areas of life—church, school, trade, recreation. There is a marked unwillingness to use English at all; some people even opposed the housing of tourists in the area on the grounds that this would eventually corrupt the language. Despite this attitude, English makes headway among the young people with their eyes on Glasgow. Gortahork is more willingly bilingual. The people speak only Gaelic among themselves, and quite readily speak English to their English-speaking neighbors, tourists, officials, et cetera. This is a truly bilingual community in that both languages are accepted and used. My informed impression is that the young people of Gortahork maintain a fluency in both languages because they are never forced to choose between one or the other, but simply see them as different tools to be used for different purposes. English is here not a threat, but a useful adjunct to Gaelic. Of course, Gaelic is the natural first language of all concerned.

Thus, there is Tory, a community that is effectively mono-lingual but resorts to English for specific purposes and readily assimilates an English vocabulary; Gweedore, a community that is assertively monolingual but is being forced into an uneasy bilingualism; and Gortahork, which is truly bilingual—using both languages with equal facility. The second two communities, unlike Tory, are surrounded by English-speaking areas, and hence have to come to terms with English in a way that Tory can avoid.

Even in a very gross way, then, it is possible to see that the language situation and the over-all cultural and social structure mirror each other and affect each other. The most eloquent expression of this is that the Tory Islanders speak Gaelic and write English. But the constant feeding in of English vocabulary, and therefore of English concepts, is essentially a softening-up process. It prepares the groundwork for the acceptance of change, and may even act to acclerate it.

It is possible to look at the total language situation in multilingual communities and relate it to cultural interaction and cultural change. The real task of the sociology of multilingualism now is to find ways of exploring how language operates in a multilingual community and what the effects of its various operations are. I have suggested here that language is more than just a mirror of reality, that it is an effective part of the reality of social change itself. This may be totally wrong, and it may be that we talk about something in another language only when we have decided to do it anyway, and that language is totally passive in this process. I do not believe this, but I would find it hard to demonstrate the truth or falsity of my assertion. It is the criteria for such a judgment, and the methods of testing such a hypothesis, that we most need to consider.

FOURTEEN

Religion and the North American Indian

Religion

IN THIS ESSAY I will take a fairly close look at a particular example of the religious experience, that of the North American Indians. Some specific beliefs and practices are unique to North America, but most of the themes outlined here are common to the whole range of religions, even the higher religions—although the germs of some of these higher religious notions, particularly salvation, remain germs, seeds, small beginnings. The Plains Indians did not actually ask for salvation from sin, but they did pray for pity. It is a small step from there to notions of salvation, but it is a significant one. The notion of salvation—whether it be the Christian, being saved from sin and redeemed into eternal life, or the Eastern, being freed from the chains of reincarnation into reunion with the infinite (nirvana)—has as its sustaining idea a god or some other eternal principle that has ordained these things *for all men.* The higher religions also link the idea of conduct with salvation. By conducting ourselves properly in this life we gain either emancipation from existence or a place in heaven.

But in Amerindian religion, there is neither the idea that the precepts apply to all men, nor the idea that conduct in this life affects one in the next. Some religious ideas were common to all tribes, but religion was basically a tribal affair—or, if pantribal, it included only related tribes who shared the same culture. Thus two Plains tribes might join for a Sun Dance, but there was no way in which they could enter into the religion of the Pueblos. Two Pueblo tribes might exchange ceremonial services, but they could never take part in a Sun Dance. The very idea of a universal religion is not only absent; it is, when presented, actually ridiculed. "If their religion is so great," one Indian told me, referring to missionaries, "why are they trying to give it away all the time?" Those Indians who, like the Pueblos, have accepted Catholicism (they had little choice at first but now they regard it as part of their lives) accept it as an accretion. They have added it to their store of religious power in the same way that they added Apache and Comanche dances to their repertoire of rituals to obtain the power of the enemy. But there is no evidence that they regard themselves as part of a universal church valid for all men. They have added the saints to the *katsinas,* they have aligned God with the Sun Father and Mary with the Corn Mother; but all of these are in fact subordinate to the supreme deity of their pantheon, Spider Woman, who still sits in her cave spinning from her body the web of thought to fill men's heads—indeed, to make them men at all.

They have trouble with Christ. The idea that someone may

sacrifice himself for others is quite reasonable to them. The idea of sacrifice as a means of controlling the supernatural is common in North America as elsewhere: something is given up to the spirits in order to get something from them in return. But the idea that a father would require the death by torture of his son is revolting to them. "That's just a priests' story," I was told. To them, Christ was a shaman who fasted and mutilated himself on behalf of his people. By going through the rituals associated with his religion, they feel they may be able to get some of his mana (*i'anyi* —"power"). To get the power of a fetish, the medicine men will rub it and then breathe in from their cupped hands. When leaving a Catholic church, a Pueblo Indian will rub the foot of the statue of the Virgin and breathe in from his hands before crossing himself with holy water.

At least one other thing bothers the Pueblo Indians about Christ: if he was the son of the All-father (the sun itself), then he should have a brother; he should be one of a pair of hero twins. They asked me if Jesus had a brother. I said that opinion was divided but that at least one of the Gospels had mentioned siblings. They were delighted. The priests had kept this from them; there was a Younger Brother Jesus, then. I said that this conflicted with the idea that Mary was a virgin. Nonsense, they replied; there were many legends in their own tribes of girls being impregnated by the Sun Father—this in fact is how the hero twins were born.

Ethnographers who have entered the native churches in Mexico (for example, in Maya country) at Christmas, have always found the traditional crib scene of Mary and Joseph and the cows and burros in the stable set up as it would be in any European church. But, often, lying in the manger were the two figures of Older and Younger Brother Jesus.

The Pueblo concept of an apostolic succession was described to me as quite straightforward. The hero twins were still represented by the war captain and his assistant —called, like the god twins, Masewi and Oyoyewi—who were responsible for installing their successors. It would be instructive to compare all the dogmas and rites of Catholicism that have native counterparts and can be readily accepted with those that cannot, and see what is left over. That there would be enormous overlap is scarcely surprising, since much of Catholicism was derived from Eastern mystery religions, and, after Constantine made Christianity respectable (even official), it spent much of its efforts proselytizing believers in fertility religions not unlike the tribal religions of the agricultural Indians. The deliberate policy of the Church, for example under Gregory the Great, was to utilize these religions as much as possible rather than rigidly to oppose them. Thus there was two-way traffic between the mysteries and the fertility cults. And Pueblo religion, being itself a blend of mystery cult and fertility religion, could easily assimilate most of the Catholic material.

Of that which it could not, the idea of salvation through the "dying god" (who haunts the pages of *The Golden Bough*) and the idea of sinful conduct leading to eternal damnation were foreign, as has been shown. What they did accept were the primitive cosmological ideas, a good deal of the ritualism, and the idea of the existence of evil forces (in this case, witches), against which religion is a protection. In brief, the magical element is accepted; the salvation element is not. This is why Protestantism, which is really Catholicism stripped of its magic (literally), makes little headway with the Pueblos.

Catholicism is much more receptive to the magical view of the universe than Protestantism, which, in establishing itself, had to purge Christianity of magical elements. Hence, a Protestant conversion of primitive people demands a complete purge of previous ideas and values, and the substitution of a new way of life and code of conduct. Catholics can get by with indirect rule as long as the sacraments are observed and mortal sin avoided. The Catholic Church considers the dances of the Indians (as long as they are not obviously lewd or obscene) "natural" religion: simple men approaching God in their simple way, harmless and innocent.

There would not be appreciable overlap in the hunting rituals that run through much of the predominantly agricultural religion. Except for the idea of ritual slaying, there is not much here that corresponds to Catholic ideas or to the ideas of any universal religion. Hunting magic, hunting gods, hunting rituals were the property, jealously guarded, of the tribe. War rituals usually developed from hunting rites; for men the two activities were closely related. What the Indians did accept was the implication that religion was primarily a male mystery and that women were at best a help and at worst a danger. The female principle (in the Corn/Earth Mother, the Deer Maiden, Spider Woman, et cetera) was reverenced—even worshiped—but the cultists were primarily men (in some cases exclusively). Women were too close to nature, too much part of what had to be controlled to be controllers. Religion was the use of culture to control nature (in the sense of keeping nature on its course, not of conquering it), and culture was a male province because men were further removed from nature than women were. Women participated in the natural world through childbirth; men stood apart from the natural world, mostly through the hunt and war. Women created life; men destroyed it. A good deal of the male religion involved a careful attempt, through hunt rituals and scalp ceremonies, to restore this balance. To this end, the men often had to abstain for long periods from that most natural of activities, eating, and for even longer periods from sex. The Indians were impressed with fasting and abstinence, both features of the Catholic priest's life. Total abstinence from sex, however, puzzled them. It defeated its own object. If you never have it, there is nothing to abstain from and therefore no virtue. But the male monopoly on religion they understood without question, even if the priests were neither hunters nor warriors.

Are there any religious ideas that underlie even those areas that do not overlap; that unite hunting magic with doctrines of personal salvation or nirvana? What can be said generally about religion can perhaps be expressed in that most abused word—because it was itself a word of abuse—"superstition." It is an old joke that "our" beliefs are a religion while "theirs" are mere superstition. But superstition is universal, even where there is little discernible religion in the form of the worship of spirits or advanced cosmology. Superstition used to be thought characteristic of the "lower" races and religion of the "higher." Perhaps it would be better to say that superstition exists even where there is little formal religion, or even where there is a denial of religion. It exists in some very primitive groups that lack any elaborate religious ideas; but it also exists in sophisticated civilizations whose members are indifferent to, or hostile to, religion in any form. It is usually manifested in small rituals—repetitive stereotyped actions or words, or both—which can quickly become the basis for more elaborate exercises, and accretions of beliefs, stories, et cetera.

I don't want here to get into the question of the "essence" or "definition" or "function" or "origin" of religion. The literature is vast, and the debate endless. The question is perhaps wrongly posed most of the time. Religion has been "defined" as belief in spiritual beings; beliefs and actions relative to the sacred, and so on. Its "essence" is the belief in the soul; the apprehension of death or the divine; fear of the dead. Its function is to explain the universe; to ensure social unity; to preserve the power of rulers. It is probably all these, but it is probably also, in its simplest manifestation, superstition "within the meaning of the act."

What is superstition? Let us take an obvious case. When a man is about to roll the dice in a crap game, he mutters some incantation he has always used that is supposed to influence the dice in his favor. He may deny that his formula really does influence the dice, but he never leaves it out —he would not dare to leave it out. Now, dice, if they are not loaded, fall randomly. He has in fact no way of influencing the outcome. In light of that his behavior is called "superstitious." It is a way of trying to influence the uncontrollable —the essentially random—by nonnatural, noninstrumental, nonempirical means.

Even when the outcome can be influenced by empirical means, it is still probabilistic. Fighter pilots in World War II could certainly affect the outcome of their sorties by their skill, but there was still a great element of chance involved. And they carried talismans and charms (rabbit-feet were popular), and they invented gremlins—malignant sprites that caused "bad luck"—to account for failures. If not gremlins, then a jinx was invoked. "Bad luck" explained failure, and a "charmed life" success, despite recklessness. All this can be dismissed as irrational and superstitious. But here were men for whom death was just around the next cloud. They were like gamblers, except that more than money was at stake.

This shows how people, even when they are involved with superior technology, resort to superstition. It used to be held that superstition was the lowest order of thought, religion next lowest, and that science and technology finally erased both. The benighted savage was sunk in his superstition, unlike the rational scientific man. But, as Malinowski demonstrated brilliantly in the case of the Trobriand Islanders, elaborate magic could exist along with skilled technology. No Trobriander believed that magic alone could affect the outcome of a sea voyage—he also paid careful attention to the design of his outrigger canoe. No matter how well the canoe was designed, however, there was still that freak storm, that rock you didn't see in time, and magic took care of these.

It could be argued that unpredictability and the feeling of lack of control over the world are greater in advanced technological societies. Even the men running the computers are predicting that soon they will not be in control of the hardware; that only computers will be able to design and program computers. One is reminded of the joke about the perfect computer that could answer all questions. It was asked, "Is there a God?" It replied, "There is now." To those not in control of advanced technology, the universe can be as chancy a place as it was for the savage, who felt precarious in his relation to nature. Today there are more jokes than ever—always revealing anxiety—about computers and how to baffle and cheat them. The "killing" of HAL in *2001* consistently drew a bigger audience reaction than anything else in the film. Witchcraft, occultism, magic, trance induction through hallucinogens, and particularly astrology are features of our time as prevalent as the computer itself.

The extraordinary popularity of astrology has puzzled those social scientists who see the trend in modern civilization as being toward greater rationality. But rationality works only in a system where the participants feel that their actions really do have effective outcomes. Few people today feel that.

They are as anxious about the seeming indifference of the social system to their fates as primitive man was about the indifference of the universe to his. And to reduce this anxiety, to make themselves feel in control, they will do the same kinds of things he did. Astrology is different from magic in that it is totally passive and totally amoral. But it does remove a person from responsibility for his own actions, especially his failures; it gives the comfortable feeling that fate is somehow come to terms with. Our faults indeed lie in our stars, not in ourselves, and the horoscopes are usually so vaguely worded as to cover any contingency. But the astrological world is still magical, in a sense—certainly not the austere Protestant universe where conduct, or even faith, determines salvation. In astrology, salvation depends on the conjunction of heavenly bodies at the time of birth; it has nothing to do with conduct. Those who think that superstition will decline with advances in knowledge and technology will be disappointed. Not only can man not stand too much reality; he cannot stand too much rationality. The dice are not loaded, the outcome is clouded, the charms are needed.

Gambling—the attempt to fix the odds in one's favor, to do better than chance—engenders first superstitions and then rituals. There was once an anthropologist who had to abandon a piece of research because it shook his faith in human rationality too deeply. There were, in a large building on a university campus, four elevators in a central shaft serving the whole building. In order to stagger the volume of traffic in the elevators, it was decided that they be controlled by a computer program that randomized the opening and closing of the doors, thus ensuring that all four elevators did not end up on the same floor at the same time. If, say, a person entered the elevator and pushed the button for the third floor, it would eventually arrive at the third floor; but when the doors would actually close and the journey to the third floor begin was, literally, a matter of chance. It might be two seconds, it might be twenty.

The anthropologist observed the behavior of regular users of the elevators. These varied from janitors to Nobel Prize winners in physics. All of them developed a "system" for getting the doors to close and the elevator to move. Some systems were simple: "Push the floor button and the 'close door' button at the same time, and then release them separately." Others were frighteningly elaborate. One Nobel Prize winner pushed the button three times, took off his hat and turned around three times, then stamped. "That's what does it," he said. When one man does a bizarre thing, the saying goes, it is called madness; when a million do it, it is called religion.

But how is this connected with gambling? The point is that man is always facing a situation in which he wants to reduce the odds against him, and he has been facing this situation throughout human evolution. The margins of error in hunting were probably quite large, as were the chances taken in courtship. The probability of a child surviving birth, or even of coming to term, was perhaps quite low. The generosity of the seasons was relatively unpredictable; fertility was always in doubt. The dice were not loaded. And even they can be loaded a little now, with technology, but the margin for error is still there. Man is faced with the elevator doors and he cannot bear to think he is not in control. So he does things—all kinds of random things, often metaphorically related to the outcome he wishes to influence. It doesn't much matter what he does; what matters is that on two or more occasions what he does is associated with a successful outcome. And since the probabilities are not entirely random, this is justifiable. A man draws an image of a deer in the sand, and then draws an arrow sticking in the deer. Wishful thinking. But he gets a deer that trip.

He draws another image and gets another deer. Like the mutterings of the dice player, or the rabbit-foot of the pilot, or the little dance of the Nobel Prize winner, if it "works" a couple of times, then man's readiness to accept superstition —which must surely, in some way or another, be innate and connected with the need to reduce anxiety—will operate to make him feel that he is beating chance, shortening the odds, loading the dice in his favor. When all the "others" join in, it is no longer a superstition; it is ritual.

Freud saw the resemblance of ritual to neurosis, but he was perhaps wrong to emphasize it. Superstition and ritual are normal, even healthy, so long as one does not neglect the technology. The neurotic is someone who really believes that his magic will do *all* the work, someone who has retreated from technology. He depends solely on his ritual. Most people combine a judicious amount of both technology and superstition. Any Trobriander who built a square boat without a sail and trusted entirely to magic to make his voyage would rightly be considered mad.

In the transformation from superstition to ritual, then, it doesn't much matter what man does. But what he does is usually a poetic extension of what he wishes to achieve, as James Frazer saw so clearly, and there is remarkable uniformity among the beliefs and practices of the religions of the world. Once they get going, they weave symbols out of symbols, add meanings to meanings and images to images and become, after a while, self-sustaining. Religions become almost self-contained systems that worship man's capacity to make symbols; worship the thing-that-makes-him-man as an end in itself. But by the same token, superstition, as it has been examined here, is a hymn to man's capacity for foresight—his ability to see that the odds are indeed against him and then to try to shorten them in his favor.

Once launched, however, a religion begins to provide

its own probabilistic universe and create its own anxieties: Am I one of the elect or one of the damned? Will I go to Paradise or not? Have I behaved in a way that will please the ancestors or not? The better a religion is at making the outcome completely unclear, the more power it has over its subjects. In highly ritualistic religions, the individual knows that if he does the right rituals he is all right. In salvation religions, on the other hand, it is always hard to be entirely certain—although people are always finding ways to increase their sense of certainty. The whole of Max Weber's influential theory of Protestantism rests on this: certain people were saved and others not. How did one know who was saved? Simple: those who were worldly successes—that is, capitalists—had clearly found favor with God and were the elect. So, if a man invested like mad and worked hard enough, he would be seen to be saved. But he was never totally certain. Man now is heir to this ethic, as many writers have pointed out, even though its theology is strikingly anachronistic.

But whether he is reducing the real odds set by the universe, or the phony odds set up for him by culture and religion, he is building on superstition. The beginnings of superstitious behavior have been noted in some animals, and this is comforting, for it suggests the deep-rooted basis for the corresponding human response. But in this analysis, belief comes a bad second and explanation a poor third. They are after the event. The cousin of superstition is ritual; and, while beliefs and explanations come and go, rituals have, like habits, a frightening persistence. The American way of life can, in some respects, be seen as an example of exactly this. The work ethic is still, with its friends the success ethic and the self-help ethic so beloved of presidents and hard-line congressmen, the dominant theme, although it has practically no relationship today to the Calvinistic Protestant belief system that spawned it. In the long run, it doesn't much matter what man believes as long as it leads to rituals that appear to him to be reducing the odds to at least evens. This is not to underestimate the power of belief, but to question the importance of the *content* of belief for an understanding of religion. People have believed in the strangest of delusions: that by singing they could keep the sun in the sky; that human sacrifice placated spirits; that stabbing a neighbor's footprint would cause him to get sore feet; that marrying a deceased wife's sister was an offense to God; that the impotence of the king blighted the land; that spirits could possess the bodies of believers; that souls were reincarnated in the bodies of future generations; that the spirits of ancestors watch over man to punish him; that God sent his son to die for mankind's sins. The list is endless. There are patterns and consistencies and correlations. But the content is as varied as the human imagination is ingenious. There isn't much that hasn't been believed. The continuity, the link, between all these beliefs and explanations lies in the underlying superstition: in the *doing,* not the *believing.* Those theorists who have given ritual precedence over belief in the analysis of religion have been right, though not always for the right reason. They have seen that it matters much more that an individual *does* something about controlling the universe or his personal fate or the fate of his group, than that he *believes* anything in particular about what he is doing. As we saw earlier, he can do almost anything; what matters is that it would seem to be associated with beating the odds.

As I said in the introduction, however, the human imagination seems remarkably open to suggestions but the suggestions are of a finite kind; so that while the list of particular beliefs is without number, the *themes* are limited. Most agriculturalists, for example, have concerns about fertility and the seasons that lead them to fix on certain beliefs and certain operations; similarly with pastoralists and hunters. Ecology, however, is not the only determinant. Weather can never be absolutely predicted, for example, and ghosts can be held to play a larger part than gods, or witches than ancestors —and so on. But at a deeper level man is open to suggestions from the unconscious, and here another basic trend manifests itself: the paranoid streak in man. Along with his desire to shorten the odds goes the belief that someone or something out there is out to load the dice *against* him, to cheat him, even to kill him. So it is not only a matter of trying to fix the game positively in his favor, but, equally, to stop the malignant spirits—however they are defined—from stopping him. Very few people can face the possibility of being cheated with the *sang-froid* of TV's Maverick, who, when told that his opponent at two-handed poker was cheating him, replied, "Of course he is; it's his deal."

Many of the things I have talked about here are dealt with in the next section; but there I have tried to be purely descriptive and not to intrude with analysis. To appreciate the data it is not necessary to worry about the "explanation" of religion I have proposed—which is an explanation in an ultimate sense only. There are many levels before the ultimate at which religion can be viewed, just as there are many levels of analysis of matter and the universe before the structure of the atom is arrived at, and so much that can be said about life before considering the molecular structure of the gene.

The North American Indian

It is important to understand from the outset that not one religion, but many religious systems will be considered here. These vary in complexity from simple shamanistic practices to intricate calendrical ceremonies; from simple animistic concepts to elaborate pantheons. Although there is a substratum of concepts and practices common to all, a rough division can be made between the religions of the hunters and gatherers and those of the settled agriculturalists, with their extreme elaboration of belief and rite. Of these concepts, that of an impersonal amoral power (Keresan *'ianyi,* Siouan *wakan,* Algonquin *orenda,* et cetera) is perhaps the most pervasive. The notion is akin to that of mana in Polynesia. This power is usually thought of as independent of both men and supernatural beings, but it is inherent in some things and can be acquired in various ways. It can be used to good and evil ends. Perverted, it is witchcraft, a universally recognized phenomenon. The use of fetishes (images, bundles, et cetera) is also common.

The essence of the religions of the aboriginal Americans lies in the idea of harmony in the universe. Harmony between nature, man, and the supernatural brings fertility for men and crops, and success in hunting and war. Disharmony —often caused by witchcraft—leads to tribal, personal, and even cosmic disaster. And ritual is a means of maintaining or restoring harmony.

I will confine myself here to the basic elements of the religious life of the Indians of North America, but many features of their religion, such as shamanism, are to be found throughout the continent.

Most of the ancestors of the American Indians entered the continent over the Bering Strait's land bridge between twenty-five thousand and nine thousand years ago. They were upper-paleolithic hunters largely of Mongoloid extraction. Some of the beliefs, myths, and rituals of the simplest American Indian groups today have recognizable counterparts in the religions of the Siberian tribes (the creation myth of Earth Diver, for example). The original religion must have been that of simple hunters, whose rituals were concerned with hunting and warfare, and whose individual shamanistic practices centered largely around divination and curing. Even as the religions were elaborated these elements were not lost; Navaho religion is still primarily concerned with healing, and the Zuni Shalako ceremony, one of the most elaborate of the ceremonials of the settled agriculturalists, is considered essentially a hunting ritual. Among the agriculturalists, however, calendrical rites and fertility rituals began to dominate the religions, and positive pantheons appeared. The individualistic religion of the hunters became overlaid with collectivist ideologies and communal rites. With the coming of the Europeans, Catholicism in particular exerted a profound influence. In most parts of Spanish America, aspects of Catholicism were incorporated into the native religions, and in some cases (for example, the Yaqui) synthetic religions were produced.

The acquisition of the horse and the development of an extensive Buffalo-hunting culture by the Plains Indians led to an elaboration of ceremony centered on various war cults and the Sun Dance. In the late nineteenth century, after a series of military reverses, these groups developed the Ghost Dance religion—an eschatological movement aimed at restoring the old ways. More recently, a synthetic religion based on the taking of peyote has flourished among the survivors.

Belief in supernatural beings is universal in the Americas, but it varies in complexity. There is not much evidence for a belief in a supreme being, except in the higher religions; and even there the supreme god is essentially *primus inter pares.* Several tribes are reported to have had ideas concerning supreme beings, but it is difficult to know how to assess these. Missionaries who were interested in aboriginal religious ideas were ever ready to translate Indian notions of spirit and power into more familiar concepts, such as God. Also, they may have been reporting the ideas of outstanding individuals, rather than commonly held tribal beliefs. But the idea of a supreme power of some kind, associated with the sky or the sun, is certainly present in some of the agricultural tribes.

There are often creator spirits that manifest at least the creative aspect of deity. Among the northern hunter-gatherers the most common of these is Earth Diver, or a spirit associated with him. The story of Earth Diver—known also in Eastern Asia—tells how there was once only water; but then a diving animal or bird brought up earth out of which the world was made. Some versions have a spirit who guides Earth Diver and his operations. Other creator spirits are equally vague; the Zuni creator is said to have willed himself into existence and then, once his task was done, to have vanished. In most myths, the creator either vanishes or is disposed of, and lesser but more tangible deities take his place.

Of these more tangible deities three types should be mentioned: the hero twins, or culture hero; the animal spirit and especially the "owner" or "leader"; and the trickster, who can be considered either mythological or religious, although he rarely has ceremonies or prayers devoted to him. The hero twins, on the other hand, do figure in ritual in many tribes, and in some religions (Navaho, for instance) they are central deities who were instrumental in the creation and early socialization of man. The hunters obviously specialized in animal spirits (wolf, thunderbird, bear), who were powerful and had to be placated in various ways by positive ritual and the observance of taboos. Prominent among them was the owner of the animals (the Deer Maiden of the Keresans; Sedna of the eastern Eskimo). This spirit —half human, half beast—was, appropriately, the link between men and beasts, birds, and fish. Properly treated and respected, it would ensure success in hunting. It was often totemistic and hence in the care of a particular clan.

With the Plains Indians the idea of guardian spirits flourished (probably derived from Algonquian sources). These were individual animal spirits obtained in a vision quest.

As religions become more complex, the array of animal and nature spirits is supplemented by the concept of power inherent in heavenly bodies, directions, winds, rain, and the earth itself. Sometimes this power is not personalized, or not to any high degree, and sometimes it develops into a definite pantheon. The Pueblos have a sky/sun father and an earth/corn mother; for the Pawnees, it is the morning and evening stars that are personalized. Finally, there are supernaturals, which are pure spirits—like the *katsinas* of the Pueblos; they are not personifications of natural phenomena, but spiritual beings deriving from early episodes in the story of creation. They are, however, conceived in anthropomorphic form and are imitated in ritual. In a similiar category—but malevolent rather than benevolent—is the notorious windigo spirit of the Ojibwa (which has counterparts among the Northwest coast Indians)—a cannibal spirit that devours men and then regurgitates them; as a result, the men themselves become cannibals.

Sacred rulers do not occur in North America, with the possible exception of the Natchez, whose ruler was identified with the sun and carried in a litter (this echoes features found in Middle and South American religion). The most definite conception of a "high god" occurred in the supreme being of the Pawnees, Tirawa-atius. Again, this tribe shows affinities with the high religions of the South.

The idea of worship includes the various means employed by men for entering into some relationship with the supernatural, not excluding relationships of avoidance. Some tribes employed rituals of purification to rid contaminated persons of dangerous power. Warriors and murderers were usually purified in this way. The notorious scalp ceremonies were also rituals of purification. Often avoidance magic was practiced against ghosts of the dead. But it was more usual to seek a relationship of intimacy with the supernatural. To this end visions were sought; indeed, the vision quest is perhaps the most typical and fundamental aspect of Amerindian worship.

Visions as a source of ritual power were common throughout the continent, but there was considerable difference in emphasis. It is roughly true—it is difficult to generalize—that north of Mexico visions were deliberately sought (hence the concept of the quest), while south of Mexico they were not sought, but were accepted if they came through dreams or hallucinatory experience. There were exceptions, of course: on the Northwest coast spirit possession was a common mode of obtaining power, with a corresponding belief in soul loss as a cause of disease. Behind all the variations, however, lay the idea that an individual could gain spiritual power by means of a vision of a supernatural entity. In some cultural areas, like the Plains, this was the pre-eminent religious idea. Among the Plains Indians it was not only the religious practitioners (shamans or medicine men) who sought visions, but every man of the tribe; initiation into full adult status depended on the obtaining of a suitable vision in which the potential warrior saw a supernatural animal, which then became his guardian spirit. There is a misconception in some quarters that visions were sought only in order to obtain guardian spirits. This misconception led to the idea that the seeking of visions was essentially a *rite de passage,* but this was only one of its functions. It is essential to grasp that the vision itself was the basic feature and that it could be put to many uses. It was used in California by shamans wishing to effect a cure; among the Montagnais to achieve success in hunting; among the Plains Indians for a variety of purposes, including mourning, success in war or vengeance, curing, hunting, and art.

The idea that visions were peculiarly associated with both initiation and with guardian spirits derives from the extreme elaboration of the vision quest among the Algonquians and the Plains Indians. The classical quest was undertaken by a boy at puberty or by a young warrior. Among the Crow a boy would fast for four days and supplicate the spirits to "take pity on him." He would often hack off part of a finger to arouse supernatural pity. Among certain of the Sioux the suppliant would stand for two days and nights praying for a vision. Whatever the means employed—and they inevitably involved mortification of the flesh—the vision usually appeared on the fourth night; generally the spirit appeared in the form of an animal: buffalo, elk, deer, bear, eagle, and sparrow hawk were popular, but even insects, such as the mosquito, might be the vehicle of supernatural power. From the spirit the suppliant learned a song and certain taboos, and was told to obtain a token—buffalo hair, eagle's wing, and so on—which would serve as a talisman.

This vision experience was the true initiation rite for the tribes around the Great Lakes and was seen primarily as a preparation for life. On the Plains, however, a man might continue to seek supernatural aid in this way throughout his life. In doing so, he collected a number of tokens and wrapped them into a bundle. This sacred, or medicine, bundle became his most important possession, and the bundles belonging to chiefs were often thought to have special powers. These sacred packages could be opened only with special ceremony. Various versions of the sacred bundle are found all over North America—frequently described in anthropological literature as "fetishes." They are all clearly derived from the hunter's basic bundle of ceremonial objects, a kind of traveling altar appropriate to a nomadic people.

The sincerity of the vision experience cannot be doubted, for there were many instances of individuals' failing to receive supernatural communications. In some tribes, a successful visionary was allowed to sell part of his power to a less successful tribesman. He would make a replica of his bundle and teach his songs and taboos, and generally take on the role of guardian spirit to his client.

The vision is the most distinguishing feature of Amerindian religion and has rarely reached such a degree of elaboration in any other tribal peoples. Visionary experience was largely confined to men. In some tribes women sought visions, but this was not common. Among the hunters, women were regarded as powerful in their own right by virtue of their ability to give birth. But this power was antithetical to male power. Its most positive manifestation was menstruation, and many hunting tribes surrounded the menstruating woman with taboos and avoidances. Menstrual blood was particularly feared as harmful to war and hunting enterprises, but it had so much power that a fearless hunter might even turn it to advantage by "taming" it and carrying some with him on the hunt. Among some hunting peoples, particularly the Athabascans, the girl's puberty ceremony ranked as a major ceremonial.

Shamanistic practices are found in most of the hunting and gathering tribes, and in others, over the whole continent. The shaman sometimes functions primarily as a healer who sucks objects from the bodies of victims of witchcraft or ghostly attack. Sometimes he is a prophet, diviner, and visionary, rather than a healer. The best term for the "sucking shaman" is perhaps "medicine man" (French *médecin*);

the title "shaman" proper is reserved—as it is among the Tungus of Siberia, from whom the term originates—for the seer, confessor, medium, and miracle worker. In either case, the power to heal or prophesy was usually obtained in a vision, although intensive training at the hands of an experienced shaman or healer was also necessary. The shaman among the Tungus and the Eskimo received his vision without a quest and usually as the result of a mysterious illness. After a period of fasting and training, he was able to see visions regularly and to control spirits. From older shamans he learned conjuring tricks, swallowing feats, fire-walking, and the like. The Eskimo shaman could perform, among other miracles, the spirit flight, and, in spirit, visit other places. He could even go down into the sea and speak to the owners of the fish and seals, or travel overland to find caribou. (The spirit flight is also very common in central Asia.) The recovering of lost souls and the hearing of confessions were also part of the shaman's task.

The miracle-working seer was more common in the extreme North and the subarctic than elsewhere. But elements of the shaman complex proper are found among the medicine men of other culture areas. As we move south, however, the idea of the medicine man as a specialist healer (albeit with spirit aid) is pervasive. Conjuring was common in the tribes around the Great Lakes, where the medicine men formed a trans-tribal cult (especially among the Winnebago, Ojibwa, and Menominee) known as the Mide'wiwin. The Navaho and other Apachean tribes of the Southwest also incorporated wonder-working into the repertoire of the "singers" (paid specialists in the Navaho curing rite), or medicine men, thus reflecting their connections with their cousins, the Athabascans, in Northwest Canada.

The above patterns were mostly to be found among the hunters. The planters relegated the individualistic, visionary shaman to a minor place or dispensed with him altogether. They were much more concerned with calendrical fertility rituals, which were usually in the hands of priests or priestly organizations. In some cases, however, these priestly cults were obviously derived from a shamanistic source—a development perhaps foreshadowed by the Mide'wiwin. The most striking example of this is the Keres-speaking Pueblo Indians of the Rio Grande in New Mexico. The priestly societies there (which still function) are organizations of medicine men who perform the sucking cures, recover lost or stolen souls, and put on annual wonder-working performances. But their organization is essentially that of a priestly cult. Initiates do not require a vision, but they must undergo a long training in word-perfect ritual accompanied by the familiar disciplines of fasting and abstinence. One of their number is the spiritual head of the tribe, and they exercise governmental as well as ritual functions. They are also concerned with the fertility rituals. This is a clear case of the shamanistic functionaries having evolved into an organized ritual-governmental organ of the tribe.

There is also continuity between the rituals of the hunters and the agriculturalists in the areas of hunting and war; for many of the agricultural tribes continued to hunt, and some of the prairie tribes—such as the Omaha—had a completely mixed economy. The hunting and war rituals were similar in both cultures, but, as the societies became more complex, there was a definite tendency for these ceremonies to be taken over by cult groups with priestly officers. It is this growth of ritual specialization that marks out the more elaborate of the agriculturalists from their hunter cousins. At one end of the scale are the completely individualistic religions, in which each man could commune directly for his own benefit with the spirits; at the other are the collectivist religions, in which the welfare of the community at large was the aim, achieved by the ritual activity of the priests. Many of the elements and symbols may have been the same in each case, but the over-all organization was quite different.

The hunters and nomads, however, did not lack collective rituals for the benefit of the whole group. The most spectacular of these was undoubtedly the Sun Dance of the Plains Indians. Although composed of ancient elements, this ceremony must have been of fairly recent elaboration, since many of the most famous Plains tribes took to the horse only at the end of the eighteenth century, when they moved into the plains from the desert or the woodlands. Many elements —reverence for the sun, the use of a sacred pole, the obtaining of visionary power through ordeal and mortification —were woven into the ceremony, which took place during eight days in midsummer, just after the great buffalo hunt. The various scattered groups of the tribe came together to relax after their exertions. There were many variations, but some features, such as the erecting of a lodge or sacred enclosure, usually circular, were common. A center pole was the focus of attention in the rituals. The ceremony was usually sponsored by an individual as a result of a vow made in time of sickness or war, but the whole tribe joined the sponsor. Past sponsors acted as officiators. After several days of preliminary ceremonial (including much smoking, a ritual act common to most tribes), the climax was reached in the actual dance itself. Looking fixedly at the sun or the pole, the dancers blew on bone whistles as they danced. In certain tribes thongs would be attached to the top of the pole, and some dancers would fasten these through their chest muscles and pull outward on them as they danced until the muscles tore. Here one is reminded of the amputations and other mortifications practiced on the vision quest, and indeed much of the prayer involved was the same in each case: a plea for pity from the sun and other supernaturals.

The sacrificial elements are obvious, but sacrifice did

not figure as largely in North America as it did in the Middle American religions. The nearest equivalents to the human sacrifices of the Aztecs occurred in the Pawnee ceremony of the sacrifice to the morning star. A girl captive representing the evening star was shot through the heart with an arrow, pulled down, and then clubbed to death. Her spirit joined that of her "husband," the morning star. The Iroquois sacrificed brave captive warriors, but it is uncertain whether or not this was really a religious ceremony. There are hints of human sacrifice in Pueblo ceremonies where symbolic victims are slain, but there is no direct evidence that this is a substitution for real sacrifice. There is no sacrifice of animals, but among many of the planting tribes there was a first-fruits offering not unlike those of the Old World.

The settled agriculturalists—the Pueblos are a good example—represent the high point of the development of priestly religions in North America. But it was rare for these priests to be full-time professionals; they were mostly members of cult groups or medicine societies, where each group was in charge of a particular ceremony. Often the priesthoods were hereditary offices; clans were often said to "own" ceremonies. Sometimes the connection between the clan and the ceremony was direct—as among the Hopi, where the snake clan was in charge of the snake ceremonies. Among the Pueblos, the practice of putting on ceremonies at the instigation of individual sponsors still exists, but the major ceremonies are all connected with calendrical observances, and in particular with the summer and winter solstices and the spring and autumn equinoxes.

Each ceremony follows a similar pattern: the priestly society goes into retreat for a fixed period, fasts, smokes, makes sand paintings, prayer sticks, and prayer feathers. (This making of pure prayer offerings is a feature of South-western religious practice.) On the final day or days of the ceremony there is public dancing. In the winter many of these dances take place in the kiva-chamber of a society or of a moiety. Prominent among the Pueblo cults is that of the *katsinas* (*kachinas*): "masked gods," or "dancing gods," associated with the clouds and with rain, and imitated by initiates in the public dances. The Pueblos show probably the greatest complexity in North America of priesthoods, cults, medicine societies, and other ritual organizations, all of which interlock in a vast ceremonial complex. The worship of the sun and the corn (who is also Mother Earth), the hero twins, sacred tobacco, shamanism, and the sacred fires are all woven into this complex of rites, which revolve around the themes of harmony and fertility.

The Navaho, the neighbors of the Pueblo Indians, are noted as ceremonialists. They are a good example of a hunting tribe that has settled and adopted more elaborate religious practices to supplement and extend its basic shamanism. The focus of Navaho ceremonial is the curing rite sponsored by the sick person and his clansmen. It is directed by a paid specialist—the singer—who knows the chants and the appropriate sand paintings. The making of sand paintings is an art borrowed from the Pueblos and elaborated to a high degree. Masked impersonations of the Navaho deities (which include the hero twins) accompany the curing ceremony in its closing stages. These ceremonies can be for the cure of a variety of illnesses, which are diagnosed in shaman fashion. The ritual details are more reminiscent of the Pueblos, but do not reflect their concern with fertility.

Forms of prayer vary. Among the Iroquoian tribes, recorded prayers are largely of thanksgiving; the Algonquians and Plains Indians prayed, largely as individuals, for pity and for success—they were suppliants; Pueblo and Navaho prayer is much more a statement of ritual fact—nearer indeed to an incantation, the proper performance of which ensures the ends desired. Most highly developed Indian ceremonials are symbolic re-enactments of myths, especially of the myths of creation.

It is almost impossible to generalize about the ethical standards and ideas of the North American Indians; they are seldom specifically connected with ideas of religious merit or demerit. There is no hell or punishment in afterlife for wrongdoers; nor are the inducements of paradise specific, despite the notion of a "happy hunting ground" held by sentimental whites. All one can say by way of generalization is that each group has socially approved ends and modes of behavior, and that often supernatural power can be used to promote these ends. This could either be power sought for individual success, as with the Plains Indians, or power sought by communal action for the communal good, as with the Pueblos. Power utilized for socially disapproved ends is almost universally regarded as witchcraft and severely punished. In every group there are thought to be evil persons who could misuse supernatural power to harm their fellows. The ideas about sorcery and the techniques of witchcraft are not peculiar to America; they are similar to those found elsewhere in the world. Outside this sphere of the evil use of power, however, the beliefs and rituals about the supernatural are not concerned with any ethical code. (In some of the revivalist religions, strongly influenced by Christianity, ethical considerations did become important.) Kindness, honesty, forgiveness, chastity, filial duty are all enjoined in some measure, and a code of ethics is usually supposed to have been laid down "in the beginning" by a creator or the culture heroes. But the rituals are concerned with these matters only incidentally; that is, harmony in human relationships is often considered essential to a successful ritual performance. There is no idea of a code of conduct that, if kept, would ensure the favor of the deities or spirits or, if broken, incur their wrath.

The myths already mentioned, including those of creation, are only a part of the vast body of Amerindian mythology. They are, however, the most important part; most of the myths connected with rituals deal with the dawn period of creation and the activities of the culture heroes and earliest settlers. As might be expected from what has been said about ethics, these are not moral tales; indeed, the activities of many of the actors run counter to the conventional morality of the tribes. Typically, they describe the origins of natural phenomena or pieces of ritual, or the exploits of holy people. As in many other parts of the world, the theme of an all-destructive deluge crops up frequently. Other myths tend to appear in clusters with characteristic "distributions." Thus the Algonquian and Siouan tribes share a series of myths, including the story of the woman who married a sky being ("star husband") and the story of an attempt to snare the sun. Some themes are more widely distributed than others, such as the stories of the testing of the hero twins and the exploits of the trickster. Both these themes have a distribution outside North America; the latter in particular has attracted attention because the principal character shows affinities with Hermes and Loki and related figures of European mythology. He appears in many guises—on the Northwest coast as a raven, in the Eastern forests as a rabbit, and in many areas as a coyote. This great archetypical figure is at once the creator of all order and the epitome of disorder; he is both immensely clever and a simple dupe; he defies every known convention and yet is the founder of convention. Typically, he has enlarged intestines wound around him and an enormous and insatiable appetite; with

301

this goes an uncontrollable and extended penis that often becomes detached and has its own adventures. He cannot control his bowels or bladder; he stoops to low pranks and humbles proud maidens. He is, in short, the impulsive, instinctively cunning and yet simple aspect of man's nature. Jung suggests that the Winnebago trickster cycle illustrates the social and sexual maturity in the human being as he gradually grows from a completely asocial to an at least partly socialized creature. But the trickster is never completely socialized; he remains the epitome of the simple, primitive energy of human personality. The variations on this theme are legion and sometimes quite attenuated, but it is in many ways the most typical and widespread myth of the Amerindians.

There are many and various myths of the creation of man. Only in the Pueblos' do we get the classic tale of mankind being begotten by Sky Father on Earth Mother, the first humans ascending from the womb of earth through a reed. In most of the tribes around the Great Lakes it was, naturally enough, some kind of emergence from water that was involved, and often this was achieved by Earth Diver under the direction of the creator spirit or a culture hero. In other tales the first creatures were animals, some of whom later took human form. On the plains and the prairies, it was held that the first men had descended from the sky, passing through various "heavens" or "worlds" until they landed in this one—just as the Pueblo Indians had risen through several worlds. In most of these myths we have the idea of man entering into a watery world with no place to land. An animal or hero helps to find a dry place for him to settle. Where a clan organization exists, it is common to find each clan with its own origin myth and some idea of a chronology of creation that establishes an order of precedence among the clans. Perhaps the only generalization to be made about the creation of man is that there is rarely any idea of a specific act of creation by a higher being for a specific purpose. Man just emerges from various sources in various ways.

Except among a few gifted thinkers there are no philosophical ideas about human nature. By and large, the order of nature and society is assumed to be fixed. There is no idea of man striving for a better condition of life. His aim is to live harmoniously and successfully within the tribal framework. He is capable of both good and evil but is not particularly prone to either. Human nature is seen as a mixture of good and evil tendencies. If there is no notion of human beings as creatures born in sin against which they must struggle, neither is there any notion of them born essentially innocent and only later corrupted by the world. Thus there is no fall of man. In fact, man is seen as having evolved from a childlike state on the model of individual ontogeny.

The first men are thought to have been relatively helpless. The culture hero often had to complete their physical development and then teach them the rudiments of culture. The most important things he taught were the rituals and other observances; as the Indian sees it, if these rituals are performed and these observances kept, the order laid down in the beginning will be maintained. This order is seen to be essentially good, and consequently life is essentially good. The great danger lies in the misuse of this power by evil persons; hence, the greatest crime of all is witchcraft.

Most tribes had some conception, if a not very well-defined one, of an afterlife. It was thought that the soul might survive for some time and then "fade away," and most tribes believed that man possessed more than one soul. With few exceptions, such as the Sioux, the dead were feared in various degrees; their power, which was held to be dangerous, could be nullified by processes such as the adoption of a substitute relative for the dead one, the substitute taking over the soul of the dead person. The idea of reincarnation was also present in some areas—but it was not an elaborate conception of a "wheel," or reincarnation from which escape was possible, but rather a Pythagorean notion that one of the souls might return as an animal or be inherited by a kinsman. Among the Hopi, dead infants were buried in the house in the expectation that their souls would be reincarnated in the next child born. It is only among the Pueblos that a definite and at all elaborate conception of a happy afterlife appears. The dead here joined the *katsinas* and became clouds and hence bringers of rain. Among the Hopi a woman had to be buried in her bridal dress to ensure her passage to the next world.

With such an attenuated or shadowy conception of an afterlife, there could be no notion of a life on earth devoted to reward in heaven, or of a Nirvanalike escape from the toils of incarnation. Human destiny, therefore, personal or general, had no end state to be achieved. Certainly, there was no idea of supernatural reward or salvation in eternal life. As we have seen, there was no notion of mankind moving from or toward any particular state of grace. The ways or roads of life had been laid down and were followed not for reward in eternity, but because they made life on earth happy and harmonious. Death was at best a peaceful state; at worst it was a state of nothingness.

The destiny of man, therefore, was to live a successful life in harmony with the natural and moral order as conceived by his culture; an order essentially unchanging and usually unchallenged. Within this framework he found his fulfillment. The idea of salvation is clearly irrelevant in such a system.

Some of the aboriginal traits mentioned earlier still

survive in certain tribes. The Pueblo Indians have maintained a quite remarkable continuity of religious belief and practice that runs in harness with adopted Catholicism. The Navaho, the most successful of the surviving tribes, retain their rituals intact. Other groups in the Southwest, such as the Yaqui, have amalgamated Catholic and indigenous elements. The Iroquois still maintain an impressive ceremonial cycle, and among some surviving Plains groups the Sun Dance is still performed. But by and large, the aboriginal religion of the hunters and the planters of the Southeast collapsed as an integrated system when these societies were destroyed.

Two modern movements, however, should be noted: one is a religion of despair, while the other may well become the unified religion of the surviving American Indians. I allude to the Ghost Dance religion and the Peyote religion. Various "prophets" had arisen throughout the eighteenth century preaching the eventual success of the Indian in his struggle with the white man. In the nineteenth century, however, it became obvious that this could not be achieved unaided and a different brand of prophecy arose, based on the old shamanistic experience of trance and spirit message. The message usually laid down, in its strict code of ethics, an injunction for the Indian to observe the old Indian ways. Along with this code went a dance ritual that was held necessary to the survival of the red man when the whites were destroyed by flood and/or the Indian dead returned. And then the buffalo could return. The most successful of these prophets was Wovoka, a Paiute, who started his own version of the Ghost Dance religion in Nevada in 1886, which spread throughout the Plains Indians and finally reached the Sioux. In 1890, the last Sioux uprising occurred, unsuccessfully, and the Ghost Dance, with its promise of the return of the old ways, disappeared.

Another tradition of prophecy had been pacific. It produced the Shaker religion, but its most significant modern development has been the growth of the Peyote religion. The fruit and roots of the peyote cactus (*Lophophora williamsii*), which contain hallucinogens, had been used in Mexico for obtaining religious visions. It was introduced to America in the late nineteenth century by Apache tribes who raided and traded over the Mexican border. There grew up around the taking of peyote a definite series of rituals deriving from Plains sources, which involved confessions, singing, drumming, smoking, praying, and the ceremonial taking of the "button" of the peyote cactus. The movement was disseminated to the tribes of the Oklahoman Indian Territory and then to the other Plains tribes, filling the vacuum left by the Ghost Dance religion. Missionaries went out to the Utes and the Navaho, and now both have versions of the cult. It is a nationally organized religion and has been incorporated as the Native American Church of the United States. Its ethics and creed are a mixture of Indian and Christian elements, but its form and inspiration clearly derive from native sources.

The future of religion in the Amerindian tribes depends on the stability and prosperity of the traditional tribes, with their relatively unchanged religions, and the relations between the new pan-Indian political movements and the syncretic religions such as peyoteism. There are two different kinds of tensions here. The tribal religions are opposed to the syncretic as a rule, and tribal religious leaders see threats both to their own authority and to tribal integrity in these "tribeless" universalistic cults. At the same time, the more radical red-power Indians are hostile to the new cults; they maintain that these cults are an "opium of the people" that prevent the red man from asserting his political rights. Paradoxically, many of the more political and radical

Indians are in favor of the tribal religions because these are "purer" and less contaminated by Christianity. It is impossible to predict the outcome of these tensions. Much will depend on how successful pan-Indian politics turns out to be.

Man in Nature

IN THIS ESSAY—a version of a speech I gave at the Third Smithsonian International Symposium—I take up some of the themes of the introduction from another angle. I am mostly concerned with the nature/culture distinction as it has been drawn by anthropology. This is central to the work of Lévi-Strauss also, but with a slight difference. He is largely concerned with the nature/culture theme as it is reflected in myth—which in turn reflects some basic human obsessions. This is where I begin, but I go on to deplore the use of this "mythical" distinction as a description of reality.

In his earlier work, Lévi-Strauss maintained that this was a "real" distinction. Now he has revised his view somewhat to suggest that the distinction is overdrawn. He argues that we should see the nature/culture divide as an aspect of reality only in the sense that it is part of persistent human *thinking* about the world.

The position I take here has been dubbed "gradualism" by those who dislike it. It sees man gradually emerging from the primate stock and refuses to acknowledge any sharp man/animal or nature/culture break. It accepts what our founding fathers—Darwin, Tylor, Morgan—all accepted: that there is considerable continuity in behavior between man and animals, and that the main task of anthropology is to explore this continuity in order to understand the differences. It is really rather an old-fashioned point of view in this sense, much as it may sound like a call to intellectual revolution.

FIFTEEN

The Cultural Animal

PRIMITIVE MYTHOLOGIES testify to man's enduring fascination with the problem of his own relationship to the natural world. For *Homo* is burdened with being *sapiens*, and one thing this *sapientia* drives him to is a ceaseless and almost passionate inquiry about his status—what T. H. Huxley aptly called *An Enquiry into Man's Place in Nature*. And, like Darwin and Huxley, the primitive seeks an answer to the eternal paradox: he is obviously part of nature, and in particular he is part of the animal world; yet he is set apart from nature by the very fact of knowing that he is part of it. Not only does no other animal know it is going to die, but no other animal knows it is alive. And no other animal concerns itself with the problem of its uniqueness.

But man is obsessed with it. He is forever seeking to define himself—a task as yet uncompleted—and to do this he has to establish the boundaries between himself and the animal world.

In their mythologies the primitives solve the problem in various ways, usually by having man descend from various animals. It might be thought that this represents an anticipation of Darwin, but unfortunately most primitives believe in acts of special creation, so they must be disqualified. It is one of these acts of creation, however, that is usually the clue to the essential difference between man and animal. Language, fire, the art of cooking, rules about incest, and so on are the diacritics of humanity. We do not communicate, convert energy, eat, or breed quite like the animals, and hence we make that crucial breakthrough from nature to culture, and become the cultural animal.

Not only does man become cultural, he becomes divine. In many of his ego-boosting mythologies man does not differ simply in degree from the animals; he differs in kind. It is not some simple attribute—like the ability to make fire— but the possession of a divine spark that renders us *in essence* different, that carves out a gulf between man and "brute creation." Here again the matter remains stubbornly unsettled, and much argument ensues about where brute creation stops and the divine human starts. Any human group is ever ready to consign another recognizably different human group to the other side of the boundary. To be fully human, it is not enough to possess culture, one must possess *our* culture. Even universalist religions, which were happy to define man as an animal with a soul, were often not very certain how to define "soul," and categories of *Homo sylvestris* and *Homo feralis* were invented to take care of marginal cases. But at least in the Western world this definition sufficed (and for many still suffices) until the eighteenth-century savants began to look down on such arguments as perhaps too "emotional," and substituted reason as the defining characteristic of man. Linnaeus, to whom man owes his pretentious zoological title, *Homo sapiens,* was very much a child of the eighteenth century, when souls were not to be trusted because one never knew quite what they were up to, and animals may very well have them, too. But brute creation did not have reason and that was obvious enough. Soulful our furry friends might be, but rational they were not. They could probably adore God, but they could not understand Pythagoras.

Darwin undermined this stance as much as he undermined the position of the religiously orthodox. He noted what in fact many of his predecessors—including Linnaeus himself, and even Kant—had noted: the striking anatomical similarity between man and the rest of the order *Primates* and ultimately between man and the rest of the vertebrates. What Darwin added was a theory that could explain how this striking relationship came about, other than by some whim of the Almighty or by some Lamarckian effort of will. Now this caused many people other than Bishop Wilberforce to feel that human dignity and uniqueness were in danger. That great anti-cleric Samuel Butler castigated Darwin for "banishing mind from the universe," for blurring the distinctions that we had assumed were inviolable. Man had emerged gradually from the animal world by a natural process, not suddenly by a supernatural one. The moral was plain to the soul merchants and the reason merchants alike: man in fact differed only in degree, not in kind, from his cousins. The reaction was interesting. The anatomical argument was quickly adopted and became its own kind of orthodoxy. Despite a few skirmishes, the battle was over before it was fought.

The anatomist W. E. LeGros Clark said recently that it is

astonishing to think people ever doubted the anatomical continuity between man and the other primates. And, indeed, it does seem absurd today, to the extent that when I am faced with an unrepentant fundamentalist I am unable to cope with him. I have no ready-made arguments for defending the self-evident, and so fare badly, thus confirming his worst fears about the conspiracy of the ungodly.

In the hundred years between the appearance of *The Origin of Species* and today, a large (although still too limited) amount of fossil evidence has come to light documenting the gradual transition that, even in the absence of direct evidence, Darwin realized *must* have happened. As far as anatomy was concerned, then, the case rested. But human behavior was somehow exempted from this rubric.

Whatever the opinion about Darwin's specific conclusions, his message was exceedingly clear. In many areas of behavior man shows great similarities to his cousins; their behavior, like their anatomy, has evolved through the process of natural selection—and so has man's. Anatomy and behavior, structure and function, were of course intimately linked, and what was true for one was true for the other.

Even in the biological sciences, the impact of this line of thinking was not immediate, and it is only comparatively recently that biologists have been investigating in a serious way the evolution of animal-behavior systems. The reasons for this are not of concern here, although the historians of science should be working on them. But one reason should be noted: investigations of animal behavior really got going under the aegis of Pavlovian-style behaviorism, which is not evolutionary in orientation and has little respect for anything that is claimed to be "innate." There was a similar reaction (or was it even a reaction?) in the social sciences. Darwin had blurred the distinctions, all right, and even reason did not appear to be so firmly enthroned now; so anthropology became defender of the faith in human uniqueness and offered culture as the defining characteristic. Anthropologists, however, were never able to define very clearly what this was.

So, as in the older myths of the primitives, the nature of man's uniqueness remains something of a mystery. Roughly, "culture," in anthropological parlance, refers to traditional modes of behaving and thinking that are passed on from one generation to another by social learning of one kind or another. We get a little uneasy when told that animal communities also have traditions that get passed on, so we retreat into symbols. Culture is couched in symbols and it is by means of these that it is transmitted. Pre-eminent among the symbol systems is language, and, when all else fails, man can cling to language. By their speech shall ye know them.

The social and behavioral sciences thus side-stepped Darwin's challenge. This was easy to do at a time when behaviorism dominated psychology, and instinct theory had fallen into disrepute. Behaviorism was rigorous and "scientific," while instinct theory—primarily under William McDougall —seemed nothing more than a kind of thesaurus of human attributes. The eugenics movement, which put such store in biological aspects of behavior, became more and more entangled with racism, and the least attempt to show that there were important biological components in behavior was regarded as incipient racism, and still is in many quarters. In sociology, the social Darwinists had also fallen into disrepute. They were not really Darwinians; they simply used analogies from Darwinian biological theory and applied them, usually incorrectly, to social processes. Their wrongheaded use of evolutionary doctrines to support the excesses of *laissez-faire* capitalism eventually sent them into oblivion. With them, the proverbial baby went out with the proverbial bath water.

Henceforth, any explanation of a social phenomenon that was Darwinian or biological was *ipso facto* erroneous in the social sciences, and that was that. Marx and Durkheim dominated sociology, and while the latter had problems with the autonomy of the subject, his doctrine that the social must be explained in terms of the social and not "reduced" to any lower level—like the biological, of course—held almost complete sway. Anthropologists continued to pronounce. Arthur Keith even set a limit below which culture was impossible: the brain, he said, had to reach a size of seven hundred fifty cubic centimeters before any fossil primate could be considered a man. This gave substance to the anthropological belief that culture was, in the words of Malinowski, "all of a piece." People were never found with religion but no language, or law but no religion, and so on. If they had one they had them all. It must have happened at the point when the brain reached the size necessary for culture to "occur."

One can immediately see the similarities between this and the Catholic doctrine as ennunciated in the encyclical *Humani generis,* which allows that man may have evolved in body, as described by Darwin, but insists that at some point an immortal soul was injected into the painfully evolving body. God would have had to wait, it seems, until his chosen primate had crossed Keith's "Cerebral Rubicon."

Anthropologists, also, were almost maniacally preoccupied with explaining cultural differences. They were really not very interested in what made men men, but in what made one lot of them different from another lot. As a student, I had the litany chanted at me: "Biological universals cannot explain cultural differentials. . . ." And, of course, at one level they cannot. Muslims, I was told, take off their shoes to go into church, while Christians take off their hats. Now find me a biological explanation for that! I was never sure I wanted to find any kind of explanation for it. It seemed to me a pretty arbitrary thing. And anyway, what explanation was I offered?

Even in those days I was plaguing my teachers with the question: If we do not really know what biological universals there are, how can we study the cultural differentials? How can we study the variables without the constants? I was told that biological universals were simply primitive drives, like hunger and sex. But the fact that sex was universal didn't explain why some cultures were polygynous and others monogamous. Maybe not, I thought, but it might explain why they were all adulterous. After all, might not behavior resulting from something as complex as sex produce more than just these rather gray and amorphous urges? Look at the courtship of birds and animals, for example. Ah, came back the answer, but that is *genetic,* whereas human courtship is *cultural.*

When all this was going on—some eighteen years ago in London—I had no ready answer. It all depends, I thought to myself and in secret, upon what you want to explain. All human cultures have some kind of courtship ceremonies, and they all look very much alike despite the different cultural trappings. If all you want to explain is why in America girls wear their dates' fraternity pins while in Fiji they put hibiscus flowers behind their ears, that is fine. But (1) it does not seem worth explaining, and (2) there probably is no explanation, in any scientific sense; it is just what they do. These are simply ways of getting the same courtship job done, and the interesting thing to me is the universality of various similar symbolic devices. Has each culture independently invented the idea that the girl should declare her intentions in this kind of way? Or is there perhaps something more subtle about courtship than previously imagined —something uncultural, something unlearned?

Anthropology was undoubtedly fighting several real battles, often shooting at the wrong enemies. The no-links-between-biology-and-culture argument was partly an attack on the racists, who wanted to explain seeming inequalities between cultures as a result of biological differences. Again the baby went out with the soapsuds when anthropology strenuously opposed *any* connection between culture and biology, even at the universal level. At best—as, for example, in the work of Malinowski—culture could be seen as a response to a rather drab set of "biological imperatives," but then this kind of Malinowskian functionalism soon fell into disrepute as well, since it did nothing to explain cultural differences. While I am on my catalogue of complaints, let me add that as far as I could see, for all its obsession with cultural differences, anthropology did nothing to *explain* them. What it did was to take cultural differences as given and use them to explain other phenomena—largely, other cultural differences. All the things that might have explained cultural differences, such as racial variation, environment, history, and diffusion, were at one time or another ruled out of court.

All in all, for a variety of ideological reasons, anthropology, along with psychology and sociology, kept the world safe for humanity by refusing to allow that anything about culture could be "reduced" to biology, and hence kept the gap between us and the brutes nicely wide. Man was the cultural animal, but stress was entirely on the *cultural;* the animal was relegated to a few odd things like blinking, sucking, feeling hungry, and copulating. It was held that 99 per cent of human behavior was learned and hence cultural. And what was more, that there was no limit to what could be learned. The human infant was a *tabula rasa* on which culture imprinted itself, and the subsequent behavior of the infant was therefore wholly a matter of which particular culture had been imprinted on it. The differences between cultures, in their beliefs, behaviors, and institutions, were held to be so great that any considerations of common biological traits could be totally ignored.

This was all a great pity, since it was not the intention of the founding fathers of anthropology to create an unbridgeable gap between man and animal. E. B. Tylor, who is rightly credited with the invention of the anthropological concept of culture, was greatly interested in the behavior of animals. In his *Anthropology* of 1881, he included a chapter called "Man and other Animals" in which he stressed continuities. (Leslie White, in his "edited" version of this classic, cut out the chapter, since it was not, according to him, consonant with modern knowledge.) Lewis Henry Morgan, whose work on kinship systems is indisputably the starting point of American anthropology, spent many years studying the beaver and wrote the standard book on its behavior. All his life he argued for a continuity of behavior between man and animal. It is ironic that Morgan, a special creationist, should be arguing for continuity, while his successors, supposedly believers in Darwinian natural selection, should have resurrected the doctrine of special creation.

What all this leads to is the crucial question: Weren't anthropologists suffering from "ethnographic dazzle"? (I have adapted the term from linguistics, where "orthographic dazzle" refers to the difficulty some people have of sorting out pronunciation from spelling.) In some respects and at some levels—of beliefs, of formal institutions—cultures are dazzlingly different from one another. Why are the Japanese the way they are, as opposed to the Americans, the Russians, the Hottentots, and so on? This is a fascinating question. But, as I have said, the answer from anthropology is a rather lame "They are different because they do things differently." Anthropology mostly tells about the *consequences* of doing things differently, and tells it very well indeed. But are societies and

cultures really so different at the level of forms and processes? Aren't they in some ways depressingly the same?
Don't anthropologists, time after time in society after society,
come up against the same processes carried out under a
variety of symbolic disguises? I think they do, and if they
can get past the cultural or ethnographic dazzle, they can
see that this is so. Thus, if one looks at the behavior of what
my colleague Lionel Tiger has called "men in groups,"
one finds that, whatever the overt cultural male-group behavior at the level of symbolism, actual practices, beliefs,
and even emotions, one thing stands out: men form themselves into associations from which they exclude women.
These associations vary in their expressed purposes, but in
many of their processes they are remarkably uniform. Once
this is grasped, a seemingly bewildering variety of male
behavior can be reduced to a few principles.

Similarly, I have tried to show that the apparently endless
kinds of kinship and marriage arrangements known to man
are in fact variations on a few simple themes. The same can
be said of political arrangements, which, despite their cultural variety, are reducible to a few structural forms. Once
one gets behind the surface manifestations, the uniformity
of human behavior and of human social arrangements is
remarkable.

None of this should surprise a behavioral zoologist; the
subject being dealt with is, after all, a uniform species
divided into a number of populations. Since this is a species
of rather highly developed mammals, one would expect
many local differences in "traditions" between the various
populations, but one would expect these differences to reflect
species-specific units of behavior. Thus, every species has a
complex of social behavior made up of recognizable units—
a complex that distinguishes it from other species—but these
units may well be put together in different ways by different

populations adapting to different environments. A baboon troop, for all its ingenuity, does not adapt in the same way as a herd of horses (and vice versa). The baboons can adapt only by using the material in their stock of behavior units, and the same is true of man.

The degree of flexibility is obviously greater among humans, but much of it is at the symbolic level. The story can be told in many different ways, but it is still the same old story. And if it is departed from too far—which is within man's capacity—the result may well be a truly dramatic chaos. For this is man's dilemma. Unlike the baboon or the horse, he can imagine things that are different from the plot laid down for him, and he can put his dreams into practice and watch to see if they will work. If man accepts that all behavior is culturally learned and that he can learn anything, he can invent any kind of society and culture for himself. If he believes that he has a species-specific repertoire of behavior that can be combined successfully only in certain ways, then there are definite limits to what this animal can do, to the kinds of societies he can operate, to the kinds of cultures he can live with. But there is no end to man's dreams and fantasies. His social behavior may have strict limits, but his imagination has few.

I mentioned earlier that language was the chief characteristic of the human species, the crucial distinguishing feature. It is now well established that the capacity for language acquisition and use lies in the brain and speech organs, and in the complex relations between the two. Linguists, like Noam Chomsky, and psychologists, like E. H. Lenneberg, argue that the capacity for grammatical speech is somehow in the brain and matures as the child matures. Thus every human child has the capacity for grammatical speech, and is ready, as it were, to be programed with whatever actual grammar. its culture provides. We know that these grammars are astonishing in their variety, and that their variation is arbitrary. There is no explanation for why the English say "horse," the French *"cheval,"* and the Germans *"pferd."* There is no explanation for why any particular pattern of sounds signifies a particular object or action (with the possible exception of onomatopoeia). This is all quite arbitrary. Nevertheless, the speech patterns of all languages operate on a few basic principles, which linguists have worked out, and the semantic patterns may also be reducible in this way, once what Chomsky calls the "deep structures" of all languages are known. When they are, a "universal grammar" can be written that will reveal the few principles upon which all actual grammars rest. Despite the enormous variety of "surface grammars," they are all not only doing the same job, but also are constrained to do it in a limited number of ways. Thus no language exists that a linguist cannot record with the universal phonetic alphabet, and analyze with universally applicable techniques of semantic analysis. Artificial languages can be invented, based on binary signals, or other codes, which require different grammars, but natural languages can all be broken down, first into phones, then phonemes, then morphemes, then lexemes, and so on up to the higher levels of grammaticality.

The rest of culture is probably like this. The potential for culture lies in the biology of the species. Man has the kinds of cultures and societies he has because he is the kind of species he is. They are built of his behavioral repertoire and are analyzable into its elements and their combinations. Like language, the capacity for specific kinds of behavior is in man, but exactly how this will be manifested will depend on the information fed into the system. The system here is the behavior potential of the individual; the information is the culture he is socialized in. But in the same way that he can learn only a language that follows the normal rules of grammaticality for human languages, so he can learn only a grammar of behavior that follows the parallel rules in the behavioral sphere. Of course, in either case he can try departing from normal grammaticality, but he will then get gibberish, linguistic or behavioral.

People generally do not try to manipulate language because the matter is out of their hands, but with behavior they are continually producing gibbering illiterates, and until they understand the structure of the behavioral grammar within which man weaves his cultural variations, they will continue to do so. No one wants to produce linguistic gibberish, because verbal communication would break down; but behavioral gibberish is constantly being produced and then everybody wonders why social communication breaks down. The answer of those who believe that anything is possible since everything is cultural is: Try to invent yet more and more different languages with any kind of grammaticality you can think of. My answer is: Find out how the universal grammar works and then effect changes within that framework; invent new behavioral languages that do not violate the principles of basic grammaticality.

At least two monarchs in history are said to have tried the experiment of isolating children at birth and keeping them isolated through childhood to see if they would spontaneously produce a language when they matured. Both the Egyptian Psammetichos, in the seventh century B.C., and James IV of Scotland, in the fifteenth century A.D., did not doubt that untutored children would speak, although King James's hope that they would speak Hebrew was perhaps a little optimistic.

I do not doubt that they *could* speak and that, theoretically, given time, they or their offspring would invent and develop a language despite their never having been taught one. Furthermore, this language, although totally different from any known, would be analyzable by linguists on the same basis as other languages and translatable into all known languages.

I would push this further. If the new Adam and Eve could survive and breed—still in total isolation from any cultural influences—they would eventually produce a society that would be likely to have laws about property, its inheritance and exchange; rules about incest and marriage; customs of taboo and avoidance; methods of settling disputes with a minimum of bloodshed; beliefs about the supernatural and practices relating to it; a system of social status and methods of indicating it; initiation rituals for young men; courtship practices, including the adornment of females; systems of symbolic body adornment generally; certain activities and associations set aside for men from which women were excluded; gambling of some kind; a tool- and weapon-making industry; myths and legends; dancing; adultery; homicide; kinship groups; schizophrenia; psychoses and neuroses, and various practitioners to take advantage of or cure these (depending on how they are viewed).

In short, the new Adam and Eve would not only produce, as the two monarchs suspected, a recognizable language, but a recognizable human culture and society. In content it might not be quite like any other. Its religious beliefs might be different, but it would have some; its marriage rules might be unique (I doubt it), but it would have them and their type would be recognized; its status structure might be based on an odd criterion, but there would be one; its initiation rituals might be unbelievably grotesque, but they would exist. All these things would be there because man is the kind of animal that does these kinds of things.

In the same way, in a zoo one can rear infant baboons

who know nothing of how their ancestors and cousins lived in the wild, and yet who, when they reach maturity, produce a social structure with all the elements found in that wild, of which they have no experience. Their capacity to produce a unique language is of course much more limited than that of our hypothetical naïve humans, but in both cases the basic grammaticality of behavior will be operating. In the same way that a linguist could take our Garden of Eden tribe and analyze its totally unique language, so an anthropologist would be able to analyze its totally unique kinship system or mythology or whatever, because the basic rules of the universal grammar would be operating.

(In the interest of accuracy I should add that the experiment might be impossible to perform. It is one of the ground rules of the universal behavioral grammar of all primates—not just humans—that if young infants are deprived of maternal care at a critical period they will grow up to be seriously disturbed and may well perpetuate this error by maltreating their own children in turn. Thus the experiment might well produce a group of maladjusted adults. But at least this presents one element of the universal system: some method has to be found of associating mother and child closely and safely during certain critical periods. If isolated during these periods, the animal may be permanently damaged. It has to learn certain things at certain times—and this is true of language as of many other areas of behavior.)

What I am saying about the human tribe developed *de novo* in an experimental Eden may not seem particularly remarkable, but it does go against the anthropological orthodoxy. Without any exposure to cultural traditions the tribe would develop specific and highly complex patterns of behavior, and probably quickly—within a matter of a few generations, once they had got a language going. They would do so for the same reason that the baboons produce a baboon social system in captivity—because it is in the beast. And it is not just a general capacity that is in the beast—not just the capacity to learn, and to learn easily—which is all the culturalists bother to assume; it is the capacity to learn some things rather than others, to learn some things easily rather than others, to learn some things at one time rather than another, and to learn some rather specific things into the bargain.

This is an important point. I am not positing that initiation ceremonies or male rituals are instinctive, in any old sense of that term. I am positing that they are an outcome of the biology of the animal because he is programed to behave in certain ways that will produce these phenomena, given a certain input of information. If this input does not occur, the behavior will not occur or will occur only in a modified or distorted form. The human organism is like a computer that is set up or wired in a particular way. The organism is thus in a state of readiness—at various points in the life cycle—to process certain kinds of information. The information has to be of a particular type, but the actual message can vary considerably. If the information is received, the "computer" stores it and uses it to go on to the next task. If the system is confused, the "machine" very easily breaks down, and might even blow the fuses. Of course, to push this analogy to its logical conclusion, there would have to be "computers" feeding each other information. Only when they are synchronized would the total system run properly.

This, although crude, is a different model from that of the old instinctivists or the behaviorists. To the instinctivists, behavior resulted simply from the manifestation of innate tendencies that, in interaction, produced such things as territorialism, maternal behavior, or acquisitiveness. To the behaviorists the infant was a *tabula rasa* and behavior ultimately was the result of learning via conditioning. (Psychoanalysis leans to the instinctivist end, but is a special case in some ways.) I see the human organism as wired to process information about certain things, like language and rules about sex, and not about other things. It can process this information only at certain times and in certain ways. This wiring is geared to the life cycle so that at any one moment in a population of *Homo sapiens* there will be individuals with a certain store of behavior at one stage of the cycle giving out information to others at another stage who are wired to treat the information in a certain way. From the interaction of these individuals at various stages, certain typical relationships will emerge.

This may seem tortuous or obvious, but it *is* a different way of viewing human behavior and social structure from the orthodox one, which informs not only anthropology but the whole secular social ideology. The orthodox view says: When in trouble, change the program, because you can write any program you want to. What it should say is: When in trouble, find out what is in the wiring, because only then will you know what programs you can safely write.

The culturalists acknowledge only a general capacity for culture, if they acknowledge anything at all about the general characteristics of the species. To them, all culture is pure human invention, and is passed on from generation to generation by symbolic learning. Thus, logically, it follows that if ever this store of culture should be lost, it is improbable that it would be invented again in the same forms. Something as specific as totemism and exogamy—that old anthropological chestnut—has to be seen in this view as a pure intellectual invention, and it would be unlikely that it would be invented again. But I think that my naïve tribe, with no experience of any other human culture and no knowledge of totemism and exogamy, would produce both very quickly, and, moreover, that these phenomena would be immediately recognizable and analyzable by anthropologists. In fact, anthropologists who argued for the "psychic unity of mankind" were acknowledging a similar position. They held that such customs had not been invented in one area and diffused throughout the world, but were stock responses of the human psyche to external pressures. They were reflections of "human nature," a phrase that anthropologists have been discouraged from using. The argument for psychic unity also had to face the constants-can't-explain-variables charge.

The psychic unity argument, however, was never pushed as far as I am pushing it. For these anthropologists the universal psyche had no specific "content"—it was a capacity to do human things, but most of its proponents would have maintained that it was a general learning capacity and that culture was invented. At the level of specific content this is true—but there is a danger of being dazzled by this into ignoring those basic processes and forms that crop up with regularity, not to say monotony. (It is an error, however, to think that universal processes necessarily produce *uniform results*. Far from it. This is not true in the plant kingdom and is even less true in the animal.)

I can now return to the problem of the route by which I reached this conclusion. The question that had been plaguing me was really: How do we know what's in the wiring and how did it get there? For it is possible to find out what it is all about only if how it was constructed and to what end it was produced is known. It is no good trying to use an analogue computer as if it were a digital computer, because they were designed for different purposes. The answer to this should have been obvious, and soon became so. What is in the wiring of the human animal got there by the same route as it got into any other animal—by mutation and natural selection. These "great constructors," as Lorenz calls them, had produced remarkable end products in the social behavior of all kinds of animals, reptiles, birds, fish, and insects. And it is here that the message of Lorenz and his associates becomes important: behavior evolves just as structure evolves, and the evolution of the two is intimately linked.

Now we are back to Darwin's principle, from which anthropology so disastrously departed at the turn of the century. What the behavioral zoologists (in Europe usually known as "ethologists") demonstrated was that units of behavior evolve on the same principle as units of anatomy and physiology—that a head movement that was part of a bird's innate repertoire of actions has an adaptive significance as great as the evolution of the wing itself. The head movement may be precisely what inhibits the attack of another bird, for example, and over the millennia it has become fixed as a signal recognized by the species as an inhibitor. Even if one does not accept that humans have "instincts" of this kind (I think they have a few but not many), one should look at behavior as the end product of evolution and analyze it in terms of the selection pressures that produced it. If man has this marvelous flexibility in his learning patterns, then it must be a feature of the biology of the species. What should be asked is *why* he has it. What selection pressures operated to bring about this particular biological feature? The enormous dependence on culture as a mode of adaptation stands in need of explanation, for this, too, is a species-specific characteristic, and it drives man toward destruction as much as it raises him to glory. It is a two-edged weapon in the fight for survival, and the simple brutes with their instinctive head-wagging, may well live to have the last laugh.

But the brutes, it has transpired, are not so simple. Man's cousins, the other primates, have an amazing complexity of social behavior. One thing the ethologist teaches is to compare the behavior of closely related species in order to get at their "proto-behavior." The flow of excellent material on nonhuman primates in the wild shows how many and subtle are the resemblances between them and man. Wider afield, the growing science of animal behavior shows that many mammals, and vertebrates generally, have social systems that duplicate features of human society, and in which similar processes occur—and even similar social pathologies. Lorenz showed how aggression was the basis of social bonding; V. C. Wynne-Edwards postulated that the "conventionalized competition" that controlled aggression was itself rooted in the control of numbers; M. R. A. Chance demonstrated that among primates the elementary social bond was that between males rather than that between males and females, and so on. The politics of macaque monkeys suggests that Aristotle was right: insofar as he is a primate, man is by nature a political animal. (It is significant how often, when this is quoted, the phrase "by nature" is omitted.) Ants can have societies, but ants cannot have politics. Politics occurs only when members can change places in a hierarchy as a result of competition. So man is more than social; he is political, and he is political because he is that kind of primate—terrestrial and gregarious.

As a consequence it becomes more and more obvious that man has a considerable animal heritage and hence a great store of comparative data to draw on in making generalizations about his own species. It forces upon us this observation: if man finds his own species displaying certain patterns of social behavior that duplicate those of other similar species, then he must conclude prima facie that these patterns are simply what would be expected from, say, a terrestrial primate, a land-dwelling mammal, a gregarious vertebrate, or whatever. Some aspects of these patterns and a great deal of their content will be unique, but this is only to say that they will be species-specific. Every species is unique because it is the end product of a particular path of evolution.

The real question—what is the nature of the uniqueness? —brings us back to where we started. And the question cannot be answered until it is known what man has in common with all other species, and with some other species, and with only closely related species. Thus the argument that man differs from all other species as a result of the triumph of culture over biology I find false, because culture is an aspect of man's biological differences from other species. It is the name for a kind of behavior found in the human species that ultimately depends on an organ, the brain, in which man happens to have specialized. Man is different from other primates, not because he has in some way *overcome* his primate nature, but because he is a different kind of primate with a different kind of nature. At the level of forms and processes man behaves culturally, because mutation and natural selection have produced an animal that *must* behave culturally—invent rules, make myths, speak languages, and form men's clubs, in the same way as the hamadryas baboon must form harems, adopt infants, and bite his wives on the neck.

But why culture? Why didn't man's simian ancestors content themselves with a much less flexible, and perhaps at the time less vulnerable, way of coping with nature's exigencies? This is where another strand of evidence comes in—the material on human evolution. In Darwin's day this was practically nonexistent, and even now it is relatively meager. But we can trace with some confidence the general picture of man's evolution over a period of at least five million years.

This is not the place for a detailed exposition of the accumulated knowledge; all I can do here is point out some of the implications of that new knowledge. Arthur Keith set the limit of brain size below which was mere animal at 750 cubic centimeters. The modern human brain averages about 1400 cc., roughly twice that of Keith's minimum. The brain of the chimpanzee is roughly 400 cc., that of the gorilla 500 cc. Modern discoveries have shown that true hominids have existed for at least two million years and probably longer, and that at that early date in their evolution they were indulging in activities that imply the existence of cultural traditions, even if of a rudimentary form. The most striking evidence of this is the existence of toolmaking industries, first in bone and horn and then in stone (wood does not survive but was undoubtedly used), among small-brained hominids in East and South Africa. Two million years ago, our ancestors with brain sizes ranging from 435 cc. to 680 cc.—only a little better than the gorilla—were doing human things, cultural things, before having reached the Cerebral Rubicon. They were hunting, building shelters, making tools, treating skins, living in base camps, and possibly doing many other things (speaking languages perhaps?) that we cannot know directly, while their morphology was still predominantly apelike and their brains in some cases smaller than the modern ape's. What was not apelike about them was their dentition and their bipedal stance. In these features they were well launched on the road to humanity since both reflect the adaptation to a hunting way of life that differentiates these animals from their primate cousins.

I say these "animals"; I might just as easily have said these "men"—and this is the moral of the story. The record of evolution shows no sharp break between man and animal that can be pinpointed at a certain brain size or anything else. What it shows is a very gradual transition in which changes in locomotion led the way and in which the brain was something of a sluggard. The pelvis of the *Australopithecinae*—those ape men of South and East Africa—is strikingly human and totally unlike anything in an ape, because these were bipedal creatures; but the brain was, if anything, smaller than that of a gorilla—an animal not particularly noted for its cultural achievements.

The moral goes deeper. Once launched on the way to humanity through bipedalism, hunting, and the use of tools, man's ancestors became more dependent on their brains than their predecessors had been. If they were going to survive largely by skill and cunning and rapid adaptation to the changing circumstances of the Pleistocene epoch, a premium had to be put on the capacity for cultural behavior. Man took the cultural way before he was clearly distinguishable from the animals, and in consequence found himself stuck with this mode of adaptation. It turned out to be successful, although for a while it must have been touch and go. But because he became dependent on culture, mutation and na-tral selection operated to improve the organ most necessary to cultural behavior, the brain, and in particular the neo-cortex with its important functions of association and control. Those animals that were best able to be cultural were favored in the struggle for existence. Man's anatomy, physiology, and behavior are therefore in large part the *result* of culture. His large and efficient brain is a consequence of culture as much as its cause. He does not have a culture because he has a large brain; he has a large brain because several million years ago his little-brained ancestors tried the cultural way to survival. Of course, the correct way to view this is as a feedback process. As cultural pressures grew, so did selection pressures for better brains; as better brains emerged, culture could take new leaps forward, thus in turn exerting more pressures.

This is an oversimplified account; the actual picture of the evolution of the brain is much more complex. But in essential outline it is true and, for immediate purposes,

enough to make the point that man's uniqueness is a biological uniqueness and that culture does not in some mysterious sense represent a break with biology. The present human
biological make-up is a consequence, among other things, of
cultural selection pressures. Man is, therefore, biologically
constituted to produce culture, not simply because by some
accident he got a brain that could do cultural things, but because the cultural things themselves propelled him into getting a larger brain. Man is not simply the *producer* of institutions like the family, science, language, religion, warfare,
kinship systems, and exogamy; he is the *product* of them.
Hence it is scarcely surprising that man continually repro-
duces that which produced him. He was selected to do precisely this, and in the absence of tuition the mythical naïve
tribe would do it all over again in the same way. It is not
only the *capacity* for culture, then, that lies in the brain;
it is the *forms* of culture, the universal grammar of language
and behavior.

This, then, is how it all got into the wiring of the human
computer. These are the facts about human evolution, and
there need be no great mystery about the production of culture by human beings and the relative uniformity of its
processes. There are many mysteries of fact that will never
be solved, since the behavior of fossil man can only be in-
ferred. But, in principle, once it is accepted that culture
is the major selection pressure operating on the evolution
of human form and behavior, and that it has produced an
animal wired for the processing of various cultural programs, the uniqueness of man becomes a problem on the
same level as the uniqueness of any other animal species.

Combining the insights of the ethologists and the students
of human evolution, we can scan the behavior of related
species for aspects of behavior that are common to all
primates and, beyond that, look to mammals and vertebrates

for clues. For in the process of evolution man did not cease to be a primate or a mammal. Weston LaBarre has said that part of man's success lies in exaggerating certain mammalian tendencies rather than in losing them—length of suckling, for example. Much human behavior—in particular, social arrangements—can be seen as a variation on common primate and gregarious-mammalian themes. Certain "unique" aspects —such as the use of true language—can be investigated for what they are, biological specializations produced by the unique evolutionary history of the species.

This perspective enables human society and behavior to be viewed comparatively, without any necessity to propound theories of the total and essential differences between man and other animals. It puts the obvious uniqueness into perspective and does not allow man's commonality with the animal kingdom to be lost sight of. Man is indeed the cultural animal, but both terms should be given equal weight; one does not contradict the other. Culture does not represent a triumph over nature, for such a thing is impossible; it represents an end product of a natural process. It is both the producer and the product of man's human nature, and in behaving culturally he is behaving naturally.

It is often said that man has lost all his instincts. I think this is a bit too extreme. If I may paraphrase Oscar Wilde: to lose some of one's instincts is unfortunate, to lose all of them smacks of carelessness. No species could afford to be that careless. But it is true that of instincts ("innate mechanisms which produce items of behavior complete at their first performance and relatively unmodifiable by experience") man has very few. Instead, it is often claimed, he has intelligence, foresight, wisdom, and the like, and the enormous capacity to learn. In rejecting instinct for intelligence he took something of a risk, since instinct does provide a sureness of response that has been evolved from trial and error over millions of years. Ant societies are much better organized and more efficient than any human societies and are driven wholly on instinctive mechanisms. But instinct has its costs. It is too rigid. Changed circumstances cannot be met by a rapid adjustment in behavior. Insects and animals heavily dependent on instinct have to wait for processes of genetic change to effect changes in the instincts themselves before they can adjust. The higher up the phyletic scale the less true this is, and with man it is least true of all. Thus there is a cost-benefit analysis in the shedding of innate instincts in favor of more complex modes of behaving.

The crux of the matter is this: even if a species sheds its dependence on instincts, it still has to do the same things that instincts were designed to do. As Bergson saw so clearly, culture has to do the same job that instinct had been doing. This is another paradox, I suppose, but an intriguing one, because to get culture to do the same jobs that instinct had been doing, cultural behavior had been made in many ways like instinctive behavior. It had to be unconscious so that it did not require thought for its operation; it had to be automatic so that certain stimuli would immediately produce it; it had to be common to all members of the population.

How much of man's cultural behavior is in fact intelligent and conscious, and how much is at that unthinking, automatic-response level? Most human behavior is automatic, absorbed during socialization, and built into patterns of habitual thought, belief, and response. Indeed, habit is, as William James said, the great flywheel of society. Anthropologists speak of "covert" or "unconscious" culture to refer to this iceberg of assumptions, values, and habitual responses. And sitting over all of them is the great evolutionary invention of conscience, superego, moral sense, or whatever you want to call it. The sense of guilt, of having broken the taboos, the rules, the laws of the tribe, keeps most people in line most of the time. Conscience is an empty canister that culture fills; but once filled, it becomes a dynamic controller of behavior. Most of man's behavior, however, never even rises to the point where conscience and the sense of guilt need to step in. Man does what he does from habit, even down to the smallest details and gestures and twitches of the facial muscles. Most of this is never thought about; but people who do not behave "normally" are quickly recognized—and are often locked up in asylums as lunatics. Think only of Irving Goffman's example of the man walking down the road in the rain without a raincoat, smiling, shoulders back, head facing the sky. Clearly a madman. He should be hunched, hurrying, and looking miserable, with his jacket collar drawn up at least.

The genius of nature here stands revealed and the paradox is resolved. Of course most of man's learned cultural behavior operates almost exactly like instinct. This has to be the case. This is not foolproof, but neither is instinct itself. So the same effect is achieved, and those habits that have proved useful in survival become part of the behavioral repertoire. But these habits can be changed within a generation. It is not necessary to wait for the long process of natural selection to operate before these quasi-instinctual behaviors can be modified; they can be modified very rapidly to meet changing circumstances. Thus man has all the benefits of instinctive behavior without its disadvantages. At any one time the rigidity of cultural habits will be just as invulnerable to change as instincts—as a moment's reflection on the persistence of traditions will confirm—and habits are extremely conservative. Since most of them are passed on by means other than direct tuition, they tend to persist for generations despite changes in deliberate education. But they can be changed relatively rapidly compared with the time span needed for changes in genetic material. Thus man can make rapid adjustments without creating anarchy (which does not mean that he always does so).

Here again cultural behavior can be seen as yet another kind of biological adaptation. At this level, other species also display behavior of the same kind, and the higher in the scale they are, the more dependent they become on habits transferred through generations by learning rather than instincts transferred in the genetic code. But it must always be kept in mind that this is not a sharp distinction. The code is not silent about learning and habits. Instructions about habitual behavior are as much in the code as instructions about instinctive behavior.

This model of behavior sees the human actor as a bundle of potentialities rather than a *tabula rasa:* potentialities for action, for instinct, for learning, for the development of un-conscious habits. These potentialities or predispositions or biases are the end products of a process of natural selection peculiar to the human species. One consequence of this view is that much of the quasi-instinctive cultural behavior of man can be studied in more or less the same way and by many of the same methods as ethologists study the truly instinctive behavior of other animals.

I began with the theme of human uniqueness, and end with my point that it has to be interpreted in the same way as the uniqueness of any other species. Anthropologists have to ask "How come?" How did culture get into the wiring? How did the great constructors operate to produce this fea-ture, which, like everything else about man, is not antinature or superorganic or extrasomatic or any of the other dema-gogic fantasy states that science and religion imagine for him? Darwin did not banish mind from the universe as Butler feared; indeed, he gave man a basis for explaining how mind got into the universe in the first place. And it got there—as did every other natural and biological feature—by natural selection. The toolmaking animal needed mind to survive; that is, he needed language and culture and the reorganization of experience that goes with these. And, once he got the rudiments and became dependent on them, there was no turning back. There was no retreat to the perilous certainty of instinct. It was mind or nothing. It was classification and verbalization, rules and laws, mnemonics and knowledge, ritual and art that pressed upon the precarious species, demanding better and better brains to cope with this new organ—culture—that was now essential to survival. Two related processes, thought and self-control, evolved together, and their end product is the cultural animal, who speaks and rules himself because that is the kind of animal he is; because speaking and self-discipline have made him what he is; because he is what he produces and was produced by what he is.

Anthropology Tomorrow

History itself is a *real* part of *natural history*, of the development of nature into man. Natural science will one day incorporate the science of man, just as the science of man will incorporate natural science; there will be one science.

—Karl Marx, *Third Paris Manuscript: 1844*

Origin of man now proved. Metaphysics must flourish. He who understands [the] baboon would do more towards metaphysics than Locke.

—Charles Darwin, *Notebook M: 1838*

LOOKING BACK over these pieces I am left with the feeling that I have heard all the drums and trumpets but that somehow I have missed the battle. I have tried to summarize half a life spent in discovering and practicing anthropology, and to see where both the discipline and the practitioner should go next. Clearly the discipline cannot keep running on the spot; it has to move, and move in the direction of evolutionary biology and ethical theory. If it won't, then I must move without it, which is sad, because my encounter with anthropology has been happy, if sometimes frustrating.

At the conclusion of his shrewd book of lyrics, *Men and Women,* Robert Browning addressed his wife in "One Word More":

> There they are my fifty men and women
> Naming me the fifty poems finished.
> Take them, love, the book and me together.
> Where the heart lies, let the brain lie also.

Unlike poets, we "objective" scientists like to affect that only our brains lie in our less than lyrical studies of men and women—the real people who make up those awful abstractions like "social structure," "kinship system," "cultural unit," "breeding population." But even if, for professional purposes, we are able to recollect our data in tranquility, at least some of us are not so self-deceived as to believe that we are dispassionate about our material. Reason is, and ought to be, the slave of the passions; Hume was right in this. If the only motive for doing anthropology is that bleak professionalism that sees human beings as useful objects of study, the discipline has lost its connection with both its origins and its purpose. There is enough exploitation in the world without our adding intellectual exploitation. Our hearts, as well as our brains, should be with our men and women.

Like Browning, I seem to be more fascinated by the quirks, weaknesses, blemishes, and even cruelties than by the nobility, humor, kindness, and courage. Too often, anthropologists who "care," care only to preserve a nice world in which "good" people will triumph. But this would not be a human world. When I plead for "humanity," I am pleading simply for a world in which people can be human—not one in which they can be only good. A world without fighting, without witches, without jealousy, without rivalry, hatred, and fear, without pride and betrayal would not be a world I would care to live or study in. But there is a human scale for all these things. A man can be proud, jealous, and pugnacious, and live a very satisfactory life without feeling *"angst,"*

342

"alienation," "anomie," "depression," or any of the other pervasive ills of our inhuman way of civilized living. A Cochiti Indian or a Tory Islander feels really helpless only against the elements; otherwise, he has ample ways of coping. When people feel helpless to affect their own lives in their own societies, they are outside the human range. And whether the helplessness stems from slavery, economic degradation, or the demands of affluence, they have left the human scale and with it any hope of a human solution to their problems.

For my own "one word more," then, I will add a brief note about four men (alas, no women) who have offered insights into the present human dilemmas and some ideas on the way to solve them.

Here I wish to create something of a pantheon: Darwin, Marx, Freud, Lévi-Strauss. These are the foremost intellects to have turned their attention to the study of man in the last hundred and fifty years. And in the new science that will rise from the ashes of anthropology each will have his honored place. What anthropologists should be out to achieve is an understanding of the human species, and a further understanding of what the species has done to itself. Each of these men has made a brilliant contribution to this undertaking, and the new science will have to incorporate their thoughts.

Darwin established the basic pattern for understanding what man is as a species and how he got that way. He did not go far into the question of what people have done to themselves, and he did not speculate on what they might do. But the basis for such an appraisal is all there in *The Descent of Man*. The case for his approach has been argued at length here; there is no need to take it further. Marx, who greatly admired Darwin and wished to dedicate the first volume of *Das Kapital* to him, paid less attention than Darwin to what man was as a species, largely because he assumed that Darwinian science would establish this. But he was more concerned with this question than many of his followers—Pavlovians and Lysenkoists to a man—would give him credit for. Engels, too, explored, in his remarkable essay "The Role of Labor in the Transition from Ape to Man," the basic issue of the "hominization" process, as it has come to be called, and anticipated the tremendous emphasis that physical anthropologists like S. L. Washburn were later to place on the role of tools in human evolution.

But Marx was mostly concerned with what man had done to himself as a species—a species characterized by sociability and a capacity for "civil society." Even before he and Engels came upon the work of Morgan, they had formed the idea of a precivilized state of "primitive communism," a kind of "natural" society in which social relations were at one with natural relations. Thus social relations followed the lines of young/old, male/female, leader/follower, et cetera, and did not cut across these. Everyone had, in a sense, the same relationship to nature. With the advent of property and exploitation—the coming of unnatural society—social relations were dominated by the relations of production and followed the lines set up by these relations: master/slave, lord/peasant, capitalist/laborer. The dynamics of these societies rested on the conflicts inherent in the unnatural relationships so set up. The way out was to destroy these unnatural relationships and return to communism, where there would be no exploitation.

There is no question that Marx thought of class society as an "episode" that intruded into the natural state of man, and that man's business was to restore that natural state; that exploitation—with its accompanying alienation—was at the root of this unnatural state of affairs; that exploitative relationships arose from the fact that people were differently related to the means of production, which could be possible only with a productive surplus; that the very dynamics of this process were inherently unstable, making class conflict the basis of all social change of a cumulative kind. These were truly incredible insights, which any theory of the kind I am advocating must take into account. And far from being alien to a Darwinian analysis—to an analysis of the biological basis of human social nature—Marx's approach welcomes such an analysis, as indeed Marx himself welcomed Darwin.

For Freud, the understanding of the evolution of human behavior was central to an understanding of human behavior itself. Freud was a serious evolutionist who, like Engels, addressed himself to the problem of the breakthrough from ape to man: the hominization process. In *Totem and Taboo*, in *Group Psychology and the Analysis of the Ego*, he tried to wrestle with the problem of what *must* have happened to produce this kind of creature. In *Civilization and Its Discontents* he took up the question of what the creature had done to itself. Of course he and Marx looked at very different components of the process, but this is valuable. Marx concentrated on the social system, while Freud was primarily concerned with the relation of the individual to the social system. The two analyses, as many contributors have noted, are complementary. And both are well within the boundaries of a Darwinian science of man and society. What exploitation and its mechanisms were to Marx, the unconscious and its mechanisms were to Freud. And both, in a way, were saying the same thing: what appears on the surface of either individual behavior or the pattern of social relationships is only a clue to the dynamics of the individual or the society. The reality must be sought in processes that are not immediately observable—only their *effects* are observable.

Lévi-Strauss has consciously adopted this approach, but he has taken the avowedly human attribute of language, rather than economics or the individual psyche, as his entry into the argument. He, too, is concerned with establishing certain facts about the breakthrough from nature to culture; about the nature of the creature; about the hidden dynamics of the societies it creates. Man is a classifying, rule-making, exchanging, exogamic creature; his thinking processes are binary; his societies are creations of these basic processes; their "content" is relatively arbitrary, but the structuring of the content is universally the same; myths are coded messages, turning on the nature/culture distinction, about social processes and the eternal problems faced by self-conscious man; all processes of communication, whatever their units— goods, women, words—have the same structure. To dub all this "structuralism" is not to add much, as Lévi-Strauss himself sees. That he approaches the neglected dimension— the intellectual—and aims to give his account of man primarily in this dimension shows that he is a complement to Marx and Freud, and that all three are a complement to Darwin. Between them they have dealt with the biological, psychological, economic, social, and intellectual dimensions of human existence in terms of both the nature of the species and its attacks on that nature.

Lévi-Strauss quite consciously follows Marx, but with a slight difference prompted by his greater knowledge of primitive society. He divides the societies of the world into "cold" and "hot"—corresponding to Marx's natural, communistic societies and his unnatural, exploitative societies. "Cold" societies are relatively static, and have "crystalline" social structures that repeat themselves cyclically and eternally. They are therefore outside history in a sense, since history is more than just existence *in* time; it is recognizable change *through* time. "Hot" societies are the only societies with history. How do they become historical? By introducing exploitation and classes—the dynamics of this situation producing change. No exploitation, no history. During the historical episode, the energy of the society is derived from the clash between people tied into the exploitative network; repetitive, cyclical, "timeless" social structures cannot exist in this hot atmosphere. The way out? Lévi-Strauss's vision of the future is about as vague as Marx's; but, like Marx, he sees a return to the natural state, which is cold. Once automation has taken over production, there will be no more need for exploitation, since the machines will produce all that is needed. Then the society itself can stop having to act as the agent of production with the inevitable result of exploitative relationships. Society can return to its cold, crystalline, primitive, repetitive, cyclical state and can design beautiful and elegant social systems, which, freed from their role as producers, can return to their "pure" role as mediators of true social relationships.

I have dwelt on this aspect of Lévi-Strauss's thinking because of its similarity to Marx's and because it tends to get overlooked in favor of other, more exotic aspects of his work. Marx, Freud, and Lévi-Strauss are all concerned with putting an end to the distortions of truly human relationships that have occurred since the advent of "civilization" and its later, frenetic phase, industrialization. Repression, alienation, exploitation are the clues. The tragedy is clearly seen: to have the kind of "civilized" society man is now used to and committed to, he has had to turn the society itself into a productive machine in which the people themselves become machines and their relationships mechanical rather than natural. To understand what the natural relationships are that man has lost, it is necessary to look to the primitive: to man reduced to his most natural state—the state that lacks the built-in torture of exploitation. Beyond the savage is the natural world of which man is still, despite his pretensions, a part. And here I would suggest that anthropologists can go further than these thinkers have gone—further than perhaps Lévi-Strauss might want to go—and, as an intellectual exercise and as a moral commitment, start on the task of restoring man to nature.

Social anthropology is trapped because it analyzes mostly ahistorical societies or "little communities." It wants to look neither outward to the rest of nature nor upward to the consequences of class society. Its theories of "conflict" are quite ridiculous when treated as generalizations about human social systems. Conflict in preclass societies—before the whole society became the productive machine—is simply not of the same order as class conflict. Social anthropologists see conflict as "integrative"—and in some small sense it surely is in the societies they study—or as purely destructive. But what they miss (and I have been as guilty as anyone) is that conflict is the *essence* of historical society. It is neither a mechanism for restoring equilibrium nor simply a destructive force; it is a social dynamic that creates history, change, and the movement from one system of production to the next. The social anthropologists' blinkered view is lacking in real insight into where the species is or how it got that way.

It will be seen where the social anthropologists are and what they have to say when the polarization of the rich and poor nations that I spoke of in the introduction turns the social systems of the world into one vast, tumultuous society, with exploiters and exploited ready to play the last act in this drama called "civilization." Will they be talking about integrative conflict or equilibrium analysis then? Probably.

The power of ideas is such that men will cling to a vision of the world in which they have a huge investment of time and ego. In the past it has not mattered greatly what people believed about themselves and their societies, since nothing that followed from these beliefs could have endangered the species. Man is now rapidly approaching the point—and it will come in the lifetimes of his children—when, unless he takes his survival consciously into his own hands, he may not survive as a species. This requires a revolution in thinking as serious as the Copernican revolution. Man has to move to a *species-centered* view of the human world he inhabits. And he has to do it quickly—within the next fifty years or even less. Anthropology, if it chooses to fulfill its mandate, can make a more significant contribution to this change in man's view of himself than any other science.

"Magnanimity in politics," said Edmund Burke, "is not seldom the truest wisdom; and great empires and little minds go ill together." The revolution in thinking that I have called for can be nothing less than an imperial venture. It requires something more than little-minded professionalism to carry out. It requires that anthropology work constructively toward a simple end: it should try, after a hundred years, to take Darwin seriously.

References

Introduction

The work by Robert Heilbroner referred to is *Between Capitalism and Socialism* (New York: Random House, 1970). His chapter 5— "Reflections on the Future of Socialism"— should be compulsory reading for all dogmatic, utopian perfectionists of whatever political color. B. F. Skinner's book is, of course, *Beyond Freedom and Dignity* (New York: Knopf, 1971). Morris Ginsberg's views can be found in *Reason and Unreason in Society* (Cambridge: Harvard Univ. Press, 1948).

My work on the incest taboo appeared as "Sibling Incest" in *British Journal of Sociology* 13 (1962): 128-50. It was reprinted in H. Kent Geiger, ed., *Comparative Perspectives on Marriage and the Family* (Boston: Little, 1968). *The Imperial Animal*, by Lionel Tiger and myself (New York: Holt, 1971), contains an extensive bibliography that documents many of the points made here.

351

Chapter 1
This chapter is a popular version of my Malinowski Memorial Lecture, which was originally published as "In the Beginning: Aspects of Hominid Behavioural Evolution" in *Man: The Journal of the Royal Anthropological Institute* 2, no. 3 (1967) : 415-33. The themes have been further elaborated in my essay "Alliance and Constraint: Sexual Selection in the Evolution of Human Kinship Systems," which is chapter 10 of Bernard Campbell, ed., *Sexual Selection and the Descent of Man 1871-1971* (Chicago: Aldine, 1972). This book, especially the essay by Robert Trivers, "Parental Investment and Sexual Selection," is relevant to the argument, which is taken up at length in chapters 2, 3, and 4 of *The Imperial Animal.*

The work of Lorenz is best represented in Konrad Lorenz, *Studies in Animal and Human Behaviour,* tr. Robert Martin, 2 vols. (Cambridge: Harvard Univ. Press, 1970-1971) ; and that of Tinbergen in Nikolaas Tinbergen, *The Study of Instinct* (Toronto: Oxford, 1951). Desmond Morris's views, which are criticized here, can be found in popular form in *The Naked Ape* (New York: McGraw, 1968), and in *The Human Zoo* (New York: McGraw, 1969). The impressive body of ethological work on which he bases his assumptions, and for which he is rarely given proper credit, can be found in his *Patterns of Reproductive Behaviour* (New York: McGraw, 1971).

Chapter 2
On the origin of races the best compilation is undoubtedly Carleton S. Coon, *The Origin of Races* (New York: Knopf, 1962). This has been heavily criticized for lending support to the polyphyletic, hence racist, view of the human species. An opposing view, and one fairly close to the one put forward here can be found in C. L. Brace and Ashley Montagu, *Man's Evolution* (New York: Macmillan, 1965). Arthur Jensen's views on race and intelligence appeared as "How Much Can We Boost I.Q. and Scholastic Achievement?" in *Harvard Educational Review* 39 (1969) : 1-123. For a lengthy critique see Alexander Alland, *Human Diversity* (New York: Columbia Univ. Press, 1971). The best general discussion of the whole issue that I know is Sherwood L. Washburn, "The Study of Race," *American Anthropologist* 65, no. 3 (1963) : 521-31.

Chapter 3

The theme of this chapter is developed in my *Kinship and Marriage: An Anthropological Perspective* (Baltimore: Penguin, 1967), and in chapters 3 and 4 of *The Imperial Animal*. The "pro-nuclear-family" viewpoint is perhaps best expressed in G. P. Murdock, *Social Structure* (New York: Macmillan, 1949).

Chapter 4

Again, my *Kinship and Marriage* explores these issues further. The work of Claude Lévi-Strauss on kinship is available in an excellent translation as *The Elementary Structures of Kinship*, trans. J. R. von Strumer and J. H. Bell, ed. and trans. R. Needham (Boston: Beacon Press, 1969). His point about the atom of kinship can be found in *Structural Anthropology* (New York: Basic Bks., 1963).

Chapter 6

Further details on Tory can be found in my chapter on "Tory Island" in Burton Benedict, ed., *Problems of Smaller Territories* (London: Athlone, 1967), and in "Kinship and Land Tenure on Tory Island," *Ulster Folklife* 12 (1966): 1-17 (reprinted as a pamphlet by the Institute of Irish Studies and the Ulster Folk Museum, Belfast). For those who read Gaelic there is a fascinating book by an ex-parish priest of Tory, An tAthair Eoghan Ø Colm: *Toraigh na dTonn* (Dublin: Foilseacháin Náisiúnta Tta, 1971).

Chapter 7

The classical tales of the myth cycles directly translated from the original manuscripts can be found in T. P. Cross and C. H. Slover, *Ancient Irish Tales* (Dublin: Allen Figgis, 1969). The relation of these tales to the Arthurian cycle is presented in popular form by Charles Squire, *Celtic Myth and Legend* (London: Gresham Publishing Co., n.d.). Such historical facts as there are on Tory can be found in the various annals: J. O'Donovan, ed., *Annala Rioghachta Eireann* [Annals of the kingdom of Ireland by the four masters] (Dublin, 1851); W. A. Hennessey, ed., *The Annals of Ulster* (Dublin, 1887).

On the ritualization of fighting behavior, see Konrad Lorenz, *On Aggression* (New York: Harcourt, 1966). Also see I. Eibl-Eibesfelt, "The Fighting Behavior of Animals," *Scientific American*, Decem-

References

ber 1961, and his *Ethology: The Biology of Behavior* (New York: Holt, 1970).

Chapter 8
The quote from Synge is from *The Works of John M. Synge: Volume Three, The Aran Islands* (Dublin: Maunsel and Co., 1910) pp. 160-62. The reader should note the comments of C. M. Arensberg and S. T. Kimball in their *Family and Community in Ireland* (Cambridge: Harvard Univ. Press, 1940) concerning the reckoning of kin in County Clare. They note the form used in Donegal as described here but found it "only in dictionaries." The only dictionary source they could be referring to is the Rev. P. Dinneen, *Foclóir Gaedhilge agus Béarla* (Dublin: Irish Texts Society, 1927). The entry under "Ø" carries numerous illustrations from *Caisleán Øir*, by Seámus Ø Grianna ("Máire"), a Donegal story.

Bilateral or cognatic descent groups are discussed by W. H. Goodenough, "A Problem in Malayo-Polynesian Social Organization," *American Anthropologist* 57 (1955): 71-83, and by Raymond Firth, "Bilateral Descent Groups: an Operational Viewpoint," in I. Schapera, ed., *Studies in Kinship and Marriage* (London: Royal Anthropological Institute, 1963). The problem of overlapping is discussed in my "Prolegomena to the Study of British Kinship" in J. Gould, ed., *Penguin Survey of the Social Sciences* (Harmondsworth: Penguin, 1965), and in my *Kinship and Marriage*. It is worth noting that the anthropological term "clan" is derived from the Gaelic word *clann*—but in anthropology it refers to a unilineal descent group, matrilineal or patrilineal. This causes the ethnographer of Gaelic life a certain embarrassment!

The distribution shown in the fourth figure could only occur by chance in one sample out of twenty: $\chi^2_{(1)} = 4.30$: $p < .05$

Chapter 9
For general details of Cochiti see Charles H. Lange, *Cochiti: A New Mexico Pueblo Past and Present* (Austin: Univ. of Tex. Press, 1959). This contains my appendix "A Note on Cochiti Linguistics." For my own analysis of Cochiti society, see *The Keresan Bridge: A Problem in Pueblo Ethnology* (New York: Humanities Press, 1968). For a recent review of the Pueblos see Alfonso Ortiz, *New Per-*

spectives on the Pueblos (Albuquerque: Univ. of N. Mex. Press, 1972).

Chapter 10
Ruth Benedict's views are best known from her *Patterns of Culture* (Boston: Houghton, 1934). The Sun Chief of Oraibi is described in *Sun Chief: The Autobiography of a Hopi Indian,* ed. Leo W. Simmons (New Haven: Yale Univ. Press, 1942). In *The Keresan Bridge,* chapter 5, I discuss the relation of baseball recruitment to the social structure to show how the two teams are recruited from tightly bound groups composed of related matrilineages and extended paternal families.

Chapter 11
The quotations in the second paragraph are from Bernard J. Siegal and Alan R. Beals, "Pervasive Factionalism," *American Anthropologist* 62 (1960): 394-417. On Taos see W. N. Fenton, "Factionalism at Taos Pueblo, New Mexico," *Bulletins of the Bureau of American Ethnology,* no. 164 (1957). For comparative material see D. French, "Factionalism at Isleta Pueblo" *American Ethnological Society Monographs,* no. 14 (1948).

Chapter 12
The Negritos of Luzon are described by Kilton Stewart (inventor of the Stewart Emotional Response Test) in a remarkable but totally neglected book, *Pygmies and Dream Giants* (New York: Norton, 1954). On the Navaho: A. H. Leighton and D. C. Leighton, "Elements of Psychotherapy in Navaho Religion," *Psychiatry* 4 (1941): 515-23.

The quotation from White is: L. A. White, "A Comparative Study of Keresan Medicine Societies," *Proceedings of the 23rd International Congress of Americanists* (1928): 604-19.

The theory of the relationship between excessive paranoia and anxiety over aggression can be found in J. W. M. Whiting and I. L. Child, *Child Training and Personality* (New Haven: Yale Univ. Press, 1953).

The quote from Eggan is: F. Eggan, *The Social Organization of the Western Pueblos* (Chicago: Univ. of Chicago Press, 1950) p. 239.

For views on ritual and social structure, see E. Durkheim, *Les formes élémentaires de la vie religieuse* (Paris, 1912); A. R.

References

Radcliffe-Brown, *Structure and Function in Primitive Society* (London: Cohen & West, 1952), and *The Andaman Islanders* (Cambridge: Cambridge Univ. Press, 1922; new ed., Chicago: Free Press, 1948).

Chapter 13
On the general problems raised in this chapter see J. J. Gumperz and Dell H. Hymes, *The Ethnography of Communication,* American Anthropological Association, Special Publications, no. 3 (Menasha, Wis., 1964). Benjamin Lee Whorf's views can be found in *Language, Thought and Reality,* ed. John B. Carroll (Cambridge: M.I.T. Press, 1956).

On the Keresan language: Franz Boas, "A Keresan Text," *International Journal of American Linguistics* 2 (1923) : 171-80; *Keresan Texts,* Publications of the American Ethnological Society, no. 8 (New York, 1936); I. Davis, "Linguistic Clues to Northern Rio Grande Prehistory" *El Palacio* 66 (1959): 73-84; "The Language of Santa Ana Pueblo," *Bulletins of the Bureau of American Ethnology,* no. 191 (1964): 53-190; R. F. Spencer "The Phonemes of Keresan," *International Journal of American Linguistics* 12 (1946): 229-36; "Spanish Loanwords in Keresan," *Southwestern Journal of Anthropology* 3 (1947): 130-46.

On the Gaelic language: An Coimisiún um Athbheochan na Gaelge, *Summary, in English, of Final Report* (Dublin: The Stationery Office, 1963); D. Corkery, *The Fortunes of the Irish Language* (Dublin: C. J. Fallon, 1954); Brian Ø Cuív, *Irish Dialects and Irish Speaking Districts* (Dublin: Institute for Advanced Study, 1951).

Chapter 14
The main sources used in compiling the description of Amerindian religion are as follows:
Ruth Benedict, "The Vision in Plains Culture," *American Anthropologist* 24 (1922): 1-23; *The Concept of the Guardian Spirit in North America,* Memoirs of the American Anthropological Association, no. 29 (1923).
Ruth L. Bunzel, "Introduction to Zuni Ceremonialism," *47th Annual Report of the Bureau of American Ethnology* (1932).
George A. Dorsey, *Traditions of the Skidi Pawnee,* Memoirs of the American Folklore Society 8 (1904).

References

W. J. Hoffman, "The Mide'wiwin or Grand Medicine Society of the Ojibwa," *7th Annual Report of the Bureau of American Ethnology* (1891).

Ake Hultkrantz, *Conceptions of the Soul among North American Indians* (Stockholm, 1953).

Robert H. Lowie, *The Religion of the Crow Indians,* 'Anthropological Papers of the American Museum of Natural History 25, Part 2 (1922).

James Mooney, "The Ghost-Dance Religion and the Sioux Outbreak of 1890," *14th Annual Report of the Bureau of American Ethnology,* Part 2 (1896).

Willard Z. Park, *Shamanism in Western North America* (Evanston: Northwestern Univ., 1938).

E. C. Parsons, *Pueblo Indian Religion,* 2 vols. (Chicago: Univ. of Chicago Press, 1939).

Paul Radin, *The Trickster: A Study in American Indian Mythology* (New York: Philosophical Lib., 1956).

Gladys A. Reichard, *Navaho Religion,* 2 vols. (Princeton: Princeton Univ. Press, 1950).

J. S. Slotkin, *The Peyote Religion* (Chicago: Free Press, 1956).

Leslie Spier, *The Sun Dance of the Plains Indians: Its Development and Diffusion,* Anthropological Papers of the American Museum of Natural History 16, Part 7 (1921).

Sol Tax, ed., *Indian Tribes of Aboriginal America* (Chicago: Univ. of Chicago Press, 1952).

Morton I. Teicher, *Windigo Psychosis* (Seattle: Univ. of Wash. Press, 1960).

Stith Thompson, *Tales of the North American Indians* (Cambridge: Harvard Univ. Press, 1929).

Clark Wissler, *Ceremonial Bundles of the Blackfoot Indians,* Anthropological Papers of the American Museum of Natural History 7, Part 2 (1912).

For many of the ideas in the opening section of this chapter, and particularly for the example of the elevators and its implications, I am indebted to Eugenia Shanklin Fox.

Chapter 15
The following authors are all mentioned in this chapter: M. R. A. Chance, "The Nature and Special Features of the Instinctive

References

Social Bond of Primates," in S. L. Washburn, ed., *Social Life of Early Man* (New York: Wenner-Gren, 1962). Noam Chomsky, *Cartesian Linguistics: A Chapter in the History of Rationalist Thought* (New York: Harper, 1966); *Language and Mind* (New York: Harcourt, 1968); *Problems of Knowledge and Freedom,* The Russell Lectures (New York: Random House, Vintage, 1972). Arthur Keith, *A New Theory of Human Evolution* (London: Watts, 1948). W. LaBarre, *The Human Animal* (Chicago: Univ. of Chicago Press, 1957). W. E. LeGros Clark, *History of the Primates* (Chicago: Univ. of Chicago Press, 1957). E. H. Lenneberg, *Biological Foundations of Language* (New York: Wiley, 1967). K. Lorenz, *On Aggression* (New York: Harcourt, 1966). L. Tiger, *Men in Groups* (New York: Random House, 1969). V. C. Wynne-Edwards, *Animal Dispersion in Relation to Social Behaviour* (New York: Hafner Pub. Co., 1962).

The bibliography of *The Imperial Animal* provides many more references relevant to this general argument. A further development of my own views can be found in my "On the Genetics of Being Human," in Arnold R. Kaplan, ed., *Human Behavior Genetics* (Evanston: Charles C. Thomas, 1973). Very influential in the development of these ideas have been the essay by Clifford Geertz, "The Transition to Humanity," in Sol Tax, ed., *Horizons of Anthropology* (London: Allen and Unwin, 1965), and C. H. Waddington's *The Ethical Animal* (New York: Atheneum, 1961).

Epilogue
The works of the four authors discussed all appear in various standard editions. The views of Lévi-Strauss as discussed here can be found in his *Leçon Inaugurale* at the Collège de France, which has been translated into English as *The Scope of Anthropology* (New York: Humanities Press, 1968). His views are elaborated further in G. Charbonnier, ed., *Conversations with Claude Lévi-Strauss* (London: Cape, J., 1969).

Acknowledgments

I should like to thank two secretaries who helped put this book together: Elizabeth McCreary and Jeanne Dreckman. It is not too much to say that without Miss Dreckman's devoted efforts the book would never have seen the light of print.

My colleague Lionel Tiger was, as always, constructive and helpful, and my editor, Steven M. L. Aronson, can take whatever credit there is for the book's being in readable English. My research assistant, Paul Heyer, has contributed much information and many stimulating ideas. I, however, am solely responsible for the opinions expressed here.

Finally, I should like to thank two institutions for giving me the time and conditions to write: Rutgers University, Dean Henry Torrey especially, and the Harry Frank Guggenheim Foundation and its president, Mason W. Gross.

Index

Index

Index

Television: and Pueblo Indians, 193–94, 266
Temperament: and human variation, 79
Tetrapods Club, London, 35
Tewa Indians, 140, 240, 263, 264–65, 266
Tiger, Lionel, 18, 36, 320; *Imperial Animal, The* (and Fox), 36, 43
Tinbergen, Niko, 46
Tools: and evolution, 54, 55, 332, 344
Tory Island, 34, 139–89, 195, 266–67; *clann* of, 180, 181–85; culture of, 141–42, 148, 151–52, 162, 267; *dream* of, 180, 182; emigration from, 146, 149, 152; English language on, 152, 177–80, 267, 268–73; etymology of name of, 161–62; and fights, external, 163, 173–74; and fights, internal, 163, 165–73, 175; fishing on, 145, 267; Gaelic language on, 33, 141–42, 151–52, 267–73; hostile environment of, 145–46, 148–49, 266–67, 343; kinship ties on, 150–51, 172, 177, 179–89; land tenure system of, 145, 146, 188; marriage customs of, 147–48, 178, 181; migrant labor from, 149–51, 152, 178, 267, 268, 270, 271; mythology and history of, 144, 151, 154–62; naming system of, 177–89, 272; religion of, 144, 147–48, 157–58, 159–61, 163, 267, 269, 272; social system of, 146–47, 148, 255, 267; towns of, 144–45, 186
Trobriand Islanders of Melanesia, 281, 284; kinship system of, 94, 101
Tungus of Siberia, 295
Tylor, E. B., 310; *Anthropology*, 319

Ute Indians, 306

Victoria, Queen of England, 164
Violence. *See* Agonistic encounters
Voltaire, 26
Vonnegut, Kurt, Jr., 38; *Slaughterhouse Five*, 19

Wales: naming system of, 188
Washburn, S. L., 344
Watson, John, 32
Weber, Max, 285
Wellington, Duke of (Arthur Wellesley), 164
White, Leslie, 235, 319
Whiting, John, 32
Whorf, Benjamin Lee, 33, 256
Wilberforce, Bishop Samuel, 313
Wilde, Oscar, 335
Williams, W. M.: *Sociology of an English Village, The*, 188
Wilson, Woodrow, 15
Winnebago Indians, 295, 302
Witchcraft, 203, 277, 288, 300, 303; and baseball, 205, 212–13, 216, 217, 218; and fear 205, 208–09, 235, 238, 239, 250–51; and illness and curing, 204, 224, 231–32, 233–40, 250, 252, 294; and medicine societies, 202, 231–32, 233–39, 251, 254; and paranoia, 194, 239, 250–51
Wittgenstein, Ludwig, 8, 256
World War II, 221, 280
Wovoka, 305
Wright, Sewall, 10
Wynne-Edwards, V. C., 330

Yaqui Indians, 263, 289, 305
Yeats, William Butler, 192

Zoological Society, London, 35, 36
Zuckerman, Lord, 42
Zuni Indians, 191, 253, 289, 290

370